How to do this in VBA?? 202 ready-made macros: Strea proven expert solutions

I0004293

1

How to do this in VBA?? 202 ready-made macros: Streamline your tasks with proven expert solutions

Delete a row 51

Delete a sheet 53

Delete columns 54

Deselect in Excel 56

Deselect in Word 58

Dim 59

Dim array 60

Dim range 62

Dim text 64

Dim variable 66

Dim worksheet 67

Display a message 69

Excel VBA loop through alphabet 71

Exponent 72

Extract year from date in Excel Vba 73

Filter 74

Filter a column 76

Filter a table 78

Find Excel 80

Find and replace 82

Find date 84

Find duplicates 86

Find error 88

Find error code 90

Find function 91

Find last column 93

Find last row 95

Find string 97

For loop 99

Format date 100

How to do this in VBA?? 202 ready-made macros: Streamline your tasks with proven expert solutions

How to do this in VBA?? 202 ready-made macros: Streamline your tasks with proven expert solutions

How to do this in VBA?? 202 ready-made macros: Streamline your tasks with proven expert solutions

How to do this in VBA?? 202 ready-made macros: Streamline your tasks with proven expert solutions

How to do this in VBA?? 202 ready-made macros: Streamline your tasks with proven expert solutions

How to do this in VBA?

This book contains the most frequently searched operations that can be performed using VBA, according to Google.

- how to a in vba - Wyszukiwarka Google
- how to **call** a **sub** in vba
- how to **call** a **function** in vba
- how to **select** a **cell** in vba
- how to **close** a **workbook** in vba
- how to **open** a **workbook** in vba
- how to **set** a **range** in vba
- how to **delete** a **row** in vba
- how to insert a vba **code** in **powerpoint**
- how to **delete** a **sheet** in vba

To run a code in Excel:

1. Open Excel and navigate to the worksheet where you want to apply bold formatting.
2. Press **Alt + F11** to open the VBA Editor.
3. In the VBA Editor, right-click on any of the objects for your workbook in the Project Explorer window (usually on the left side) and select **Insert > Module**. This action opens a new module.
4. Copy the subroutine code into the module window.
5. Close the VBA Editor and return to your Excel worksheet.
6. Run the macro by pressing **Alt + F8**, selecting subroutine's name, and then clicking **Run**.

To run a code in Word:

1. Open Microsoft Word and either open an existing document or create a new one.
2. Press **Alt + F11** to open the VBA Editor.
3. In the VBA Editor, insert a new module by right-clicking on **ThisDocument** or any other object in your Project Explorer, then select **Insert > Module**.
4. Copy and paste subroutine into the module window.
5. Close the VBA Editor and return to your Word document.
6. You can run the macro by pressing **Alt + F8**, selecting the desired subroutine and clicking Run.

How to do this in VBA?? 202 ready-made macros: Streamline your tasks with proven expert solutions

Some entries appear in a similar form in several places in the book. Thanks to this, I was consistent with the queries entered into Google. Moreover, different solutions to a similar problem have educational value. I encourage you to study them. Thank you for purchasing the book. I hope you enjoy using it.

Block comment

Below is an example of how to use block comments in VBA (Visual Basic for Applications) with explanations included in the code. VBA doesn't support block comments in the same way that languages like C++ or Java do, where you can enclose a block of text within a specific symbol or keyword to comment out multiple lines at once. Instead, VBA uses the single quote (`'`) at the beginning of each line to mark it as a comment. However, you can simulate block comments by using conditional compilation arguments, which is a more advanced technique. I'll show you both the standard method using single-line comments and the conditional compilation method for block commenting.

➢Standard method using single-line comments

```
Sub ExampleStandardComment()
    ' This is a single line comment in VBA
    ' Each line must start with a single quote to be
considered a comment
    ' This method is straightforward and is used for brief
explanations or to comment out code line by line

    Dim exampleVariable As Integer
    exampleVariable = 5 ' Setting the value of
exampleVariable to 5

    ' The following line of code has been commented out
and will not execute
    ' MsgBox "The value of exampleVariable is: " &
exampleVariable
    End Sub
```

➢ Advanced method using conditional compilation for block comments

```
Sub ExampleConditionalCompilation()
    #Const BlockComment = False
    #If BlockComment Then
        ' This entire block is considered a comment when
BlockComment is set to False
        ' You can include multiple lines of code or
comments here and they will be ignored during execution
```

```
        ' This method is useful for temporarily disabling
large blocks of code

        Dim exampleVariable As Integer
        exampleVariable = 5
        MsgBox "The value of exampleVariable is: " &
exampleVariable
    #End If
End Sub
```

In the conditional compilation method, changing `#Const BlockComment = False` to `True` would "uncomment" the block, making it active code again. This method is handy for larger blocks of code that you might want to enable or disable for debugging or development purposes.

Remember, the use of conditional compilation for commenting is more of a workaround and is generally used for toggling large sections of code during testing or debugging rather than for actual commenting for explanatory purposes. The standard single-line comment method is more straightforward and widely used for adding explanations or disabling specific lines of code.

Bold text in Excel

To demonstrate how to apply bold formatting to text in VBA, let's use an example where we make the text in a specific cell of an Excel spreadsheet bold. This example assumes you are familiar with the basics of Excel VBA and how to run VBA scripts within Excel.

```
Sub MakeTextBold()
    ' This line of code sets the ActiveSheet property to
refer to the worksheet that is currently active.
    ' The Range object is then used to specify the cell
(or cells) we want to modify. Here, we're focusing on cell
"A1".
    ' The .Font property of the cell allows us to access
various font attributes, including .Bold.
    ' Setting .Bold = True applies bold formatting to the
text in cell A1.

    ActiveSheet.Range("A1").Font.Bold = True
```

```
              ' If you want to apply bold formatting to a range of
cells, you can modify the Range reference as follows:
              ' ActiveSheet.Range("A1:B3").Font.Bold = True
              ' This would make the text in cells A1 through B3
bold.
          End Sub
```

This script will make the text in cell A1 of the active sheet bold. You can adapt this example to apply bold formatting to different cells or ranges as needed by adjusting the `**Range**` property in the code.

Bold text in Word

Let's look at an example where we use VBA to make text bold within a Microsoft Word document. This example assumes you have basic knowledge of how to run VBA scripts within the Word environment.

The following VBA code snippet demonstrates how to make the entire text of the active document bold, as well as how to make specific text bold within a Word document. For clarity and learning purposes, I'll break it into two parts.

➢ Part 1: making the entire text of a document bold

```
          Sub MakeAllTextBold()
              ' This subroutine will make all the text in the active
Word document bold.

              ' The ActiveDocument property refers to the document
currently open and active in Word.
              ' The .Content property accesses all the content
within the active document.
              ' The .Font property allows access to font attributes,
including .Bold.
              ' Setting .Bold = True applies bold formatting to all
text content in the document.

          ActiveDocument.Content.Font.Bold = True
          End Sub
```

➢ Part 2: Making specific text bold

How to do this in VBA?? 202 ready-made macros: Streamline your tasks with proven expert solutions

```vba
Sub MakeSpecificTextBold()
    ' This subroutine demonstrates how to make a specific
    range of text bold within the active document.

    ' The .Range method is used here to specify the start
    and end positions within the document's text.
    ' The arguments (0, 5) specify that the range starts
    at the beginning of the document and extends up to the 5th
    character.
    ' Adjust these values to select different portions of
    the text.
    ' The .Font.Bold property is then set to True to apply
    bold formatting to the selected range.

    ActiveDocument.Range(Start:=0, End:=5).Font.Bold =
True

    ' You can also search for specific text and make it
    bold by using the .Find property and executing a search.
    ' Here's a simple way to do this:

    With ActiveDocument.Content.Find
        .Text = "example" ' Replace "example" with the
    text you're searching for
        .Font.Bold = False ' Search for text that is not
    already bold
        .Execute Replace:=wdReplaceAll, ReplaceWith:="",
    Format:=True, Font.Bold:=True
        ' This will replace the found text with itself,
    but modifies the formatting to make it bold.
    End With
End Sub
```

Remember, the `Start` and `End` parameters in the `Range` method, as well as the search text in the `Find` property, can be adjusted based on the specific requirements of your document and the text you wish to format.

Break code

In VBA (Visual Basic for Applications), "**breaking code**" usually means interrupting the execution of a running subroutine or function. This can be done programmatically by using the `Exit Sub` or `Exit Function` statements to immediately terminate the execution of the subroutine or function in which they are placed. These statements are particularly useful for controlling the flow of your code under certain conditions, such as when an error occurs or a specific condition is met.

Here's an example that demonstrates how to use `Exit Sub` to break out of a subroutine, and `Exit Function` to exit a function prematurely. The comments within the code will explain their usage in detail.

➤ Example 1: Using `Exit Sub` to break a subroutine

```
Sub CheckValueAndExit()
    ' This subroutine checks the value of a variable and
    exits if the condition is met.

    Dim value As Integer
    value = 10 ' Assign a value to the variable

    ' Check if the value is greater than 5. If so, display
    a message and exit the subroutine.
    If value > 5 Then
        MsgBox "Value is greater than 5, exiting
    subroutine."
        Exit Sub ' This statement immediately ends the
    execution of the subroutine.
    End If

    ' If the condition is not met, this message will be
    displayed.
    MsgBox "Value is 5 or less."
End Sub
```

➤ Example 2: Using `Exit Function` to break a function

```
Function CalculateValue(inputValue As Integer) As Integer
```

```
      ' This function attempts to calculate and return a
value based on the input.
      ' If the input value is negative, the function will
exit prematurely.

      If inputValue < 0 Then
            MsgBox "Input is negative. Exiting function."
            Exit Function ' This exits the function without
completing the rest of the code.
            ' Note: When Exit Function is used, the function
returns the default value for its return type.
            ' In this case, as the return type is Integer, the
default return value is 0.
      End If


      ' If the input is non-negative, perform some
calculations (as an example, doubling the input).
      CalculateValue = inputValue * 2


      ' This message will not show if the function has
exited via Exit Function.
      MsgBox "Calculation complete."
End Function
```

These examples show how to use `Exit Sub` and `Exit Function` to control the execution flow of your VBA code effectively.

Break for loop

In VBA you can break out of a `For` loop before it naturally terminates by using the `Exit For` statement. This is useful when you have a condition within the loop that, if met, should terminate the loop's execution immediately rather than continuing through the rest of the iterations. Here's how you can use `Exit For` within a `For` loop in VBA, with explanations in the comments:

```
Sub BreakForLoopExample()
      ' This subroutine demonstrates how to break out of a
For loop before its natural termination.
```

15

```vba
Dim i As Integer


' A simple For loop that is supposed to run from 1 to
10.
For i = 1 To 10
    ' Check if the loop variable (i) equals 5.
    If i = 5 Then
        ' If i is 5, display a message and then use
Exit For to break out of the loop.
        MsgBox "Breaking out of the loop at i = " & i
        Exit For
    End If
    ' If the condition is not met, this message will
show the current value of i.
    MsgBox "Current value of i: " & i
Next i


' After breaking out of the loop or completing all
iterations, execution continues here.
MsgBox "Loop complete. Execution continued after the
loop."
End Sub
```

This example demonstrates a `For` loop that iterates from 1 to 10. Inside the loop, there's a check to see if the loop counter `i` equals 5. If `i` equals 5, the program displays a message box indicating that it will break out of the loop and then uses `Exit For` to do so. This stops the loop prematurely, and execution continues with the next line of code after the `Next i` statement. If `i` does not equal 5, a message box shows the current value of `i`, demonstrating the loop's progression.

This technique is very useful for optimizing performance and control flow in your VBA scripts by avoiding unnecessary iterations once a specific condition has been met.

Break line

In VBA breaking a line or continuing a line of code onto the next line is done using the underscore character (`_`) as a line continuation marker. This is useful

How to do this in VBA?? 202 ready-made macros: Streamline your tasks with proven expert solutions

for improving the readability of your code, especially when dealing with long lines of code that would otherwise extend far off the screen. Below is an example demonstrating how to use the line continuation character in VBA, along with explanations in the comments.

```vba
Sub LineBreakExample()
    ' This subroutine demonstrates how to use the line
continuation character
    ' to break long lines of code into more manageable,
readable pieces.

    ' Let's say we have a long line of code that sets a
variable to a long string:
    Dim longString As String
    longString = "This is a very long string that might
not fit nicely on the screen " & _
                    "when you are coding, so it's a good idea
to break it up."

    ' In the above assignment, the underscore (_) at the
end of the first line
    ' indicates that the line of code continues on the
next line.
    ' Note: There must be a space before the underscore,
and the underscore must
    ' be the last character on the line (except for the
space before it).

    MsgBox longString ' Display the long string to show it
works as intended

    ' You can also use line continuation for calling
functions or methods with many parameters:
    Call SomeFunctionWithLotsOfParameters("parameter1",
"parameter2", _
                        "parameter3",
"parameter4", _
```

How to do this in VBA?? 202 ready-made macros: Streamline your tasks with proven expert solutions

```
                                          "parameter5")


        ' Note: The Call keyword is optional in modern VBA but
    included here for clarity.
    End Sub


    Sub SomeFunctionWithLotsOfParameters(ByVal param1 As
    String, ByVal param2 As String, _
                              ByVal param3 As
    String, ByVal param4 As String, _
                              ByVal param5 As
    String)
        ' Dummy function to demonstrate line continuation with
    multiple parameters
        MsgBox "Function called with parameters: " & param1 &
    ", " & param2 & ", " & _
                param3 & ", " & param4 & ", " & param5
    End Sub
```

In this example, the `longString` variable assignment demonstrates how to use the underscore to break a long string across multiple lines for better readability. The `SomeFunctionWithLotsOfParameters` subroutine call further illustrates using the line continuation character to split a function call with many parameters across several lines, making the code easier to read and maintain.

This approach is beneficial for maintaining clean and readable code, especially when dealing with complex or lengthy statements.

Break line in MsgBox

When working with message boxes (`MsgBox`) in VBA, you might often need to break text onto multiple lines to improve readability or present information in a structured format. To break a line within a `MsgBox`, you can use the `vbNewLine` constant, the `Chr(10)` function for a line feed, or `Chr(13)` for a carriage return. In most cases, `vbNewLine` is preferred for its readability and because it's specifically designed for this purpose.

Here's an example showing how to use `vbNewLine` to break lines in a message box, along with explanations in the comments:

```vba
Sub MessageBoxLineBreakExample()
    ' This subroutine demonstrates how to break lines in a
    message box using vbNewLine.

    Dim message As String

    ' Constructing a message string with line breaks.
    ' vbNewLine is used here to insert a new line between
    each piece of information.
    message = "This is the first line of the message." & _
    vbNewLine & _
                "Here is the second line, showing how to
    break lines." & vbNewLine & _
                "And this is the third line."

    ' Displaying the message box with the constructed
    message.
    ' The message will appear with each sentence on a new
    line, thanks to vbNewLine.
    MsgBox message, vbInformation, "Message Box with Line
    Breaks"

    ' The vbInformation argument adds an information icon
    to the message box,
    ' and "Message Box with Line Breaks" is the title of
    the message box.
End Sub
```

This method of inserting line breaks can be very useful for creating more readable and organized message boxes in your VBA applications.

Break out of loop

To break out of a loop in VBA, you can use the `Exit For` statement within a `For` loop, or the `Exit Do` statement within a `Do While` or `Do Until` loop. This technique is useful for exiting a loop prematurely when a certain condition is met, instead of waiting for the loop to reach its natural termination

How to do this in VBA?? 202 ready-made macros: Streamline your tasks with proven expert solutions

condition. Here's how you can use these statements in both `For` loops and `Do While`/`Do Until` loops, with explanations provided in the comments.

➢ Breaking out of a `For` loop example

```vba
Sub BreakOutOfForLoop()
    ' This subroutine demonstrates how to break out of a
    For loop.

    Dim i As Integer

    ' A For loop that is intended to run from 1 to 10.
    For i = 1 To 10
        ' Check if the loop counter (i) is equal to 5.
        If i = 5 Then
            ' If i is 5, then exit the For loop
            prematurely.
            MsgBox "Exiting the loop at i = " & i
            Exit For
        End If
        ' If i is not equal to 5, this line will execute.
        Debug.Print "i = " & i
    Next i

    ' Code execution continues here after the loop exits.
    MsgBox "Loop exited. Now outside the loop."
End Sub
```

➢ Breaking out of a `Do While` loop example

```vba
Sub BreakOutOfDoWhileLoop()
    ' This subroutine demonstrates how to break out of a
    Do While loop.

    Dim i As Integer
    i = 1 ' Initialize the loop counter

    ' A Do While loop that in theory runs as long as i is
    less than or equal to 10.
```

20

```
Do While i <= 10
        ' Check if the loop counter (i) is equal to 5.
        If i = 5 Then
                ' If i is 5, then exit the Do While loop
prematurely.
                MsgBox "Exiting the loop at i = " & i
                Exit Do
        End If
        ' If i is not equal to 5, this line will execute.
        Debug.Print "i = " & i

        i = i + 1 ' Increment the counter
    Loop

    ' Code execution continues here after the loop exits.
    MsgBox "Loop exited. Now outside the loop."
End Sub
```

These examples show how to use `Exit For` and `Exit Do` to control the flow of your loops based on specific conditions, allowing for more flexible and efficient VBA code execution.

Break while loop

In VBA, while loops are typically constructed using `Do While` or `Do Until` loops. To demonstrate breaking out of a "while" loop, which in VBA terms would be a `Do While` loop, I'll show you how to use the `Exit Do` statement. This statement allows you to exit the loop prematurely when a certain condition is met, instead of waiting for the loop's condition to become False (or True, in the case of `Do Until`). Here's how it works, with detailed comments explaining each part of the code.

➢ Example: Breaking out of a `Do While` loop in VBA

```
Sub BreakOutOfWhileLoop()
    ' This subroutine demonstrates how to break out of a
Do While loop in VBA.

    Dim counter As Integer
    counter = 1 ' Initialize the counter to 1
```

```
    ' Start the Do While loop. This loop will continue as
long as counter is less than or equal to 10.
    Do While counter <= 10
        ' Check if the counter has reached 5.
        If counter = 5 Then
            ' If the counter is 5, display a message and
exit the loop.
            MsgBox "Counter is 5. Exiting the loop."
            Exit Do
        End If


        ' If the counter is not 5, print the counter value
to the Immediate Window (Debug Window in the VBA Editor).
        Debug.Print "Counter = " & counter


        ' Increment the counter by 1.
        counter = counter + 1
    Loop


    ' Once the loop is exited (either naturally or via
Exit Do), execution continues here.
    MsgBox "Loop exited. Counter is " & counter
End Sub
```

This example demonstrates the use of `Exit Do` to break out of a `Do While` loop in VBA. The `Exit Do` statement is particularly useful for controlling the execution flow of your loop when you need to stop the loop based on a condition other than the one specified in the `Do While` statement.

Call a function

In VBA, calling a function involves invoking the function by its name and passing any required parameters to it. Functions can return values, so you can assign the result of a function call to a variable. Below is an example that demonstrates defining a simple function and then calling it from a subroutine. The comments within the code will guide you through the process.

➢ Example: Defining and calling a function in VBA

```
' This function calculates the square of a given number.
' It takes an integer as an input parameter and returns
the square of that number as an integer.
Function SquareNumber(ByVal num As Integer) As Integer
    ' Calculate the square of the input parameter.
    SquareNumber = num * num
End Function


' This subroutine demonstrates how to call the
SquareNumber function.
Sub CallSquareNumberFunction()
    Dim originalNumber As Integer
    Dim squaredNumber As Integer

    ' Assign a value to the originalNumber variable.
    originalNumber = 5

    ' Call the SquareNumber function, passing
originalNumber as the argument.
    ' Assign the result of the function (the squared
number) to the squaredNumber variable.
    squaredNumber = SquareNumber(originalNumber)

    ' Display the result using a message box.
    MsgBox "The square of " & originalNumber & " is " &
squaredNumber
End Sub
```

This example demonstrates defining a simple function that performs a calculation and returns a result, along with a subroutine that calls this function, processes its return value, and displays the result to the user.

Call a sub

In VBA, calling a subroutine (Sub) is a straightforward process. A subroutine is a block of code that performs a specific task but does not return a value. You can call a subroutine directly by its name from another subroutine or function within the same module or from a different module (if the called subroutine is accessible, meaning it's not declared as Private in a different module). Here's an example that illustrates how to define a subroutine and call it from another subroutine, with comments explaining each step.

➢ Example: Defining and calling a subroutine in VBA

```
' This subroutine displays a simple message to the user.
Sub DisplayMessage()
    ' Display a message box with a greeting.
    MsgBox "Hello from DisplayMessage Sub!"
End Sub


' This subroutine demonstrates how to call the
DisplayMessage subroutine.
Sub CallDisplayMessageSub()
    ' Call the DisplayMessage subroutine. When called, it
will execute the code within DisplayMessage.
    DisplayMessage

    ' The code execution continues here after
DisplayMessage Sub has been executed.
    ' Let's display another message box to indicate we're
back in CallDisplayMessageSub.
    MsgBox "Back in CallDisplayMessageSub, after calling
DisplayMessage."
End Sub
```

In this example, `DisplayMessage` is a simple subroutine that shows a message box with a greeting. The `CallDisplayMessageSub` subroutine demonstrates how to invoke the `DisplayMessage` subroutine. When `CallDisplayMessageSub` is executed, it calls `DisplayMessage`, which then executes and shows its message box. After `DisplayMessage` finishes execution, the control returns to `CallDisplayMessageSub`, and the execution continues from the point right after the call was made, showing another message box indicating the return to `CallDisplayMessageSub`.

This example showcases the basic structure and execution flow when calling one subroutine from another in VBA, allowing for organized, modular code development.

Check if a sheet exists

In VBA, checking if a sheet exists in an Excel workbook before trying to access it is a common task, which helps avoid runtime errors if the specified sheet is not found. Below is an example of how to write a function that checks for the existence of a sheet by its name and then a demonstration of calling this function. The code is annotated with comments for clarity.

➢ Example: Function to check if a sheet exists

```
' This function checks if a sheet with a specified name
exists in the active workbook.
' It takes a sheet name as a parameter and returns True if
the sheet exists, False otherwise.
Function SheetExists(sheetName As String) As Boolean
    Dim sheet As Worksheet
    On Error Resume Next ' Disable error reporting
    ' Attempt to assign the sheet with the given name to
the sheet variable.
    ' If the sheet does not exist, an error will occur,
and Nothing will be assigned to sheet.
    Set sheet = ThisWorkbook.Sheets(sheetName)
    On Error GoTo 0 ' Re-enable error reporting

    ' Check if the sheet variable is Nothing. If it is
not, the sheet exists.
    If Not sheet Is Nothing Then
        SheetExists = True
    Else
        SheetExists = False
    End If
End Function

' This subroutine demonstrates how to use the SheetExists
function.
Sub CheckSheet()
    Dim sheetNameToCheck As String
```

How to do this in VBA?? 202 ready-made macros: Streamline your tasks with proven expert solutions

```
            sheetNameToCheck = "MySheet" ' Change "MySheet" to the
        name of the sheet you want to check.


            ' Call the SheetExists function and pass the name of
        the sheet to check.
            If SheetExists(sheetNameToCheck) Then
                MsgBox "Sheet '" & sheetNameToCheck & "' exists."
            Else
                MsgBox "Sheet '" & sheetNameToCheck & "' does not
        exist."
            End If
        End Sub
```

In this code, the `SheetExists` function tries to reference a sheet by its name. If the sheet does not exist, an error will occur, but the `On Error Resume Next` statement prevents the error from stopping the execution of the code. After attempting to set the `sheet` variable, error reporting is re-enabled with `On Error GoTo 0`. The function then checks if the `sheet` variable was successfully set to a sheet object. If `sheet` is not `Nothing`, the function returns `True`, indicating the sheet exists; otherwise, it returns `False`.

The `CheckSheet` subroutine demonstrates how to call the `SheetExists` function and inform the user whether a specific sheet exists within the active workbook. This approach is particularly useful for avoiding errors in macros that perform operations on specific sheets by ensuring the sheet is present before attempting to access or modify it.

Close a workbook

Closing a workbook in VBA can be achieved using the `Close` method of the `Workbook` object. This action can be performed without saving changes, with saving changes, or by prompting the user to save changes. Here's an example demonstrating each approach, complete with comments to guide you through the process.

➢ Example: Closing a workbook in VBA

```
        ' This subroutine demonstrates how to close a specific
        workbook.
        Sub CloseWorkbookExample()
            Dim wb As Workbook
```

```
    ' Attempt to assign the workbook you want to close to
the wb variable.
    ' Make sure to replace 'WorkbookName.xlsx' with the
actual name of your workbook.
    ' Note: The workbook must be open in the same Excel
instance for this to work.
    On Error Resume Next ' Use this to avoid error if the
workbook is not open.
    Set wb = Workbooks("WorkbookName.xlsx")
    On Error GoTo 0 ' Turn back on the default error
handling.

    ' Check if the wb variable was successfully set.
    If Not wb Is Nothing Then
        ' Close the workbook without saving changes.
        wb.Close SaveChanges:=False

        ' To close the workbook and save changes, use:
        ' wb.Close SaveChanges:=True

        ' To prompt the user to save changes (if any),
simply omit the SaveChanges parameter:
        ' wb.Close
    Else
        MsgBox "The workbook is not open or does not
exist."
    End If
End Sub
```

This script attempts to close a workbook named "**WorkbookName.xlsx**". It first tries to reference the workbook by its name. If the workbook is open, it will be assigned to the `wb` variable. The script then checks if this assignment was successful to determine if the workbook is open. If `wb` is not `Nothing`, the script proceeds to close the workbook.

The example demonstrates three ways to close the workbook:

- Without saving changes: `wb.Close SaveChanges:=False`

How to do this in VBA?? 202 ready-made macros: Streamline your tasks with proven expert solutions

- Saving changes: `wb.Close SaveChanges:=True`
- Prompting the user to decide whether to save changes: `wb.Close` (without specifying the `SaveChanges` parameter).

This flexibility allows you to tailor the workbook closing behavior to fit the needs of your VBA project or script.

Close a workbook

Closing a workbook in VBA is a common task, especially when automating processes that involve opening, modifying, and then closing workbooks. Below is a succinct example of how to close a workbook. The code comments provide explanations and context for each operation performed.

➢ Example: Closing a workbook in VBA

```
Sub CloseSpecificWorkbook()
    ' Define a variable to hold the workbook object for
easier reference.
    Dim wb As Workbook

    ' Assign the workbook you wish to close to the
variable.
    ' Replace 'MyWorkbook.xlsx' with the name of your
workbook.
    Set wb = Workbooks("MyWorkbook.xlsx")

    ' Check if the workbook object was successfully set.
    If Not wb Is Nothing Then
        ' Close the workbook.
        ' Use SaveChanges:=False to close without saving
changes.
        ' Use SaveChanges:=True to save changes before
closing.
        ' Omitting SaveChanges or setting it to True
prompts the user if there are unsaved changes.
        wb.Close SaveChanges:=False
```

```
                        ' If you wanted to prompt the user to save if
                there are unsaved changes, you could use:
                        ' wb.Close
                        ' Or to save changes without prompting:
                        ' wb.Close SaveChanges:=True
                Else
                        ' If the workbook was not found or could not be
                set, display a message.
                        MsgBox "Workbook not open or does not exist."
                End If
        End Sub
```

This subroutine, `CloseSpecificWorkbook`, demonstrates how to close a workbook named "**MyWorkbook.xlsx**". It first attempts to assign the workbook to a variable for easy reference. The script checks if the workbook is actually open (the variable is successfully set) and then proceeds to close it based on the specified `SaveChanges` parameter. The `SaveChanges` parameter controls whether changes should be saved before closing, with options to save, not save, or prompt the user, providing flexibility based on the specific needs of your task.

Comment multiple lines

In VBA, there isn't a built-in feature to comment out multiple lines of code with a single command like block comments in some other programming languages. Instead, each line of code that you wish to comment out must be prefixed with a single quote (`'`). However, for a more efficient way to handle multiple lines, you can use the VBA editor's ability to comment and uncomment blocks of code manually through its interface. Here's how you might manually add comments to multiple lines and an example to illustrate this:

➢ Example: Manually commenting multiple lines

```
        ' This is an example of manually commenting multiple lines
        in VBA.
        ' Each line is prefixed with a single quote to make it a
        comment.
        ' The following lines of code are commented out to prevent
        them from executing.
        ' Dim exampleVariable As Integer
        ' exampleVariable = 10
```

```
' MsgBox "The value of exampleVariable is: " &
exampleVariable
```

➤ Using the VBA editor for multiple line comments

To comment out multiple lines without adding a single quote to each line individually in the VBA Editor:

1. Highlight the lines of code you wish to comment out.
2. Right-click the highlighted section.
3. Choose **"Comment Block"** from the context menu (depending on your version of the VBA Editor, you might need to add this option to the toolbar via customization).

To uncomment, you'd highlight the commented lines, right-click, and choose **"Uncomment Block"**.

This method is a manual workaround rather than a coding solution. It's useful for quickly disabling sections of your code for testing purposes without permanently altering the codebase.

Concatenate

Concatenation in VBA is the process of joining two or more strings together. This can be achieved using the `&` operator, which combines string expressions into a single string. Below is an example that demonstrates how to concatenate strings in VBA, with detailed comments explaining each step.

➤ Example: Concatenating strings in VBA

```
Sub ConcatenateStrings()
    ' Declare variables for holding strings.
    Dim firstName As String
    Dim lastName As String
    Dim fullName As String

    ' Assign values to the first and last name strings.
    firstName = "John"
    lastName = "Doe"

    ' Concatenate the firstName and lastName variables
with a space in between.
    fullName = firstName & " " & lastName
```

```
        ' Display the concatenated fullName string in a
    message box.
        MsgBox "The full name is: " & fullName
    End Sub
```

This subroutine, `ConcatenateStrings`, creates two strings (`firstName` and `lastName`), and then concatenates them into a `fullName` string, with a space between the first and last names. The final `fullName` string is displayed in a message box.

The `&` operator is used here for concatenation, ensuring that the operation treats the operands as strings. This approach is straightforward and effective for combining strings in VBA, whether for displaying messages, creating combined strings for processing, or other purposes where string manipulation is required.

Convert column number to letter

Converting a column number to its corresponding letter(s) in Excel can be quite useful, especially when working with Excel objects in VBA that require a column letter reference. Here's a straightforward example of how to achieve this conversion using a custom VBA function. The function handles columns from 1 (A) to 16384 (XFD), covering the entire range of possible columns in Excel.

➢ Example: Function to convert column number to letter

```
    Function ColumnNumberToLetter(columnNumber As Long) As
    String
        ' This function converts a column number to its
    corresponding Excel column letter.

        Dim columnLetter As String
        Dim modulo As Integer

        ' Check if the column number is within the valid range
    (1 to 16384 for Excel).
        If columnNumber > 0 And columnNumber <= 16384 Then
            ' Loop until columnNumber is 0.
            Do While columnNumber > 0
```

How to do this in VBA?? 202 ready-made macros: Streamline your tasks with proven expert solutions

```vba
            modulo = (columnNumber - 1) Mod 26
            ' Prepend the new letter in front of the
previous ones.
            columnLetter = Chr(65 + modulo) & columnLetter
            columnNumber = (columnNumber - modulo) \ 26
        Loop
    Else
        columnLetter = "Invalid Column"
    End If


    ' Return the calculated column letter.
    ColumnNumberToLetter = columnLetter
End Function

Sub TestColumnNumberToLetter()
    ' Test the function with a sample column number.
    Dim testColumnNumber As Long
    testColumnNumber = 28 ' Example column number to
convert.

    ' Display the result using a message box.
    MsgBox "Column " & testColumnNumber & " is " &
ColumnNumberToLetter(testColumnNumber)
End Sub
```

This code snippet includes a `ColumnNumberToLetter` function that takes a column number as input and returns the corresponding column letter as a string. The function works by repeatedly dividing the column number by 26 (the number of letters in the alphabet) and using the remainder to find the correct letter. Letters are determined by adding the remainder to the ASCII code for 'A' (65), then converting this to a character with the `Chr` function.

The `TestColumnNumberToLetter` subroutine demonstrates how to use this function and displays the result in a message box. This setup is ideal for various applications, such as dynamically generating cell references in Excel through VBA.

Convert number stored as text to number

Converting a number stored as text to an actual numeric value in VBA can be essential for performing mathematical operations or comparisons. Here's an example demonstrating how to accomplish this conversion. The code includes comments to explain each step in detail.

➢ Example: Converting text to number

```
Sub ConvertTextToNumber()
    ' This subroutine demonstrates how to convert a number
stored as text to a numeric data type in VBA.

    ' Assume we have a number stored as text.
    Dim textNumber As String
    textNumber = "123.45"

    ' Convert the text to a Double using CDbl.
    ' You could use CLng for long integers, CInt for
integers, etc., depending on your needs.
    Dim numericValue As Double
    numericValue = CDbl(textNumber)

    ' Now, numericValue holds the numeric representation
of textNumber, and you can perform mathematical
operations.
    ' For example, let's add 10 to this number.
    numericValue = numericValue + 10

    ' Display the result to verify the conversion and
operation.
    MsgBox "The converted number plus 10 is: " &
numericValue
End Sub
```

This subroutine, `ConvertTextToNumber`, starts by defining a string `textNumber` that represents a number stored as text. It then uses the `CDbl` function to convert this text to a `Double`, which is a data type suitable for holding numbers with decimals. After the conversion, you can perform any mathematical operation on the `numericValue`. The example adds 10 to the converted value and displays the result.

The choice of conversion function (`CDbl`, `CLng`, `CInt`, etc.) depends on the specific type of number you're working with (e.g., integers, long integers, floating-point numbers) and the requirements of your application. This method ensures that numbers initially stored as text are correctly treated as numerical data in your VBA code.

Convert number to letter

If by **"convert number to letter"** you mean mapping numerical values to their corresponding alphabetical representations (e.g., 1 -> A, 2 -> B, ..., 26 -> Z), you can accomplish this using a simple function in VBA. This function will be useful for scenarios where you need to generate alphabetic sequences based on numeric input. Here's how you can do it:

➢ Example: Function to convert number to letter

```
Function NumberToLetter(number As Integer) As String
    ' This function converts a number to its corresponding
letter in the alphabet.
    ' For example, 1 -> A, 2 -> B, ..., 26 -> Z.
    ' Inputs outside the range 1-26 will result in an
empty string.

    If number >= 1 And number <= 26 Then
        ' The ASCII code for uppercase A is 65. Subtract 1
from the number to align with this (e.g., 1 -> 65 (A)).
        NumberToLetter = Chr(64 + number)
    Else
        ' Return an empty string if the number is outside
the valid range.
        NumberToLetter = ""
    End If
End Function


Sub TestNumberToLetter()
    ' Test the NumberToLetter function with a sample
number.
```

```
Dim testNumber As Integer
testNumber = 3 ' Example number to convert.


' Display the result using a message box.
MsgBox "The letter corresponding to number " &
testNumber & " is " & NumberToLetter(testNumber)
End Sub
```

This code snippet provides a `NumberToLetter` function that takes an integer as input and returns a string representing the corresponding letter of the alphabet. The function checks if the input number is within the valid range (1-26), calculates the corresponding letter using the `Chr` function, and returns it. If the input number is outside the valid range, the function returns an empty string.

The `TestNumberToLetter` subroutine demonstrates how to call the `NumberToLetter` function with a sample number and display the result. This example showcases a basic but useful operation that can be expanded or modified for more complex alphanumeric mapping tasks in VBA.

Convert string to number

Converting a string to a number in VBA is a common task, especially when dealing with values input as text that need to be processed numerically. VBA provides several functions to perform this conversion, such as `CInt`, `CLng`, `CSng`, `CDbl`, etc., depending on the type of number you're working with (integer, long, single, double, etc.). Below is an example that demonstrates how to convert a string to a double-precision floating-point number, which is one of the more commonly required conversions.

➢ Example: Converting string to number

```
Sub ConvertStringToNumber()
    ' This subroutine demonstrates how to convert a string
to a Double in VBA.


    ' Assume we have a string that represents a floating-
point number.
    Dim strNumber As String
    strNumber = "123.45"
```

```
' Use CDbl to convert the string to a Double.
' CDbl is used here for demonstration; you may use
CInt, CLng, CSng, etc., based on your specific needs.
Dim dblNumber As Double
dblNumber = CDbl(strNumber)

' Now, dblNumber holds the numeric representation of
strNumber, allowing for numerical operations.
' For instance, let's multiply the number by 2.
dblNumber = dblNumber * 2

' Display the result to verify the conversion and
multiplication.
MsgBox "The result of multiplying the string-converted
number by 2 is: " & dblNumber
End Sub
```

This subroutine, `ConvertStringToNumber`, first defines a string `strNumber` containing a numeric value in text form. It then uses the `CDbl` function to convert this text to a `Double`, which is a numeric data type suitable for holding numbers with decimals. After conversion, it performs a multiplication operation on the resulting numeric value to demonstrate that it's now a number, not a text string. The result of this operation is then displayed in a message box.

The conversion function you choose (`CInt`, `CLng`, `CSng`, `CDbl`, etc.) depends on the type of number you expect to work with. This ensures the converted value is appropriate for your calculations or data processing needs.

Convert string to text

In VBA, strings are already treated as text, meaning there's no explicit conversion required to treat a string variable as text. Strings can hold any text content, including numbers, symbols, and letters. However, it might be useful to demonstrate how to work with strings in ways that are commonly needed, such as formatting or manipulating string content. Here's an example that shows how to take a numeric value stored as a string, format it, and then use it within a more complex string (text) context. This could be interpreted as converting and using "string to text" in a practical scenario.

➢ Example: Formatting and using strings as text

```vba
Sub FormatAndUseStringAsText()
    ' This subroutine demonstrates working with a numeric
string,
    ' formatting it, and then using it within a textual
context.

    ' Start with a numeric value in string format.
    Dim strNumber As String
    strNumber = "1234.56"

    ' Perhaps we want to format this number for display
purposes.
    ' Convert the string to a Double then format it to
include commas and two decimal places.
    Dim formattedNumber As String
    formattedNumber = Format(CDbl(strNumber), "#,##0.00")

    ' Now, use this formatted number in a textual context.
    Dim messageText As String
    messageText = "The formatted value is: " &
formattedNumber

    ' Display the result to verify the formatting and
concatenation.
    MsgBox messageText
End Sub
```

This subroutine, `FormatAndUseStringAsText`, demonstrates taking a numeric value stored as a string, converting it to a numeric type for formatting purposes, and then formatting it as a string with commas and two decimal places. This is a common need when preparing numeric strings for display or reporting purposes. The formatted string is then concatenated with additional text to form a more complex message, showcasing how strings (text) can be manipulated and presented in VBA. This process can be thought of as taking a raw string (number as text) and converting or preparing it for use as part of a more meaningful text output.

Convert string yyyymmdd to date

Converting a string in the format "yyyymmdd" to a date type in VBA requires parsing the string to extract the year, month, and day components, and then constructing a date from these components. Below is a straightforward example that demonstrates how to perform this conversion. The code includes comments for clarity.

➢ Example: Converting string "yyyymmdd" to date

```
Function ConvertStringToDate(strDate As String) As Date
    ' This function converts a string in "yyyymmdd" format
to a Date type.

    ' Extract the year, month, and day from the string.
    ' The Left, Mid, and Right functions are used to parse
the string.
    Dim yearPart As Integer: yearPart = CInt(Left(strDate,
4))
    Dim monthPart As Integer: monthPart =
CInt(Mid(strDate, 5, 2))
    Dim dayPart As Integer: dayPart = CInt(Right(strDate,
2))

    ' Use the DateSerial function to construct the date
from year, month, and day parts.
    ConvertStringToDate = DateSerial(yearPart, monthPart,
dayPart)
End Function

Sub TestConvertStringToDate()
    ' Test the ConvertStringToDate function with a sample
string date.
    Dim testDateString As String
    testDateString = "20240311" ' Example string date to
convert.

    ' Convert the string to a Date and store the result.
```

How to do this in VBA?? 202 ready-made macros: Streamline your tasks with proven expert solutions

```
Dim resultDate As Date
resultDate = ConvertStringToDate(testDateString)


' Display the result to verify the conversion.
' The Format function is used to display the date in a
more readable form.
MsgBox "The converted date is: " & Format(resultDate,
"mmmm dd, yyyy")
End Sub
```

This code snippet consists of a function `ConvertStringToDate` that takes a string parameter in "yyyymmdd" format and returns a `Date` type. It uses the `Left`, `Mid`, and `Right` functions to parse the year, month, and day parts of the input string, respectively. These parts are then converted to integers and passed to the `DateSerial` function, which constructs and returns the corresponding date.

The `TestConvertStringToDate` subroutine demonstrates how to use the `ConvertStringToDate` function, passing a test string as input and displaying the converted date using a message box. This example showcases a basic yet effective approach to handling date strings in custom formats in VBA.

Convert xls to xlsx

Converting an Excel file from the older `.xls` format to the newer `.xlsx` format can be accomplished using VBA by opening the `.xls` workbook and then saving it in the `.xlsx` format. Below is an example that demonstrates this process. Note that to run this example, you'll need to have access to Excel and the VBA editor within Excel.

➤ Example: Converting `.xls` to `.xlsx` using VBA

```
Sub ConvertXLSToXLSX()
    ' This subroutine demonstrates how to convert an .xls
    file to .xlsx format.


    ' Define the path to the source .xls file.
    ' Update this path to the actual location of your .xls
    file.
    Dim sourceFilePath As String
    sourceFilePath = "C:\Path\To\Your\File.xls"
```

```vba
    ' Define the path and filename for the .xlsx file to
be created.
    ' Ensure this directory exists or the script will
error.
    Dim destinationFilePath As String
    destinationFilePath = "C:\Path\To\Your\File.xlsx"

    ' Open the .xls workbook.
    Dim xlsWorkbook As Workbook
    Set xlsWorkbook = Workbooks.Open(sourceFilePath)

    ' Save the workbook in .xlsx format.
    ' The FileFormat parameter for .xlsx is 51.
    xlsWorkbook.SaveAs Filename:=destinationFilePath,
FileFormat:=xlOpenXMLWorkbook

    ' Close the workbook.
    xlsWorkbook.Close SaveChanges:=False

    ' Optionally, you can inform the user that the
conversion is complete.
    MsgBox "Conversion complete. The file was saved to: "
& destinationFilePath
    End Sub
```

To use this code, you'll need to:

1. Open Excel and press `Alt + F11` to open the VBA editor.
2. Insert a new module by right-clicking on any of the objects in the Project Explorer and selecting `Insert` > `Module`.
3. Copy and paste the `ConvertXLSToXLSX` subroutine into the module window.
4. Update the `sourceFilePath` and `destinationFilePath` variables in the script to reflect the actual paths to the `.xls` file you want to convert and where you want to save the `.xlsx` file.
5. Run the subroutine by pressing `F5` or by using the Run button.

This script opens the specified `.xls` file, saves it as an `.xlsx` file using the `SaveAs` method with the appropriate `FileFormat` parameter, and then closes the original workbook. It's a straightforward way to automate the conversion process for multiple files if needed.

Copy and paste

Copying and pasting data within an Excel workbook is a common task automated with VBA. Below is an example that demonstrates how to copy a range from one worksheet and paste it into another worksheet within the same workbook. The comments in the code explain each step of the process.

➢ Example: Copy and paste in Excel VBA

```
Sub CopyAndPasteRange()
    ' This subroutine copies a range from one worksheet
    and pastes it into another.

    ' Define variables for the source and destination
    worksheets.
    Dim sourceSheet As Worksheet
    Dim destinationSheet As Worksheet

    ' Set the source and destination worksheets.
    ' Adjust "Sheet1" and "Sheet2" to the actual names of
    your worksheets.
    Set sourceSheet = ThisWorkbook.Sheets("Sheet1")
    Set destinationSheet = ThisWorkbook.Sheets("Sheet2")

    ' Copy a specific range from the source sheet.
    ' Here, we're copying the range A1:A10. Adjust this
    range as needed.
    sourceSheet.Range("A1:A10").Copy

    ' Paste the copied range into the destination sheet at
    a specific starting cell.
    ' This example pastes into cell B1 of the destination
    sheet.
```

```
    ' PasteSpecial allows you to specify different paste
types like values, formats, etc.
    ' For example, to paste only values use
Paste:=xlPasteValues.
    ' Here, we're using xlPasteAll to paste everything
(including formats, values, formulas).
    destinationSheet.Range("B1").PasteSpecial
Paste:=xlPasteAll


    ' Optional: Clear the clipboard to remove the
"marching ants" around the copied range.
    Application.CutCopyMode = False
End Sub
```

This subroutine, `CopyAndPasteRange`, uses the `Copy` method to copy a specified range from one worksheet and the `PasteSpecial` method to paste it into a specific location on another worksheet. The `PasteSpecial` method is versatile, allowing for various paste options (e.g., pasting values only, formats, formulas, etc.). After pasting, the `Application.CutCopyMode = False` statement is used to clear the clipboard and remove the selection outline (the "marching ants") from the copied range.

This example showcases a basic but fundamental operation in Excel VBA, serving as a foundation for more complex data manipulation tasks.

Create a JSON file

Creating a JSON file in VBA involves formatting your data as a JSON string and then saving that string to a file. VBA does not have built-in JSON support, so you manually format the JSON string. Here's an example that demonstrates how to create a simple JSON string and write it to a file. This example uses a hard-coded JSON string, which represents an object with a couple of properties, for demonstration purposes.

➢ Example: Creating and writing a JSON file in VBA

```
    Sub CreateJSONFile()
        ' This subroutine creates a JSON string and writes it
    to a file.

        ' Define the JSON string.
```

How to do this in VBA?? 202 ready-made macros: Streamline your tasks with proven expert solutions

```vba
    ' Here, we're creating a JSON string that represents
an object with two properties.
    Dim jsonString As String
    jsonString = "{""name"":""John Doe"",""age"":30}"

    ' Set the path and filename where the JSON file will
be saved.
    ' Update the path as needed.
    Dim filePath As String
    filePath = "C:\Path\To\Your\file.json"

    ' Create a FileSystemObject to handle the file
creation and writing.
    Dim fs As Object
    Set fs = CreateObject("Scripting.FileSystemObject")

    ' Create the file (or open it if it already exists)
and write the JSON string.
    Dim jsonFile As Object
    Set jsonFile = fs.CreateTextFile(filePath, True)
    jsonFile.Write jsonString

    ' Close the file.
    jsonFile.Close

    ' Clean up.
    Set jsonFile = Nothing
    Set fs = Nothing

    ' Notify the user that the file has been created.
    MsgBox "JSON file created at: " & filePath
End Sub
```

This subroutine uses the `FileSystemObject` (part of the Microsoft Scripting Runtime) to create a text file and write a JSON string to it. The JSON string (`jsonString`) is manually formatted to represent a simple object with a name and age. The file path (`filePath`) is where the JSON file will be saved, and you should adjust this to an appropriate location on your system.

Before running this example, make sure the path exists or adjust the `filePath` variable to point to a valid directory on your machine. This example provides a basic template for creating and saving JSON data from VBA, which you can expand upon to include more complex data structures or to dynamically generate the JSON string based on your application's data.

Create xml file

Creating an XML file in VBA involves leveraging the `Microsoft XML, v6.0` library (or similar) to construct the XML structure and then saving it to a file. Below is an example that demonstrates how to create a simple XML document representing a list of users, each with a name and age, and save this document to an XML file. This example uses comments to guide you through each step.

➢ Example: Creating and writing an XML file in VBA

```
Sub CreateXMLFile()
    ' This subroutine demonstrates how to create an XML
file in VBA.
    ' It requires a reference to the Microsoft XML, v6.0
library.
    ' You can set this reference by going to Tools ->
References in the VBA editor
    ' and checking "Microsoft XML, v6.0".


    ' Create a new XML DOM document instance.
    Dim xmlDoc As MSXML2.DOMDocument60
    Set xmlDoc = New MSXML2.DOMDocument60


    ' Create the root element 'Users' and append it to the
document.
    Dim usersNode As MSXML2.IXMLDOMNode
    Set usersNode = xmlDoc.createElement("Users")
    xmlDoc.appendChild usersNode
```

How to do this in VBA?? 202 ready-made macros: Streamline your tasks with proven expert solutions

```vba
    ' Add a user element to the 'Users' node.
    Dim userNode As MSXML2.IXMLDOMNode
    Dim nameNode As MSXML2.IXMLDOMNode
    Dim ageNode As MSXML2.IXMLDOMNode

    ' Create and append the first user.
    Set userNode = xmlDoc.createElement("User")
    ' Create a 'Name' element, set its text, and append it
to the 'User' node.
    Set nameNode = xmlDoc.createElement("Name")
    nameNode.Text = "John Doe"
    userNode.appendChild nameNode
    ' Create an 'Age' element, set its text, and append it
to the 'User' node.
    Set ageNode = xmlDoc.createElement("Age")
    ageNode.Text = "30"
    userNode.appendChild ageNode
    ' Append the 'User' node to the 'Users' node.
    usersNode.appendChild userNode

    ' Optionally, create and append more users in a
similar way...

    ' Save the XML document to a file.
    ' Specify your desired path and file name here.
    Dim filePath As String
    filePath = "C:\Path\To\Your\users.xml"
    xmlDoc.Save filePath

    ' Notify the user that the XML file has been created.
    MsgBox "XML file created at: " & filePath
End Sub
```

➢ Steps to use this example:

1. Enable the Microsoft XML Library:

How to do this in VBA?? 202 ready-made macros: Streamline your tasks with proven expert solutions

- Open the VBA editor in Excel (or another Office application) by pressing `Alt + F11`.
- Go to `Tools` -> `References...` in the menu.
- Scroll down and check `Microsoft XML, v6.0` (or a similar version if 6.0 is not available).
- Click `OK` to add the reference to your project.

2. Add the VBA code:

- Insert a new module by right-clicking on any of the items in the `Project` window, then select `Insert` -> `Module`.
- Copy and paste the provided code into the new module.

3. Run the Code:

- Press `F5` or click `Run` -> `Run Sub/UserForm` and select `CreateXMLFile`.

4. Check the Output:

- Navigate to the specified `filePath` on your system to view the created XML file.

This example outlines creating a basic XML structure with VBA and saving it to a file. You can modify the element names, attributes, and text content to fit your specific requirements.

Declare a variable

Declaring variables in VBA is fundamental for writing clear and maintainable code. Variables are declared using the `Dim` statement, and it's best practice to specify the data type of the variable to ensure your code works as expected. Below are examples that demonstrate how to declare variables of different data types in VBA. Each example includes comments that explain the purpose and usage of the variable being declared.

➢ Example: Declaring variables in VBA

```
Sub DeclareVariables()
    ' Declare a variable as an Integer.
    Dim myInteger As Integer
    myInteger = 10
```

How to do this in VBA?? 202 ready-made macros: Streamline your tasks with proven expert solutions

```vba
    ' Declare a variable as a Double for fractional
numbers or larger ranges.
    Dim myDouble As Double
    myDouble = 123.456

    ' Declare a variable as a String for textual data.
    Dim myString As String
    myString = "Hello, World!"

    ' Declare a variable as a Boolean for true/false
values.
    Dim myBoolean As Boolean
    myBoolean = True

    ' Declare a Date variable for date and time values.
    Dim myDate As Date
    myDate = Now

    ' Declare an Object variable. Can be used for Excel
objects like Range, Worksheet, etc.
    Dim myRange As Range
    Set myRange =
ThisWorkbook.Sheets("Sheet1").Range("A1")

    ' Use MsgBox to display values for demonstration.
    MsgBox "Integer: " & myInteger & vbNewLine & _
           "Double: " & myDouble & vbNewLine & _
           "String: " & myString & vbNewLine & _
           "Boolean: " & myBoolean & vbNewLine & _
           "Date: " & myDate & vbNewLine & _
           "Range Address: " & myRange.Address
    End Sub
```

This subroutine, `DeclareVariables`, showcases the declaration of variables with different data types: `Integer`, `Double`, `String`, `Boolean`, `Date`, and an `Object` (specifically a `Range` object in Excel). For object variables (like `myRange`), the `Set` keyword is used to assign the object reference.

How to do this in VBA?? 202 ready-made macros: Streamline your tasks with proven expert solutions

➢ Running the Example:

1. Open the VBA Editor in Excel by pressing `Alt + F11`.
2. Insert a new module into your VBA project by right-clicking on any of the project items and selecting `Insert` -> `Module`.
3. Copy and paste the code example into the new module.
4. Run the subroutine by pressing `F5` while the cursor is within the code or by using the Run menu.

This example illustrates the basics of variable declaration in VBA, setting the foundation for writing more complex and functional macros.

Declare array

Declaring arrays in VBA is a powerful way to work with a set of variables under a single name, where each item in an array is accessed by an index. Below are examples showing how to declare different types of arrays in VBA, including fixed-size arrays, dynamic arrays, and multi-dimensional arrays. The comments explain the purpose and usage of each array declaration.

➢ Example: Declaring arrays in VBA

```
Sub DeclareArrays()
    ' Declare a fixed-size array.
    ' Here, a fixed-size array of 5 integers is declared.
    Dim fixedArray(4) As Integer

    ' Assign values to the fixed-size array by index.
    fixedArray(0) = 10
    fixedArray(1) = 20
    fixedArray(2) = 30
    fixedArray(3) = 40
    fixedArray(4) = 50

    ' Declare a dynamic array.
    ' Initially, the dynamic array does not have a size.
    Dim dynamicArray() As Integer

    ' Later in the code, the size of the dynamic array can
    be set or resized using ReDim.
```

```
ReDim dynamicArray(4)


' Assign values to the dynamic array.
dynamicArray(0) = 100
dynamicArray(1) = 200
dynamicArray(2) = 300
dynamicArray(3) = 400
dynamicArray(4) = 500


' Declare a multi-dimensional array.
' This example creates a 2D array with 2 rows and 3
columns.
Dim multiArray(1, 2) As Integer


' Assign values to the multi-dimensional array by
specifying row and column indexes.
multiArray(0, 0) = 1
multiArray(0, 1) = 2
multiArray(0, 2) = 3
multiArray(1, 0) = 4
multiArray(1, 1) = 5
multiArray(1, 2) = 6


' MsgBox to display a value from each array for
demonstration.
MsgBox "Fixed Array first element: " & fixedArray(0) &
vbNewLine & _
        "Dynamic Array first element: " &
dynamicArray(0) & vbNewLine & _
        "Multi-dimensional Array first element: " &
multiArray(0, 0)
End Sub
```

➤ Explanation:

- **Fixed-Size Array**: Declared with a specific number of elements. The size cannot be changed after the declaration. In the example, `fixedArray` is declared to hold 5 integer values.

How to do this in VBA?? 202 ready-made macros: Streamline your tasks with proven expert solutions

- **Dynamic Array**: Declared without a size, allowing it to be set or changed at runtime using `ReDim`. `dynamicArray` is an example, resized to hold 5 elements.
- **Multi-Dimensional Array**: Declared with more than one dimension. `multiArray` is a 2-dimensional array with 2 rows and 3 columns.

These examples demonstrate the flexibility of arrays in VBA, enabling efficient storage and manipulation of collections of values.

Delete a file

Deleting a file in VBA can be accomplished by using the `Kill` statement, which allows you to delete files from your file system. Below is an example that demonstrates how to safely attempt to delete a file with error handling to prevent the program from crashing if the file does not exist or another error occurs.

➢ Example: Deleting a file with error handling

```
Sub DeleteFile()
    ' This subroutine demonstrates how to delete a file
using VBA.

    ' Define the path of the file to be deleted.
    ' Ensure you replace this with the actual path to the
file you want to delete.
    Dim filePath As String
    filePath = "C:\Path\To\Your\File.txt"

    ' Attempt to delete the file with error handling to
catch any problems like file not found.
    On Error Resume Next ' Ignore errors and continue
execution.
    Kill filePath ' Delete the file.

    ' Check if an error occurred during file deletion.
    If Err.Number <> 0 Then
        ' Display an error message if there was a problem
deleting the file.
```

```
            MsgBox "Error deleting file: " & Err.Description,
    vbCritical
            Err.Clear ' Clear the error.
        Else
            ' Notify the user that the file was successfully
    deleted.
            MsgBox "File successfully deleted: " & filePath,
    vbInformation
        End If
        On Error GoTo 0 ' Turn back on default error handling.
    End Sub
```

➢ Notes:

- **Error Handling**: This example uses `On Error Resume Next` to prevent the subroutine from stopping if the `Kill` statement fails (e.g., if the file does not exist). After attempting to delete the file, it checks `Err.Number` to see if an error occurred.
- **Safety**: Be cautious when deleting files programmatically. Once deleted, the file cannot be easily recovered. Always ensure the file path is correct and consider implementing additional checks before deletion if necessary.
- **File Path**: The `filePath` variable should be updated to reflect the actual path of the file you intend to delete. Make sure the path is correct to avoid unintended data loss.

By following these guidelines and modifying the `filePath` variable to target the correct file, you can use this subroutine to delete files as needed in your VBA projects.

Delete a row

Deleting a row in an Excel worksheet using VBA can be accomplished by specifying the row number and using the `Delete` method on the `Rows` collection. Below is a simple example that demonstrates how to delete a specific row from an active worksheet. This example includes comments for clarity and to explain each step of the process.

➢ Example: Deleting a row in Excel VBA

```
    Sub DeleteSpecificRow()
```

```
    ' This subroutine demonstrates how to delete a
specific row in an Excel worksheet.


    ' Define the row number you want to delete.
    ' For this example, we will delete row 5. Adjust this
value as needed.
    Dim rowNumber As Long
    rowNumber = 5


    ' Use the Rows object and the Delete method to remove
the specified row.
    ' The Rows object represents all the rows in the
worksheet, and by specifying
    ' a row number, you can reference a single row.
    Rows(rowNumber & ":" & rowNumber).Delete


    ' Alternatively, for a single row, you can simplify it
as:
    ' Rows(rowNumber).Delete


    ' Note: This action cannot be undone via VBA once
executed.
    ' It's a good practice to prompt the user for
confirmation before deleting.
    End Sub
```

➢ Key points:

- **Row Number**: The `rowNumber` variable specifies the row to delete. You can adjust this to target a different row.
- **Delete Method**: The `Delete` method is called on the `Rows` collection to remove the row. The syntax `Rows(rowNumber & ":" & rowNumber).Delete` allows for deleting a range of rows if needed; however, for deleting a single row, simply `Rows(rowNumber).Delete` is also valid.
- **Caution**: Deletion is permanent within the context of the macro's execution, and users cannot undo this action via Excel's undo feature once the macro completes. Implementing a confirmation dialog box

How to do this in VBA?? 202 ready-made macros: Streamline your tasks with proven expert solutions

(`MsgBox` with `vbYesNo`) before performing the delete operation can prevent accidental data loss.

➢To use this code:

1. Open Excel and the VBA editor (`Alt + F11`).
2. Insert a new module into your VBA project (right-click any object in the **Project Explorer > Insert > Module**).
3. Copy and paste the provided code into the new module.
4. Run the subroutine by pressing `F5` while the cursor is within the code or via the Run menu.

This approach provides a straightforward method for programmatically managing row deletions within Excel sheets, enhancing the automation of data organization and cleanup tasks.

Delete a sheet

Deleting a worksheet in an Excel workbook using VBA involves the `Delete` method of the `Worksheet` object. It's important to handle this action with care, as once a worksheet is deleted, it cannot be recovered programmatically. Below is a simple example demonstrating how to delete a worksheet by name, with appropriate error handling to avoid disrupting the user if the specified sheet does not exist or if the user decides not to proceed with the deletion.

➢ Example: Deleting a worksheet in Excel VBA

```
Sub DeleteWorksheetByName()
    ' This subroutine demonstrates how to safely delete a
    worksheet by name in Excel using VBA.

    ' Specify the name of the worksheet you want to
    delete.
    Dim sheetName As String
    sheetName = "SheetToDelete"

    ' Disable alerts to prevent Excel from showing
    messages asking for delete confirmation.
    Application.DisplayAlerts = False

    ' Attempt to delete the worksheet.
```

```
    On Error Resume Next ' Use error handling to catch if
the sheet does not exist.
    Dim ws As Worksheet
    Set ws = ThisWorkbook.Sheets(sheetName)
    If Not ws Is Nothing Then
        ws.Delete
        MsgBox sheetName & " has been deleted.",
vbInformation
    Else
        MsgBox "Sheet '" & sheetName & "' does not
exist.", vbExclamation
    End If
    On Error GoTo 0 ' Turn back to the default error
handling.


    ' Re-enable alerts after deletion attempt.
    Application.DisplayAlerts = True
End Sub
```

➢ Key points:

- **Sheet Name**: Replace `"SheetToDelete"` with the actual name of the sheet you wish to delete.
- **Display Alerts**: `Application.DisplayAlerts = False` temporarily disables Excel's confirmation dialog when deleting sheets, making the deletion process smoother. It's crucial to set `Application.DisplayAlerts` back to `True` afterwards to ensure Excel behaves normally for other actions.
- **Error Handling: On Error Resume Next** is used to gracefully handle the scenario where the specified sheet does not exist. This prevents the macro from crashing. After attempting to delete the sheet, error handling is reset with `On Error GoTo 0`.
- **Confirmation Message**: After deleting the sheet, a message box confirms the action. If the sheet wasn't found, the user is informed.

➢ Safety considerations:

- **Irreversible Action**: Sheet deletion is permanent within the context of the VBA macro's execution. Consider adding a confirmation dialog (`MsgBox` with `vbYesNo`) before executing the delete operation.

- **Sheet Existence Check**: The code checks if the worksheet exists before attempting deletion, minimizing errors and unintended consequences.

This example provides a basic framework for deleting worksheets within Excel via VBA, illustrating key practices for safe operation, including error handling and user alerts management.

Delete columns

Deleting columns in Excel using VBA is a straightforward task that can greatly help in automating data manipulation and cleanup processes. Below is an example demonstrating how to delete a specific column by its letter identifier. This method can easily be adapted to delete multiple columns or columns identified by their numeric index.

➢ Example: Deleting a specific column in Excel VBA

```
Sub DeleteSpecificColumn()
    ' This subroutine demonstrates how to delete a
specific column in an Excel worksheet.

    ' Define the column letter you want to delete.
    ' For this example, we'll delete column "C".
    ' You can change "C" to any column letter you need to
delete.
    Dim columnLetter As String
    columnLetter = "C"

    ' Use the Columns property to reference the column and
call the Delete method.
    ' This deletes the entire column from the worksheet.
    Columns(columnLetter & ":" & columnLetter).Delete

    ' Note: You could also delete columns by their numeric
index. For example,
    ' Columns(3).Delete would delete the third column
(which is "C" in a default sheet).
```

```
        ' Optional: If you're deleting multiple contiguous
    columns, you can specify a range.
        ' For example, to delete columns "B" to "D", you would
    use:
        ' Columns("B:D").Delete

        ' Warning: Deleting columns cannot be undone with VBA
    once the macro finishes.
        ' Consider adding a confirmation message before
    executing the delete command.
    End Sub
```

➢ Key considerations:

- **Column letter**: the `columnLetter` variable holds the letter of the column you wish to delete. Modify this according to the column you're targeting.
- **Deletion command**: the `Delete` method is used on the `Columns` object to remove the specified column. This action is immediate and affects all rows in the column.
- **Numeric index**: columns can also be referenced by their numeric index (e.g., `Columns(3).Delete`), which can be useful in loops or when column positions are calculated dynamically.
- **Contiguous columns**: to delete a range of contiguous columns, specify the start and end columns in the format `"StartColumn:EndColumn"` within the `Columns` property.
- **Irreversibility**: once executed, the deletion action cannot be reversed by VBA. Implementing user confirmation (e.g., via `MsgBox` with `vbYesNo`) can prevent accidental data loss.

This code provides a basic template for column deletion tasks in Excel VBA, showcasing both direct column reference and deletion methods. Adjustments can be made to accommodate different scenarios, such as deleting non-contiguous columns or incorporating user confirmations for safety.

Deselect in Excel

Deselecting cells or ranges in Excel VBA isn't directly supported in the way selection is, because the `Select` method doesn't have a direct inverse. However, you can achieve a "deselect" effect by either selecting a single cell, typically `A1` or any other cell you prefer, or by using the `Activate` method on a single cell, which moves the focus but doesn't highlight the cell as `Select` does. This can effectively "deselect" any previously selected range. Below is an example showing both approaches.

➤ Example: Deselecting cells/ranges in Excel VBA

```
Sub DeselectCells()
    ' This subroutine demonstrates two methods to
effectively deselect cells/ranges in Excel VBA.

    ' Method 1: Select a single cell, often A1, to
deselect any other selection.
    ' This changes the selection to just this cell.
    Range("A1").Select

    ' Do some tasks...

    ' Method 2: Use the Activate method to move the focus
without selecting.
    ' This doesn't highlight the cell as Select does, but
moves the cursor and deselects any range.
    ' Note: Only one cell or object can be active at a
time, so this method effectively deselects other
cells/ranges.
    Range("A1").Activate

    ' After running this, you'll notice that any previous
selection is no longer highlighted,
    ' effectively achieving a "deselect" action.

    ' Note: Using Activate is a more subtle way to remove
focus from a selection without
    ' making it obvious that a specific cell is now
selected.
End Sub
```

Important considerations:

- **Method choice**: if you prefer not to change the current selection visibly but need to ensure no range is selected for subsequent operations, using `Activate` on a single cell is more subtle than `Select`.

- **Selection side effects**: both methods change the active cell, which might not always be desirable, especially if you have a complex worksheet where the active cell is important for context or formulas.
- **Action reversal**: unlike many actions in Excel, there's no direct way to "undo" a deselection because it doesn't affect the content or structure of your worksheet, only the current focus or selection state.

This approach is handy in macros where you need to clear selections without significantly disrupting the user's view or the current state of the workbook. Adjust the target cell for `Select` or `Activate` as necessary for your specific use case.

Deselect in Word

Deselecting text or objects in Word via VBA involves a different approach compared to Excel. In Word, you can achieve a "deselect" effect by collapsing the selection. This essentially removes any text selection and places the cursor at the start or end of the original selection. Here's how to do it:

➤ Example: Deselecting in Word VBA

```
Sub DeselectText()
    ' This subroutine demonstrates how to deselect text in
Word by collapsing the selection.

    ' Check if anything is selected in the document.
    If Selection.Type <> wdSelectionNone Then
        ' Collapse the selection to the start position,
effectively deselecting text.
        ' Use wdCollapseStart to collapse to the beginning
of the selection.
        ' Use wdCollapseEnd to collapse to the end of the
selection.
        Selection.Collapse Direction:=wdCollapseStart

        ' Alternatively, to collapse to the end, you could
use:
        ' Selection.Collapse Direction:=wdCollapseEnd
```

How to do this in VBA?? 202 ready-made macros: Streamline your tasks with proven expert solutions

```
      End If


      ' After this, the selection is cleared (deselected),
   and the cursor is placed
      ' at the beginning or the end of the original
   selection, based on your choice.
   End Sub
```

➤ Key points:

- **Selection check**: it's good practice to check if there is a selection (`wdSelectionNone`) before attempting to collapse it. This ensures that the macro won't run into errors if there's nothing selected.
- **Collapse direction**: the `Collapse` method takes a `Direction` parameter that can be either `wdCollapseStart` or `wdCollapseEnd`, determining where the cursor will be placed after deselecting. This gives you control over the resulting cursor position.
- **Cursor placement**: this method does not remove or alter the selected text; it simply clears the selection and moves the cursor, making it ready for the next action without any text being actively selected.

This code snippet provides a straightforward way to clear any text selection in Word with VBA, useful in various macro-driven text processing or document editing tasks where you need to reset the selection state as part of the workflow.

Dim

In VBA, the `Dim` statement is used for variable declaration, allowing you to specify the name and type of a variable. Declaring variables is a fundamental aspect of writing clear and efficient VBA code, as it helps with readability and can prevent type-related errors. Here's an example demonstrating how to declare variables of different types using `Dim`, along with comments explaining each declaration.

➤ Example: Using `Dim` to declare variables in VBA

```
   Sub DeclareVariablesUsingDim()
      ' Declare an integer variable.
      Dim myInteger As Integer
      myInteger = 10
```

```vba
' Declare a double precision floating point variable.
Dim myDouble As Double
myDouble = 3.14159

' Declare a string variable.
Dim myString As String
myString = "Hello, VBA!"

' Declare a boolean variable.
Dim myBoolean As Boolean
myBoolean = True

' Declare a date variable.
Dim myDate As Date
myDate = #12/31/2023#

' Declare an object variable. Here, using it to hold a
reference to a Worksheet object.
Dim mySheet As Worksheet
Set mySheet = ThisWorkbook.Sheets("Sheet1")

' Displaying the values assigned to the variables in a
message box.
MsgBox "Integer: " & myInteger & vbCrLf & _
       "Double: " & myDouble & vbCrLf & _
       "String: " & myString & vbCrLf & _
       "Boolean: " & myBoolean & vbCrLf & _
       "Date: " & myDate & vbCrLf & _
       "Worksheet Name: " & mySheet.Name
End Sub
```

➤ Key points:

- **Type specification**: each variable is declared with a specific data type (`Integer`, `Double`, `String`, `Boolean`, `Date`, `Worksheet`), which determines the kind of data it can hold.
- **Object variables**: for object variables like `**mySheet**`, use the `Set` keyword to assign an object reference to the variable.

- **Initialization**: variables can be initialized (assigned a value) immediately after declaration or at any point later in the code before they're used.

This example covers basic variable declaration and initialization in VBA, illustrating how to use the `Dim` statement to define variables of various types. Understanding and using proper variable types is crucial for developing robust VBA applications and macros.

Dim array

In VBA, arrays are a useful way to store multiple items under a single name, accessible by indices. You can declare arrays using the `Dim` statement, similar to how you declare other variables, but you also specify the size or use dynamic sizing. Here are examples demonstrating how to declare both fixed-size and dynamic arrays using `Dim`, with comments to guide you.

➢ Example: Declaring fixed-size and dynamic arrays

```
Sub DeclareArrays()
    ' Declare a fixed-size array.
    ' Here, a fixed-size array of 5 elements (indices 0 to
4) is declared.
    Dim fixedArray(4) As Integer

    ' Initialize the fixed-size array elements.
    Dim i As Integer
    For i = 0 To 4
        fixedArray(i) = (i + 1) * 10 ' Assign values 10,
20, 30, 40, 50
    Next i

    ' Declare a dynamic array.
    ' At this point, the array does not have a size.
    Dim dynamicArray() As String

    ' Later in the code, define the size of the dynamic
array using ReDim.
    ' Here, sizing the array to hold 3 elements (indices 0
to 2).
```

```vba
ReDim dynamicArray(2)


' Initialize the dynamic array elements.
dynamicArray(0) = "Red"
dynamicArray(1) = "Green"
dynamicArray(2) = "Blue"


' Example of resizing a dynamic array while preserving
its content using ReDim Preserve.
' Resize the array to hold 4 elements.
ReDim Preserve dynamicArray(3)
dynamicArray(3) = "Yellow" ' Add a new color to the
array.


' Display the last element of each array to
demonstrate they have been initialized.
MsgBox "Last element of fixedArray: " & fixedArray(4)
& vbCrLf & _
        "Last element of dynamicArray: " &
dynamicArray(3)
End Sub
```

➢ Key concepts:

- **Fixed-size array**: declared with a specific number of elements. Its size cannot be changed once declared. Useful when you know in advance how many elements you need.
- **Dynamic array**: its size isn't specified at declaration. Instead, use `ReDim` to set or change its size within the code, which allows for flexibility. `ReDim Preserve` lets you resize the array while retaining its existing values.
- **Initialization**: arrays can be populated with values immediately after declaration. For fixed-size arrays, this often occurs in a loop. For dynamic arrays, you typically set initial values after sizing the array with `ReDim`.

This example showcases basic array declarations and initializations, demonstrating how VBA allows for both statically and dynamically sized arrays to suit different programming needs.

Dim range

Declaring a `Range` object in VBA is essential when you're working with cells or ranges in Excel. This allows you to programmatically manipulate these ranges, such as reading or writing values, formatting cells, and more. Below is an example that demonstrates how to declare a `Range` variable and assign it to a specific range in a worksheet. The comments in the code provide guidance on each step.

➤ Example: Declaring and using a range Variable

```
Sub DeclareAndUseRange()
    ' Declare a Range object variable.
    Dim myRange As Range

    ' Assign the Range object to a specific range of cells
in the active worksheet.
    ' Here, the range consists of cells from A1 to B2.
    Set myRange = ActiveSheet.Range("A1:B2")

    ' Now, you can manipulate the range using the
variable.
    ' For example, let's write values to this range.
    myRange.Value = "Hello, VBA!"

    ' Formatting the range - setting the font to bold.
    myRange.Font.Bold = True

    ' Setting the background color of the cells in the
range to yellow.
    ' The Color property takes RGB values - RGB(255, 255,
0) represents yellow.
    myRange.Interior.Color = RGB(255, 255, 0)

    ' It's also possible to refer to a single cell within
a range using the Cells property.
    ' For instance, changing the value of the first cell
in the range to "First Cell".
```

```
myRange.Cells(1, 1).Value = "First Cell"

    ' You can also resize and reposition the range. Here's
how to shift it one row down.
    ' Note: This does not move the content, but changes
the range reference itself.
    Set myRange = myRange.Offset(1, 0)

    ' After offsetting, let's clear the contents of the
new range to demonstrate.
    myRange.ClearContents

    ' This subroutine showcases basic operations with
Range objects:
    ' assigning ranges, writing values, formatting, and
manipulating range references.
    End Sub
```

➤ Key concepts:

- **Declaring a range**: the `Dim` statement is used to declare a variable of type `Range`.
- **Assigning a range**: the `Set` keyword assigns a specific range of cells to the `Range` variable. The range can be specified in various ways, including A1 notation, using the `Cells` method, or other `Range` methods.
- **Manipulating ranges**: Once declared and assigned, you can perform a variety of operations on the range, including modifying values, applying formatting, and adjusting the range's size or position.

This example provides a basic overview of working with `Range` objects in VBA, illustrating how to declare, assign, and use ranges for cell manipulation and data processing in Excel sheets.

Dim text

Declaring a text variable in VBA typically involves using the `String` data type, as it allows for the storage of textual data. Here's a simple example that demonstrates how to declare a `String` variable, assign text to it, and then use it within a subroutine. The comments in the code explain each step and provide additional context.

How to do this in VBA?? 202 ready-made macros: Streamline your tasks with proven expert solutions

➢ Example: Declaring and using a text variable

```
Sub DeclareAndUseTextVariable()
    ' Declare a variable with the String data type to hold
text.
    Dim myText As String

    ' Assign a text value to the variable.
    ' Strings in VBA are enclosed in double quotes.
    myText = "Hello, this is a text string in VBA!"

    ' Now that myText holds a string, you can use it in
various ways.
    ' For example, displaying the text in a message box.
    MsgBox myText

    ' Strings can also be manipulated and combined.
    ' Here's how to append more text to the original
string.
     myText = myText & " Let's add some more text."

    ' Display the updated text in a message box to see the
changes.
    MsgBox myText

    ' Additionally, you can perform operations like
finding the length of the string.
    Dim textLength As Integer
    textLength = Len(myText)

    ' Display the length of the updated text.
    MsgBox "The length of the text is: " & textLength & "
characters."
End Sub
```

➢ Key points:

- **String declaration**: the `Dim` statement is used alongside the `String` data type to declare a variable that will hold text.
- **Assigning text**: text is assigned to the variable using the `=` operator and must be enclosed in double quotes.
- **Manipulating text**: the example shows basic text manipulation, including appending additional text to the existing string and calculating the string's length using the `Len` function.

This straightforward example outlines the basics of working with text (strings) in VBA, demonstrating declaration, assignment, display, and simple manipulation. These operations form the foundation for more complex text processing and manipulation tasks in VBA programming.

Dim variable

Declaring variables in VBA is essential for writing clear and efficient code. The `Dim` statement is used to declare variables in VBA, allowing you to specify a variable's name and type. Declaring the type of a variable is highly recommended as it makes your code more robust, easier to understand, and often more efficient. Below is an example demonstrating how to declare variables of different types using `Dim`, along with comments explaining the purpose of each type.

➢ Example: Declaring various types of variables in VBA

```
Sub DeclareVariables()
    ' Declare an Integer variable. Integers are used to
store whole numbers.
    Dim myInteger As Integer
    myInteger = 100


    ' Declare a Double variable. Doubles are used for
fractional numbers or very large numbers.
    Dim myDouble As Double
    myDouble = 3.14159


    ' Declare a String variable. Strings are used to store
text.
    Dim myString As String
    myString = "Hello, VBA!"
```

```vba
    ' Declare a Boolean variable. Booleans can only hold
True or False values.
    Dim myBoolean As Boolean
    myBoolean = True

    ' Declare a Date variable. Dates are used to store
date and time.
    Dim myDate As Date
    myDate = Now() ' Assigns the current date and time to
the variable

    ' Declare a Variant variable. Variants can hold any
type of data, including numbers, text, or objects.
    ' It's more flexible but less efficient and should be
used judiciously.
    Dim myVariant As Variant
    myVariant = "This can be anything"

    ' Displaying some of the variable values
    MsgBox "Integer: " & myInteger & vbCrLf & _
           "Double: " & myDouble & vbCrLf & _
           "String: " & myString & vbCrLf & _
           "Boolean: " & myBoolean & vbCrLf & _
           "Date: " & myDate
End Sub
```

➤ Key concepts:

- **Data type specification**: when declaring variables, specifying the data type (e.g., `Integer`, `Double`, `String`, `Boolean`, `Date`, `Variant`) helps VBA manage memory more efficiently and reduces errors.
- `Dim` **Statement**: used at the beginning of a procedure to declare local variables. Variables declared with `Dim` at the module level are private to the module by default.
- **Initialization**: variables can be initialized (assigned a value) immediately after declaration or later in the code. For example, `myInteger = 100` assigns the value `100` to `myInteger`.

How to do this in VBA?? 202 ready-made macros: Streamline your tasks with proven expert solutions

This example covers the basics of variable declaration in VBA, illustrating how to use the `Dim` statement to define variables of various types. Understanding and using the correct data types is crucial for developing effective VBA solutions.

Dim worksheet

Declaring a `Worksheet` variable in VBA allows you to work with specific worksheets in an Excel workbook by referring to them through your code, making it easier to read and maintain. Here's an example demonstrating how to declare a `Worksheet` variable, assign a worksheet to it, and then use this variable to access properties and methods of the worksheet.

➢ Example: Declaring and using a worksheet variable in VBA

```
Sub DeclareAndUseWorksheet()
    ' Declare a Worksheet variable to reference a specific
worksheet.
    Dim mySheet As Worksheet

    ' Assign the worksheet named "Sheet1" to the mySheet
variable.
    ' Replace "Sheet1" with the actual name of the
worksheet you want to work with.
    Set mySheet = ThisWorkbook.Sheets("Sheet1")

    ' Now, you can use the mySheet variable to interact
with the "Sheet1".
    ' For example, write a value in cell A1 of this
worksheet.
    mySheet.Range("A1").Value = "Hello, VBA!"

    ' You can also use the Worksheet variable to change
properties, such as the name of the worksheet.
    ' Let's rename "Sheet1" to "MySheet". Ensure that the
new name does not conflict with existing sheet names.
    mySheet.Name = "MySheet"
```

```
        ' Worksheets can also be referenced by their index
number.
        ' For instance, the first worksheet in the workbook
can be referenced as follows:
        ' Set mySheet = ThisWorkbook.Sheets(1)
        ' This is useful if you know the position of the
worksheet but not its name.

        ' Using a variable to interact with worksheets
simplifies tasks such as reading from or writing to cells,
        ' manipulating worksheet properties, and navigating
through the workbook.
        End Sub
```

➢ Key Points:

- **Worksheet variable**: the `Dim` statement is used alongside the `Worksheet` type to declare a variable that can reference a worksheet within the workbook.
- **Assignment**: the `Set` keyword is necessary to assign an object (like a worksheet) to a variable in VBA.
- **Usage**: once assigned, the `mySheet` variable can be used to access and manipulate the worksheet, such as changing cell values or the worksheet's properties.
- **Sheet reference**: worksheets can be referenced by name (`Sheets("SheetName")`) or by index (`Sheets(1)`), depending on your specific needs.

This example provides a foundation for working with worksheets in VBA, illustrating how to declare, assign, and utilize a `Worksheet` variable for various tasks.

Display a message

Displaying a message in VBA is commonly achieved using the `MsgBox` function. This function can display a message box with a message, an optional title, and buttons to interact with. Here's a basic example demonstrating how to display a simple message box. The comments in the code explain the usage and purpose of each parameter.

➢ Example: Displaying a message with `MsgBox` in VBA

```vba
Sub DisplayMessage()
    ' Use the MsgBox function to display a message box to
the user.
    ' The simplest form of the MsgBox function only
requires one argument: the message string.

    MsgBox "Hello, World!"

    ' You can also add a title to the message box by
specifying a second argument.
    ' The following example includes a message and a title
for the message box.

    MsgBox "This is a basic example of using MsgBox to
display messages in VBA.", vbOKOnly, "Message Box Title"

    ' The MsgBox function can also display different types
of icons and buttons.
    ' This is specified by the second argument, which
determines the buttons to display and the icon style.
    ' For example, to display an information icon and an
OK button, you can use the vbInformation constant along
with vbOKOnly.

    MsgBox "This message box includes an information icon
and an OK button.", vbInformation + vbOKOnly,
"Information"

    ' There are several other constants that can be used
to customize the message box, including:
    ' vbExclamation, vbQuestion, vbCritical, vbYesNo,
vbYesNoCancel, vbOKCancel, and many others.
    ' These can be combined using the + operator to
achieve the desired effect.
```

```
        ' Displaying a message box with Yes and No buttons and
    a question icon.
        Dim response As VbMsgBoxResult
        response = MsgBox("Do you like VBA programming?",
    vbQuestion + vbYesNo, "Question")

        ' Handling the response from the message box.
        If response = vbYes Then
            MsgBox "Glad to hear you like VBA!",
    vbInformation, "Response"
        Else
            MsgBox "VBA can be challenging at first. Keep
    learning!", vbInformation, "Response"
        End If
    End Sub
```

This subroutine, `DisplayMessage`, showcases various ways to use the `MsgBox` function in VBA, from displaying simple messages to asking questions with custom icons and handling user responses. The `MsgBox` function is versatile and provides immediate feedback or interaction with the user, making it invaluable for debugging, notifications, and user-guided decision-making in VBA scripts.

Excel VBA loop through alphabet

Looping through the alphabet in Excel VBA can be achieved by leveraging the ASCII character codes corresponding to letters. For example, the ASCII code for uppercase '**A**' is 65, and for uppercase '**Z**' is 90. You can use a `For` loop to iterate through these codes, converting each to its corresponding character with the `Chr` function. Below is an example demonstrating how to loop through the alphabet and print each letter in the Immediate Window (accessed in the VBA editor by pressing `Ctrl+G`).

➢ Example: Looping through the Alphabet

```
    Sub LoopThroughAlphabet()
        ' This subroutine loops through the alphabet from A to
    Z
        ' and prints each letter to the Immediate Window.
```

```vba
Dim i As Integer ' Variable to hold the ASCII code.

' Loop from 65 (ASCII for 'A') to 90 (ASCII for 'Z').
For i = 65 To 90
    ' Convert the ASCII code to its character
representation and print it.
    Debug.Print Chr(i)
Next i

' If you want to loop through lowercase letters, use
97 ('a') to 122 ('z').
' For example:
' For i = 97 To 122
'     Debug.Print Chr(i)
' Next i
End Sub
```

➢ Key concepts:

- **ASCII codes**: the `For` loop iterates through the numeric ASCII codes that represent uppercase letters (65 to 90). For lowercase letters, you would loop from 97 to 122.
- **Character conversion**: the `Chr` function converts each ASCII code to its corresponding character, allowing the loop to process each letter of the alphabet.
- **Output**: the `Debug.Print` statement outputs each letter to the Immediate Window, providing a simple way to observe the loop's operation.

This code snippet offers a basic method for iterating over all the letters in the alphabet, demonstrating control structures, character encoding, and debugging output in VBA. This approach can be adapted for various tasks, such as generating alphabetic lists, processing letter-based data, or any scenario where you need to work with the letters of the alphabet sequentially.

Exponent

Calculating an exponent in VBA, which involves raising a number to the power of another number, can be accomplished using the `^` operator. This operator is used to perform exponential calculations. Below is an example that

How to do this in VBA?? 202 ready-made macros: Streamline your tasks with proven expert solutions

demonstrates how to use this operator to calculate the result of a number raised to an exponent, along with comments explaining each step.

➤ Example: Calculating an exponent in VBA

```
Sub CalculateExponent()
    ' This subroutine demonstrates how to calculate the
exponent of a number in VBA.

    ' Declare variables for the base number and the
exponent.
    Dim baseNumber As Double
    Dim exponent As Double
    Dim result As Double

    ' Assign values to the base number and the exponent.
    ' For example, calculating 2 raised to the power of 3
(2^3).
    baseNumber = 2
    exponent = 3

    ' Calculate the exponent using the ^ operator.
    result = baseNumber ^ exponent

    ' Display the result in a message box.
    MsgBox baseNumber & " raised to the power of " &
exponent & " is " & result
End Sub
```

➤ Key points:

- **Base number and exponent**: the `baseNumber` and `exponent` variables hold the values for the calculation. These can be modified to compute different exponential expressions.
- **Exponential operator `^`**: this operator is used to perform the exponential calculation, effectively raising `baseNumber` to the power of `exponent`.
- **Result display**: the result of the calculation is shown in a message box, providing a clear demonstration of the operation's outcome.

How to do this in VBA?? 202 ready-made macros: Streamline your tasks with proven expert solutions

This example provides a straightforward demonstration of performing exponential calculations in VBA, showcasing the use of the `^` operator. Such calculations are common in various mathematical, financial, and scientific applications developed with VBA.

Extract year from date in Excel Vba

Extracting the year from a date in Excel VBA can be easily accomplished using the `Year` function. This function takes a date as its argument and returns the year portion as a four-digit number. Below is a simple example demonstrating how to use this function within a VBA subroutine. The comments in the code provide further explanations and context.

➢ Example: Extracting the year from a date

```
Sub ExtractYearFromDate()
    ' This subroutine demonstrates how to extract the year
    from a date in Excel VBA.

    ' Declare a variable to hold the date.
    Dim exampleDate As Date

    ' Assign a date to the variable. Change this to any
    date you need to work with.
    exampleDate = #12/31/2023#

    ' Use the Year function to extract the year from the
    date.
    Dim extractedYear As Integer
    extractedYear = Year(exampleDate)

    ' Display the extracted year in a message box.
    MsgBox "The year extracted from " & exampleDate & " is
    " & extractedYear
End Sub
```

➢ Key points:

74

- **Date variable**: the `exampleDate` variable is declared as a `Date` type and is assigned a specific date using the date literal (enclosed in `#` signs).
- **Year function**: the `Year` function is used to extract the year part of the `exampleDate` variable and store it in the `extractedYear` variable, which is declared as an `Integer`.
- **Displaying results**: the `MsgBox` function displays the result, showing both the original date and the extracted year.

This code snippet is a straightforward way to work with dates in VBA, specifically focusing on extracting the year component from a date value. It illustrates the use of built-in date functions and how to display results using message boxes.

Filter

Applying a filter to a range or table in Excel using VBA involves the `AutoFilter` method. This method can filter data based on specific criteria, making it a powerful tool for data analysis and manipulation. Below is an example demonstrating how to apply a filter to a column in a worksheet to show only rows that meet certain criteria. The comments in the code explain each step.

➤ Example: Filtering a range by criteria

```
Sub ApplyFilterToRange()
    ' This subroutine demonstrates how to apply a filter
    to a range in Excel using VBA.

    ' Assume we have data in columns A to D, with row 1
    containing header names.
    ' We will apply a filter to column B to show only the
    rows where column B's value is greater than 50.

    ' Specify the range to apply the filter to. Adjust the
    range as necessary for your data.
    Dim targetRange As Range
    Set targetRange =
ThisWorkbook.Sheets("Sheet1").Range("A1:D100")
```

```vba
    ' Ensure any existing filters are cleared before
applying a new one.
    If targetRange.Worksheet.AutoFilterMode Then
targetRange.Worksheet.AutoFilterMode = False


    ' Apply the filter.
    ' The first argument of AutoFilter is the field
(column) number, relative to the range's first column.
    ' In this case, 2 represents the second column in the
specified range (Column B).
    ' The Criteria1 argument defines the condition. Here,
we're filtering for values greater than 50.
    targetRange.AutoFilter Field:=2, Criteria1:=">50"


    ' Now, only the rows in the range that meet the
criteria (values in column B > 50) will be visible.
    ' Other rows are hidden by the filter, not deleted.


    ' Note: To remove the filter, you can turn off
AutoFilterMode as follows:
    ' targetRange.Worksheet.AutoFilterMode = False
    End Sub
```

➤ Key points:

- **Target range**: the `targetRange` variable specifies the range to apply the filter to. It's important that this range includes all columns you want to remain visible after applying the filter, and it should start with the row containing your column headers.
- **AutoFilter method**: the `AutoFilter` method is called on the `targetRange`. The `Field` parameter specifies the column to filter based on its position within the range, and `Criteria1` defines the filtering criteria.
- **Clearing existing filters**: before applying a new filter, existing filters are cleared using `AutoFilterMode = False` to ensure the new filter is applied correctly.
- **Visibility of rows**: the filter will hide rows that do not meet the specified criteria. These rows are not deleted or removed; they're simply hidden and can be made visible again by clearing the filter.

This example provides a basic framework for applying filters to ranges in Excel via VBA, showcasing how to dynamically narrow down data visibility based on specific conditions.

Filter a column

Applying a filter to a specific column in Excel using VBA is a common task for data analysis, allowing you to quickly narrow down your data set based on specific criteria. Here's an example demonstrating how to filter a column to show only rows that meet certain criteria. The example will use the `AutoFilter` method to filter column "A" to display only the rows where the value in column "A" is greater than 50.

➤ Example: Filtering a column by criteria

```
Sub FilterColumnByCriteria()
    ' This subroutine demonstrates how to filter a
specific column in Excel using VBA.
    ' The goal is to display only the rows in which the
value in column "A" is greater than 50.

    ' Specify the range to apply the filter to, including
the header.
    ' It's important to include the entire range that
might contain the data you're filtering.
    ' Adjust the "A1:A100" range according to your actual
data range.
    Dim dataRange As Range
    Set dataRange =
ThisWorkbook.Sheets("Sheet1").Range("A1:A100")

    ' Ensure any existing filters are cleared to avoid
conflicts.
    If dataRange.Worksheet.AutoFilterMode Then
        dataRange.Worksheet.AutoFilterMode = False
    End If

    ' Apply the filter to column "A".
```

```
          ' Since our range starts with column "A", we use
      Field:=1 to indicate the first column in the range.
          ' Criteria1:=">50" sets the condition to display only
      rows with values greater than 50 in column "A".
          dataRange.AutoFilter Field:=1, Criteria1:=">50"


          ' After applying the AutoFilter, only rows with values
      greater than 50 in column "A" will be visible.
          ' Rows that do not meet the criteria are hidden, not
      deleted.
      End Sub
```

➢ Key points:

- **Defining the data range**: the `dataRange` variable is set to encompass the column you want to filter, including the header. This range can be adjusted to fit your dataset's specific size and location.
- **Clearing existing filters**: before applying a new filter, it's a good practice to clear any existing filters on the worksheet to ensure the new filter works as expected.
- **Applying the filter**: the `AutoFilter` method is used to filter the data. The `Field` parameter specifies the column within the defined range (starting with 1), and `Criteria1` sets the filter condition.
- **Visibility of rows**: the filter action will hide rows that don't meet the specified criteria, making it easier to focus on the data of interest. These rows are not removed from the worksheet; their visibility is simply toggled.

This code snippet offers a straightforward method for filtering data in a single column based on a specified condition, demonstrating the flexibility and power of using VBA to manage and analyze data in Excel.

Filter a table

Filtering a table in Excel using VBA can significantly streamline data analysis processes. The `ListObject` and its `AutoFilter` method provide a robust framework for applying filters programmatically to tables (also known as ListObjects in VBA). Below is an example that demonstrates how to apply a filter to a table column, showing only rows that meet specific criteria. This example focuses on filtering a table based on a value in one of its columns.

➢ Example: Filtering a table by column criteria

```vba
Sub FilterTableByColumn()
    ' This subroutine demonstrates how to apply a filter
    to a specific column in an Excel table using VBA.
    ' The goal is to filter the table to show only rows
    where the value in a specific column matches the criteria.

    ' First, declare a variable to reference the table
    (ListObject).
    Dim myTable As ListObject

    ' Set the myTable variable to the specific table on a
    worksheet.
    ' Replace "MyTableName" with the actual name of your
    table.
    ' Tables in Excel can be named and referenced by name
    in the VBA.
    Set myTable =
    ThisWorkbook.Sheets("Sheet1").ListObjects("MyTableName")

    ' Apply the filter to a specific column in the table.
    ' Replace "ColumnName" with the actual name of the
    column you want to filter.
    ' Here, we filter the column to show only rows where
    the column value is greater than 50.
    With myTable
        ' Ensure any existing filters are cleared to avoid
    conflicts.
        .AutoFilter.ShowAllData

        ' Apply the filter. The field number is determined
    by the column's position in the table.
        ' Criteria1 is set to ">50", indicating that only
    rows with values greater than 50 in the specified column
    should be shown.
        .Range.AutoFilter
    Field:=.ListColumns("ColumnName").Index, Criteria1:=">50"
```

```
End With
```

```
' The specified column of the table is now filtered
according to the criteria,
    ' and only matching rows are visible. Other rows are
hidden.
End Sub
```

➤ Key concepts:

- **Table reference**: the `ListObject` represents the table, and it's important to reference the correct table by its name.
- **Clearing existing filters**: the `.AutoFilter.ShowAllData` method clears any existing filters on the table, ensuring the new filter is applied correctly.
- **Specifying the column**: the column to filter is specified by its name through the `ListColumns("ColumnName").Index` property, making the code more readable and maintainable.
- **Filter criteria**: the `Criteria1` parameter defines the condition that the rows must meet to be visible after the filter is applied.

This code snippet provides a clear example of how to programmatically filter a table in Excel based on column values using VBA, facilitating data analysis and management by allowing for dynamic data views based on specified criteria.

Find Excel

Finding specific data in Excel using VBA can be accomplished with the `Find` method of the `Range` object. This method is powerful for searching through a range for a value, returning the cell where the value is found. Here's an example demonstrating how to use the `Find` method to search for a specific value within a worksheet and report whether and where the value was found. The comments in the code explain each step for clarity.

➤ Example: Using `Find` to locate data in Excel

```
Sub FindValueInWorksheet()
    ' This subroutine demonstrates how to find a specific
value within an Excel worksheet using VBA.

    ' Specify the value to search for.
    Dim searchValue As String
```

```vba
    searchValue = "Excel"

    ' Define the range to search in. Here, we'll search
the entire worksheet.
    Dim searchRange As Range
    Set searchRange =
ThisWorkbook.Sheets("Sheet1").UsedRange

    ' Use the Find method to search for the value.
    Dim foundCell As Range
    Set foundCell = searchRange.Find(What:=searchValue, _

After:=searchRange.Cells(1, 1), _
                                LookIn:=xlValues, _
                                LookAt:=xlPart, _

SearchOrder:=xlByRows, _

SearchDirection:=xlNext, _
                                MatchCase:=False)

    ' Check if something was found.
    If Not foundCell Is Nothing Then
        ' If found, report the address of the first cell
that contains the search value.
        MsgBox "Value '" & searchValue & "' found at " &
foundCell.Address
    Else
        ' If the value was not found, inform the user.
        MsgBox "Value '" & searchValue & "' not found in
the worksheet."
    End If
End Sub
```

➢ Key concepts:

- **Search value**: this is the value you're looking for in the worksheet. You can modify `searchValue` to fit your needs.

- **Search range**: the range where you want to perform the search. In this example, `UsedRange` is used to search the entire worksheet, but you can specify a more limited range if needed.
- `Find` **method parameters**:
  - `What`: the value to search for.
  - `After`: specifies the cell after which the search begins. This example starts searching after cell A1.
  - `LookIn`: specifies whether to search in values, formulas, etc. `xlValues` is used here to search in the cell values.
  - `LookAt`: can be `xlWhole` (for the whole match) or `xlPart` (for partial match). `xlPart` is used in this example.
  - `SearchOrder`: determines whether the search proceeds by rows or columns. `xlByRows` is used here.
  - `SearchDirection`: can be `xlNext` (forward) or `xlPrevious` (backward). `xlNext` is used in this example.
  - `MatchCase`: specifies whether the search is case-sensitive. Set to `False` in this example for case-insensitive search.

This example provides a foundational approach to searching for data within an Excel worksheet using VBA, illustrating how to utilize the `Find` method effectively.

Find and replace

Performing a find and replace operation in Excel using VBA is a common task for automating the modification of data within your worksheets. The `Replace` method of the `Range` object can be used for this purpose. Here's an example demonstrating how to use this method to search for a specific value and replace it with a new one across an entire worksheet. The comments within the code provide guidance on each step.

➢ Example: Using `Find and Replace` in Excel VBA

```
Sub FindAndReplaceInWorksheet()
    ' This subroutine demonstrates how to perform a find
    and replace operation across an entire worksheet using
    VBA.

    ' Specify the worksheet you're working with.
    ' Adjust "Sheet1" to the name or index of your target
    worksheet.
    Dim ws As Worksheet
```

How to do this in VBA?? 202 ready-made macros: Streamline your tasks with proven expert solutions

```vba
Set ws = ThisWorkbook.Sheets("Sheet1")


    ' Define the value to find and the value to replace it
with.
    Dim findValue As String
    Dim replaceValue As String
    findValue = "OldValue"
    replaceValue = "NewValue"


    ' Use the Replace method to find all instances of
findValue and replace them with replaceValue.
    ' The following parameters are being used:
    '    What: The value you want to find.
    '    Replacement: The value you want to replace the
found value with.
    '    LookAt: Can be xlWhole (match the whole cell
content) or xlPart (match part of the cell content).
    '    SearchOrder: Can be xlByRows or xlByColumns.
xlByRows is used here.
    '    MatchCase: Specifies whether the search is case-
sensitive.
    ws.Cells.Replace What:=findValue,
Replacement:=replaceValue, _
                    LookAt:=xlPart,
SearchOrder:=xlByRows, _
                    MatchCase:=False,
SearchFormat:=False, _
                    ReplaceFormat:=False


    ' Inform the user that the operation has been
completed.
    MsgBox "All instances of '" & findValue & "' have been
replaced with '" & replaceValue & "'.", vbInformation
    End Sub
```
➤ Key points:

- **Worksheet reference**: the `ws` variable is set to reference the worksheet where the find and replace operation will be performed. Adjust this to target the correct worksheet in your workbook.
- **Find and Replace values**: `findValue` and `replaceValue` hold the strings for the find and replace operation. Modify these variables based on your specific needs.
- `Replace` **method parameters**:
  - `What`: the text or value to find.
  - `Replacement`: the text or value to use as a replacement.
  - `LookAt`: determines if the whole cell must match (`xlWhole`) or if partial matches are acceptable (`xlPart`).
  - `SearchOrder`: specifies the order to search (`xlByRows` is common).
  - `MatchCase`: when `True`, makes the search case-sensitive.
- **User notification**: a message box notifies the user upon completion of the operation, providing feedback that the task has been executed.

This code snippet showcases how to automate the process of finding and replacing text or values in an Excel worksheet, a valuable tool for data cleaning and management tasks.

Find date

Finding a specific date within a range in an Excel worksheet using VBA involves leveraging the `Find` method, similar to searching for text or numbers. Dates in Excel are stored as numbers, so it's crucial to ensure the date you're searching for is properly formatted. Here's an example that demonstrates how to find a cell containing a specific date, with comments explaining each step.

➢ Example: Finding a specific date in Excel VBA

```
Sub FindSpecificDate()
    ' This subroutine demonstrates how to find a cell
containing a specific date within a worksheet.

    ' Define the specific date you are looking for.
    ' Dates in VBA can be assigned using the DateValue
function or the #mm/dd/yyyy# format.
    Dim targetDate As Date
    targetDate = DateValue("12/31/2023")
```

```vba
    ' Specify the range where you want to search for the
date.
    ' In this example, we'll search the entire used range
of the worksheet.
    Dim searchRange As Range
    Set searchRange =
ThisWorkbook.Sheets("Sheet1").UsedRange

    ' Use the Find method to search for the target date.
    ' Note: Excel stores dates as numbers, so it's
important to ensure the date formats match.
    Dim foundCell As Range
    Set foundCell = searchRange.Find(What:=targetDate,
LookIn:=xlValues, _

                                    LookAt:=xlWhole,
SearchOrder:=xlByRows, _

SearchDirection:=xlNext, MatchCase:=False)

    ' Check if the target date was found.
    If Not foundCell Is Nothing Then
        ' If found, display a message with the address of
the cell containing the date.
        MsgBox "The date " & Format(targetDate,
"mm/dd/yyyy") & " was found at " & foundCell.Address
    Else
        ' If the target date is not found, inform the
user.
        MsgBox "The date " & Format(targetDate,
"mm/dd/yyyy") & " was not found in the specified range."
    End If
End Sub
```

➢ Key points:

- **Target date**: the `targetDate` variable holds the date you're searching for. Use `DateValue` or direct assignment with `#mm/dd/yyyy#` format for clarity.
- **Search range**: the `searchRange` is where the subroutine looks for the date. Adjust this range according to your specific needs.
- `Find` method parameters:
  - `What`: the value you're searching for, in this case, `targetDate`.
  - `LookIn`: set to `xlValues` to search in cell values.
  - `LookAt`: use `xlWhole` to find cells that exactly match the date.
  - `SearchOrder` & `SearchDirection`: controls the order and direction of the search.
  - `MatchCase`: not directly applicable to dates but required for the `Find` method syntax.
- **Result handling**: the script checks if a cell was found and displays its location or informs the user if the date was not found.

This example provides a foundational approach for searching dates within a worksheet, demonstrating how VBA can interact with Excel's date storage mechanism to locate specific data points.

Find duplicates

Finding duplicates in a range or column in Excel using VBA involves iterating through the cells and using a method to track previously seen values. A common approach is to use a `Dictionary` object to store and check for duplicates. Below is an example demonstrating how to find duplicates in a specific column and highlight them. This code includes comments for clarity and understanding of each step.

➢ Pre-requisites:

Before running this example, ensure the reference to the Microsoft Scripting Runtime is enabled in your VBA editor for the `Dictionary` object to work. This can be done by going to **Tools > References** in the VBA editor and checking "Microsoft Scripting Runtime."

➢ Example: Highlighting duplicates in a column

```
Sub HighlightDuplicates()
    ' This subroutine finds and highlights duplicate
values in a specific column.
```

```vba
    Dim ws As Worksheet
    Set ws = ThisWorkbook.Sheets("Sheet1") ' Specify the
worksheet to work on

    Dim checkRange As Range
    Set checkRange = ws.Range("A1:A100") ' Specify the
range to check for duplicates

    Dim cell As Range
    Dim dict As Scripting.Dictionary
    Set dict = New Scripting.Dictionary

    ' Loop through each cell in the specified range
    For Each cell In checkRange
        If Not cell.Value = "" Then ' Ignore empty cells
            If dict.Exists(cell.Value) Then
                ' If the value is already in the
dictionary, it's a duplicate. Highlight the cell.
                cell.Interior.Color = RGB(255, 255, 0) '
Yellow highlight
            Else
                ' If the value is not in the dictionary,
add it.
                dict.Add cell.Value, Nothing
            End If
        End If
    Next cell

    ' Inform the user that the process is complete.
    MsgBox "Duplicates have been highlighted in yellow.",
vbInformation
End Sub
```

➤ Key concepts:

- **Worksheet and range setup**: the code specifies which worksheet and range to work on. Adjust `ws` and `checkRange` to match your data.

- **Using a dictionary**: the `Dictionary` object is used to track values that have been encountered. It's efficient for checking the existence of keys (cell values in this case).
- **Loop through each cell**: the subroutine iterates through each cell within the specified range, checking for duplicates by looking up each cell's value in the dictionary.
- **Highlight duplicates**: when a duplicate value is found (i.e., it already exists in the dictionary), the cell is highlighted in yellow.
- **Microsoft scripting runtime reference**: this reference is required for the `Dictionary` object to work. It needs to be enabled through the VBA editor's References dialog.

This method provides a clear example of how to identify and visually indicate duplicate values within a specified range or column in Excel using VBA, offering a practical approach to data cleaning and validation tasks.

Find error

Finding and handling errors in Excel VBA is crucial for developing robust and user-friendly applications. VBA provides structured error handling using the `On Error GoTo` statement, which directs the code execution to an error-handling routine when an error occurs. Below is an example demonstrating how to find and handle errors in a subroutine. This approach ensures that your program can gracefully manage unexpected issues, enhancing its reliability.

➤ Example: Error handling in VBA

```
Sub FindAndHandleError()
    ' This subroutine demonstrates basic error handling in
VBA.
    ' It attempts to perform a division operation that
might result in an error (e.g., division by zero).

    ' Declare variables for demonstration.
    Dim numerator As Double
    Dim denominator As Double
    Dim result As Double

    ' Initialize variables.
    numerator = 10
```

```vba
        denominator = 0 ' This will cause a division by zero
    error.

        ' Set up structured error handling.
        On Error GoTo ErrorHandler

        ' Attempt to perform the division.
        result = numerator / denominator

        ' If no error occurs, display the result.
        MsgBox "The result is: " & result

        ' Exit the subroutine before reaching the error
    handling code.
        Exit Sub

ErrorHandler:
        ' Error handling code.
        ' Check the Err object to identify the specific error.
        If Err.Number = 11 Then ' Error 11 corresponds to
    division by zero.
            MsgBox "Error encountered: Division by zero.
    Please check your inputs.", vbCritical
        Else
            ' Handle other errors.
            MsgBox "An unexpected error occurred. Error
    number: " & Err.Number, vbCritical
        End If

        ' Optional: Resume execution or exit.
        ' Resume Next ' Proceeds to the next line of code.
        ' Or simply exit the subroutine if error handling is
    complete.
        End Sub
```
➢ Key concepts:

- **Structured error handling**: `On Error GoTo ErrorHandler` directs VBA to jump to the `ErrorHandler` label when an error occurs.
- **Performing operations**: the subroutine attempts operations that might fail, such as division, where `denominator` might be zero.
- **Exiting subroutine**: `Exit Sub` ensures that the subroutine exits before reaching the error-handling code under normal circumstances.
- **Error handler routine**: the `ErrorHandler` section checks `Err.Number` to identify the specific error and respond accordingly. Common errors like division by zero are handled with tailored messages.
- **Resume or exit**: after handling the error, you can choose to `Resume Next`, which continues execution with the next line of code, or exit the subroutine if error handling is deemed complete.

This example illustrates fundamental error handling in VBA, allowing for graceful error management and improved user experience by providing clear feedback on issues encountered during execution.

Find error code

Detecting and handling specific error codes in VBA allows for more precise control over error management, enabling tailored responses to different issues that may arise during execution. Below is an example demonstrating how to identify a specific error code when an error occurs, and how to respond accordingly. This example includes comments to explain each step and provide context.

➤ Example: Handling specific error codes in VBA

```
Sub HandleSpecificErrorCode()
    ' This subroutine demonstrates how to catch and handle
a specific error code in VBA.


    On Error GoTo ErrorHandler ' Direct the code to jump
to ErrorHandler when an error occurs.


    ' Example operation that could cause an error.
    ' Attempting to open a non-existent file will generate
error 53 - File not found.
    Dim fileName As String
```

```vba
fileName = "C:\NonExistentFile.txt"
Open fileName For Input As #1


' Normal code execution resumes here if no error
occurs.
Close #1 ' Close the file if it was successfully
opened.
Exit Sub ' Ensure the subroutine exits before reaching
the ErrorHandler if no error occurs.


ErrorHandler:
' Error handling code.
If Err.Number = 53 Then ' Check if the error code is
53 - File not found.
    MsgBox "File not found: " & fileName,
vbExclamation, "Error"
Else
    ' Handle other unexpected errors.
    MsgBox "An unexpected error occurred. Error #" &
Err.Number & ": " & Err.Description, vbCritical, "Error"
End If


' Resume at next line, or you can use Resume to retry
a specific operation, or Exit Sub to end.
Resume Next
End Sub
```

➢ Key concepts:

- **Error handling setup**: using `On Error GoTo ErrorHandler` to define where the code should jump if an error occurs.
- **Triggering an error**: the example intentionally includes a scenario likely to produce an error (trying to open a non-existent file), which is a common source of runtime errors in applications that interact with the filesystem.
- **Specific error handling**: in the `ErrorHandler`, `Err.Number` is used to identify the specific error. Here, error 53 corresponds to "File not found", allowing for a tailored response to this anticipated issue.

- **General error handling**: the `else` clause catches and handles any other unexpected errors, providing the error number and description to help with debugging.
- **Resuming execution**: after handling the error, `Resume Next` is used to proceed with the next line of code following the one that caused the error. Alternatives include `Resume` (to retry the operation that failed) or simply ending the subroutine with `Exit Sub`.

This structured approach to error handling enables VBA developers to create more robust and user-friendly applications by anticipating and responding to specific issues that may arise during execution.

Find function

Creating and using custom functions in Excel VBA allows you to perform specific tasks and calculations that can be reused throughout your workbook or across multiple workbooks. Below is an example demonstrating how to define a custom function named `FindFunction`, which searches for a specified value within a given range and returns the address of the first cell that contains the value, if found. This example includes comments to guide you through each step.

➢ Example: Creating a custom `FindFunction` in VBA

```
Function FindFunction(SearchRange As Range, ValueToFind As
Variant) As String
    ' This custom function searches for a specified value
within a given range
    ' and returns the cell address where the value is
found. If the value is not found,
    ' it returns "Not Found".


    ' Declare a variable to hold the found cell.
    Dim FoundCell As Range


    ' Use the Find method of the Range object to search
for the value.
    Set FoundCell = SearchRange.Find(What:=ValueToFind, _
                            LookIn:=xlValues, _
                            LookAt:=xlPart, _
```

```
SearchOrder:=xlByRows, _

SearchDirection:=xlNext, _
                                    MatchCase:=False)

    ' Check if anything was found.
    If Not FoundCell Is Nothing Then
        ' If found, return the address of the cell.
        FindFunction = FoundCell.Address
    Else
        ' If the value is not found, return "Not Found".
        FindFunction = "Not Found"
    End If
End Function
```

➤ How to use the `FindFunction` in Excel:

- After adding this code to a standard module in the VBA editor, you can use the `FindFunction` directly in your Excel worksheets similar to how you would use built-in functions.
- For example, if you want to find the value "Excel" in the range A1:A100, you would enter the following formula in a cell:

```
=FindFunction(A1:A100, "Excel")
```

- This formula will return the address of the first cell within the range A1:A100 that contains the value "Excel". If "Excel" is not found, the function returns "Not Found".

➤ Key concepts:

- **Function parameters**: `SearchRange` specifies the range to search within, and `ValueToFind` is the value you're looking for.
- **Using the `Find` method**: this method is part of the `Range` object and is used to search for `ValueToFind` within `SearchRange`.
- **Return value**: the function returns the address of the first cell where the value is found or "Not Found" if the value does not exist within the specified range.

This example illustrates how to create a useful custom function in VBA that extends Excel's native capabilities, allowing for more flexible data searches directly from worksheet formulas.

Find last column

Finding the last column with data in a specific row or throughout a worksheet is a common task in Excel VBA, useful for dynamically adjusting the range your macros work with based on the actual data present. Below is an example that demonstrates how to find the last used column in a particular row and in the entire worksheet. This approach uses the `Find` method, which is more reliable across different versions of Excel than other methods like `UsedRange`. The comments in the code explain each step for clarity.

➢ Example: Finding the last used column

```vba
Sub FindLastColumn()
    ' This subroutine demonstrates how to find the last
    used column in a worksheet.

    Dim ws As Worksheet
    Set ws = ThisWorkbook.Sheets("Sheet1") ' Specify your
    sheet here.

    ' Find the last used column in a specific row. Here,
    we're checking row 1.
    Dim lastColInRow As Long
    lastColInRow = ws.Cells(1,
    ws.Columns.Count).End(xlToLeft).Column

    ' Display the last used column in row 1.
    MsgBox "The last used column in row 1 is: " &
    lastColInRow

    ' Find the last used column in the entire sheet.
    ' This method uses the Find function, looking from the
    last cell backwards.
    Dim lastColInSheet As Long
    Dim lastCell As Range
    Set lastCell = ws.Cells.Find(What:="*", _
                        After:=ws.Range("A1"), _
                        LookAt:=xlPart, _
```

```
                                    LookIn:=xlFormulas, _
                                    SearchOrder:=xlByColumns,

        _

    SearchDirection:=xlPrevious, _
                                    MatchCase:=False)

        If Not lastCell Is Nothing Then
            lastColInSheet = lastCell.Column
        Else
            lastColInSheet = 1 ' Default to 1 if the sheet is
    empty.
        End If


        ' Display the last used column in the entire sheet.
        MsgBox "The last used column in the entire sheet is: "
    & lastColInSheet
    End Sub
```

➢ Key concepts:

- **Specific row**: to find the last used column in a specific row, the `End(xlToLeft)` method is used starting from the last possible column of the row. This method moves left until it finds a cell with content.
- **Entire sheet**: the `Find` method searches the entire worksheet for any cell with content, starting from "A1" and searching backwards (`xlPrevious`). It's reliable for finding the last cell with content in formulas or values.
- **Error handling**: if no cell with content is found, implying an empty sheet, the code defaults to using column 1 as the last used column to avoid errors.

This subroutine provides a solid foundation for determining the extent of data within a worksheet, allowing for dynamic range selections in your VBA projects.

Find last row

Finding the last used row in an Excel worksheet is a frequent task when automating data processes with VBA, allowing for dynamic adjustments based on the data present. Below is an example demonstrating how to find the last used row in a worksheet. This approach uses the `End(xlUp)` method from a cell in the last row of the worksheet, which is similar to pressing CTRL+UP in Excel to find the last non-empty cell. Comments in the code provide additional explanations.

➢ Example: Finding the last used row in a worksheet

```vba
Sub FindLastRow()
    ' This subroutine demonstrates how to find the last
used row in an Excel worksheet.


    ' Define the worksheet variable. Adjust "Sheet1" to
your worksheet's name.
    Dim ws As Worksheet
    Set ws = ThisWorkbook.Sheets("Sheet1")


    ' Finding the last used row in the worksheet.
    ' The .Cells property is used with .Rows.Count to
start at the last possible row,
    ' and .End(xlUp) moves upwards to the first non-empty
cell.
    Dim lastRow As Long
    lastRow = ws.Cells(ws.Rows.Count, "A").End(xlUp).Row


    ' Display the last used row to the user.
    MsgBox "The last used row in the worksheet is: " &
lastRow


    ' If you need to find the last row of the entire sheet
regardless of the column,
    ' you can use the Find method, which is more
comprehensive but slower:
    Dim lastCell As Range
    Set lastCell = ws.Cells.Find(What:="*", _
                            After:=ws.Cells(1, 1), _
                            LookIn:=xlFormulas, _
                            LookAt:=xlPart, _
                            SearchOrder:=xlByRows, _
```

```
SearchDirection:=xlPrevious, _
                              MatchCase:=False)


    If Not lastCell Is Nothing Then
        ' Display the row number of the last cell with
content.
        MsgBox "The last row with content in the entire
sheet is: " & lastCell.Row
    Else
        MsgBox "The worksheet appears to be empty."
    End If
End Sub
```

➤ Key concepts:

- **Worksheet variable**: specifies which worksheet the macro operates on.
- **Last used row in a column**: using `ws.Cells(ws.Rows.Count, "A").End(xlUp).Row` finds the last used row in column A. Change `"A"` to another column letter if necessary.
- **Last used row in entire sheet**: the `Find` method searches for any cell with content in the worksheet and returns the last row with data. This approach is useful when data is spread across multiple columns and you need the very last row used.

This example provides two methods for finding the last used row: one for a specific column and another for the entire worksheet, demonstrating flexibility in addressing different scenarios you might encounter in your data processing tasks with VBA.

Find string

Finding a string within a range in Excel using VBA can be effectively done using the `Find` method of the `Range` object. This method searches for specific text within the range and returns a `Range` object that represents the first cell where that text is found. Here's an example demonstrating how to use the `Find` method to search for a string and report its location. Comments in the code explain each step for clarity.

➤ Example: Finding a string in a range

```vba
Sub FindStringInWorksheet()
    ' This subroutine demonstrates how to find a specific
string within a range on a worksheet.

    ' Define the string you're searching for.
    Dim searchString As String
    searchString = "SampleText"

    ' Define the range where you want to search for the
string.
    ' In this example, we search in the entire worksheet.
    Dim searchRange As Range
    Set searchRange =
ThisWorkbook.Sheets("Sheet1").UsedRange

    ' Use the Find method to search for the string.
    Dim foundCell As Range
    Set foundCell = searchRange.Find(What:=searchString, _

After:=searchRange.Cells(1, 1), _
                                    LookIn:=xlValues, _
                                    LookAt:=xlPart, _

SearchOrder:=xlByRows, _

SearchDirection:=xlNext, _
                                    MatchCase:=False)

    ' Check if the string was found.
    If Not foundCell Is Nothing Then
        ' If found, display a message box with the address
of the first cell that contains the string.
        MsgBox "String '" & searchString & "' found at " &
foundCell.Address
    Else
```

```
        ' If the string is not found, display a message
indicating it was not found.
        MsgBox "String '" & searchString & "' not found in
the specified range.", vbExclamation
    End If
End Sub
```

> Key points:

- **Search string**: the `searchString` variable holds the text you're looking for within the specified range.
- **Range to search**: the `searchRange` is set to the `UsedRange` of `Sheet1`, which includes all cells that have ever been used. Adjust this range as needed.
- **Using the `Find` method**: this method is invoked on `searchRange` with various parameters to specify how the search should be conducted. These include:
    - `What`: the text to find.
    - `After`: specifies the cell after which to begin searching (starting point).
    - `LookIn`: specifies to search in values (`xlValues`).
    - `LookAt`: can be set to `xlWhole` (match whole cell contents) or `xlPart` (allow partial matches).
    - `SearchOrder` and `SearchDirection`: define the order and direction of the search.
    - `MatchCase`: specifies whether the search should be case-sensitive.
- **Handling search results**: the script checks if the `Find` method returned a cell (`Not foundCell Is Nothing`) and displays its location or a message indicating the string was not found.

This example offers a foundational approach to searching for text strings within Excel worksheets using VBA, illustrating key aspects of using the `Find` method for effective data searching and analysis.

For loop

The `For` loop in VBA is a powerful construct that allows you to execute a block of code a specific number of times. This is particularly useful for iterating over collections, arrays, or simply repeating actions. Below is an example demonstrating how to use a `For` loop to iterate through a range of numbers, perform a calculation, and print the results to the Immediate Window. The code includes comments to guide you through the process.

How to do this in VBA?? 202 ready-made macros: Streamline your tasks with proven expert solutions

➢ Example: Using a `For` loop in VBA

```vba
Sub DemoForLoop()
    ' This subroutine demonstrates the use of a For loop
in VBA.
    ' It calculates the square of numbers from 1 to 10 and
prints the results.

    Dim i As Integer ' Loop counter variable
    Dim result As Integer ' Variable to hold the
calculation result

    ' Start the For loop. i is the loop counter, starting
at 1 and ending at 10.
    For i = 1 To 10
        ' Calculate the square of the current value of i.
        result = i * i

        ' Print the result to the Immediate Window (Ctrl +
G to view the Immediate Window in VBA editor).
        Debug.Print "The square of "; i; " is "; result
    Next i ' Move to the next value of i and repeat the
loop until i reaches 10.
End Sub
```

➢ Key points:

- **Initialization**: the loop counter variable `i` is initialized at the start of the `For` loop with the value 1.
- **Condition**: the loop continues as long as the condition `i <= 10` is true. After each iteration, `i` is incremented by 1 automatically.
- **Body**: inside the loop, the square of the current value of `i` is calculated and printed to the Immediate Window.
- **Iteration**: the `Next i` statement at the end of the loop block causes the loop to iterate, automatically incrementing `i` by 1 and then checking the loop condition again.

This example showcases the basic structure and functionality of a `For` loop in VBA, illustrating how to use it for repetitive tasks and iterations over a fixed range of values.

Format date

Formatting dates in Excel VBA can be done using the `Format` function, which allows you to convert a date into a specified format. This function is incredibly useful for displaying dates in a more readable or customized manner. Here's an example demonstrating how to use the `Format` function to format a date variable in various common formats. The comments in the code explain each formatting operation.

➢ Example: Formatting dates in VBA

```vba
Sub FormatDateExample()
    ' This subroutine demonstrates various ways to format
    dates in VBA using the Format function.

    ' Define a date variable.
    Dim exampleDate As Date
    exampleDate = DateSerial(2023, 12, 31) ' Setting a
    specific date (December 31, 2023).

    ' Format the date in the "Month Day, Year" format.
    Dim formattedDate1 As String
    formattedDate1 = Format(exampleDate, "mmmm dd, yyyy")
    Debug.Print "Formatted Date 1: " & formattedDate1 '
    Output: Formatted Date 1: December 31, 2023

    ' Format the date as "dd/mm/yyyy".
    Dim formattedDate2 As String
    formattedDate2 = Format(exampleDate, "dd/mm/yyyy")
    Debug.Print "Formatted Date 2: " & formattedDate2 '
    Output: Formatted Date 2: 31/12/2023

    ' Format the date as "yyyy-mm-dd" (often used in
    databases and sorting).
    Dim formattedDate3 As String
    formattedDate3 = Format(exampleDate, "yyyy-mm-dd")
    Debug.Print "Formatted Date 3: " & formattedDate3 '
    Output: Formatted Date 3: 2023-12-31
```

```
' Format the date to include day of the week.
Dim formattedDate4 As String
formattedDate4 = Format(exampleDate, "dddd, mmmm dd, yyyy")
Debug.Print "Formatted Date 4: " & formattedDate4 '
Output: Formatted Date 4: Sunday, December 31, 2023

' Format the date as a short date string.
Dim formattedDate5 As String
formattedDate5 = Format(exampleDate, "Short Date")
Debug.Print "Formatted Date 5: " & formattedDate5 '
The output will depend on the system's short date
settings.
End Sub
```

➢ Key concepts:

- `Format` function: used to convert dates into various string formats.
- **Date variable**: a specific date is assigned to `exampleDate` for demonstration.
- **Custom formats**: the `Format` function allows for custom date formatting strings, such as `"mmmm dd, yyyy"` for full month name, day, and four-digit year.
- **Debug.Print**: each formatted date string is output to the Immediate Window in the VBA editor, allowing you to see the results of the formatting.

This example provides a foundation for using the `Format` function to create custom date presentations in VBA, catering to different formatting requirements and enhancing the readability of dates in your VBA-driven applications.

Format text

Formatting text in VBA involves using functions to manipulate strings to achieve the desired format. This can include changing the case of text, padding strings with characters, or combining text in specific ways. Below is an example demonstrating several common text formatting operations in VBA, such as concatenation, uppercase, lowercase, and adding padding to a string. Comments in the code explain each step for clarity.

How to do this in VBA?? 202 ready-made macros: Streamline your tasks with proven expert solutions

➤ Example: Formatting text in VBA

```vba
Sub FormatTextExample()
    ' This subroutine demonstrates various ways to format
    text in VBA.

    ' Concatenate two strings.
    Dim firstName As String
    Dim lastName As String
    firstName = "John"
    lastName = "Doe"
    Dim fullName As String
    fullName = firstName & " " & lastName ' Concatenates
    firstName and lastName with a space.
    Debug.Print "Full Name: " & fullName

    ' Convert text to uppercase.
    Dim upperCaseText As String
    upperCaseText = UCase("hello world") ' Converts "hello
    world" to uppercase.
    Debug.Print "Uppercase Text: " & upperCaseText

    ' Convert text to lowercase.
    Dim lowerCaseText As String
    lowerCaseText = LCase("HELLO WORLD") ' Converts "HELLO
    WORLD" to lowercase.
    Debug.Print "Lowercase Text: " & lowerCaseText

    ' Left pad a number with zeros. Useful for formatting
    numbers or codes.
    Dim paddedNumber As String
    paddedNumber = Right("0000" & 123, 5) ' Pads the
    number 123 with zeros to ensure it has a length of 5.
    Debug.Print "Padded Number: " & paddedNumber

    ' Combine and format a date into a string.
```

How to do this in VBA?? 202 ready-made macros: Streamline your tasks with proven expert solutions

```
Dim formattedDate As String
formattedDate - Format(Now, "yyyy-mm-dd") ' Formats
the current date as "YYYY-MM-DD".
Debug.Print "Formatted Date: " & formattedDate


' Note: The Debug.Print statements output text to the
Immediate Window in the VBA editor.
End Sub
```

➢ Key points:

- **String concatenation**: uses the `&` operator to combine strings, such as creating a full name from first and last names.
- **Case conversion**: the `UCase` and `LCase` functions convert text to uppercase and lowercase, respectively.
- **Padding strings**: demonstrates how to left-pad a string, often used for displaying numbers or codes with a fixed length.
- **Formatting dates**: the `Format` function can also format dates (and numbers) as strings in a specific pattern.

This example covers basic but essential text formatting techniques in VBA, showing how to manipulate and present text data effectively. These operations are fundamental for creating user-friendly displays of data in macros and applications.

Freeze panes

Freezing panes in Excel using VBA allows you to keep certain rows and/or columns visible while scrolling through the rest of your worksheet. This feature is particularly useful for navigating large datasets. Below is an example demonstrating how to freeze panes programmatically in VBA. This code freezes the top row of the active worksheet, but I'll also explain how to adjust it for different freezing scenarios. Comments in the code provide further guidance.

➢ Example: Freezing the top row

```
Sub FreezeTopRow()
    ' This subroutine demonstrates how to freeze the top
row of the active worksheet.


    ' Ensure no cells are selected to avoid unexpected
behavior.
```

```
ActiveWindow.Panes(1).Activate
ActiveWindow.ActivePane.SmallScroll


' Freeze the top row. This is done by selecting the
first cell in the second row
' and then using the FreezePanes property.
With ActiveWindow
    .SplitColumn = 0
    .SplitRow = 1
    .FreezePanes = True
End With


' Inform the user that the top row has been frozen.
MsgBox "The top row has been frozen.", vbInformation
End Sub
```

➤ Adjusting the code for different scenarios:

- **To freeze the first column instead of the top row**:
  - set `.SplitColumn = 1` and `.SplitRow = 0`.
- **To freeze both the top row and the first column**:
  - set `.SplitColumn = 1` and `.SplitRow = 1`.
- **To freeze a different number of rows and/or columns (e.g., the top two rows)**:
  - adjust `.SplitRow` to `2` (for rows) or `.SplitColumn` to the number of columns you wish to freeze.

➤ Key concepts:

- **Activation and scrolling**: activating the pane and performing a small scroll ensures that the worksheet is in a suitable state for freezing panes.
- **Splitting and freezing**: the `.SplitColumn` and `.SplitRow` properties determine where the split occurs, and `.FreezePanes = True` applies the freeze based on those splits.

This code snippet provides a foundation for using VBA to control the freeze panes feature in Excel, enhancing the usability of worksheets with large datasets or important header information.

Get cell value

Retrieving the value from a specific cell in Excel using VBA is straightforward and can be accomplished in various ways, depending on the context and the specific requirements of your task. Below is an example that demonstrates how to get the value from a cell by referencing it directly through its row and column numbers. This example also shows how to access a cell using its address (e.g., "A1") and how to work with named ranges. Comments within the code provide further explanations and context.

➢ Example: Getting cell values in VBA

```
Sub GetCellValueExamples()
    ' This subroutine demonstrates different methods to
get the value from a cell in Excel VBA.

    ' Method 1: Using row and column numbers.
    ' Get the value from the cell in the first row and
first column (A1).
    Dim valueByRowColumn As Variant
    valueByRowColumn =
ThisWorkbook.Sheets("Sheet1").Cells(1, 1).Value
    Debug.Print "Value in cell A1 (by row and column): " &
valueByRowColumn

    ' Method 2: Using the cell's address.
    ' Get the value from a specific cell using its
address.
    Dim valueByAddress As Variant
    valueByAddress =
ThisWorkbook.Sheets("Sheet1").Range("B2").Value
    Debug.Print "Value in cell B2 (by address): " &
valueByAddress

    ' Method 3: Using a named range.
    ' Assume you have a named range "MyNamedRange"
referring to a specific cell.
```

```
    ' This method shows how to get the value from that
named range.
    Dim valueByNamedRange As Variant
    valueByNamedRange =
ThisWorkbook.Sheets("Sheet1").Range("MyNamedRange").Value
    Debug.Print "Value in MyNamedRange: " &
valueByNamedRange

    ' Note: Replace "Sheet1" with the actual name of your
sheet.
    ' The Debug.Print statements output the values to the
Immediate Window in the VBA editor.
    End Sub
```

➢ Key concepts:

- **Row and column numbers**: the `.Cells` property allows you to access a cell by specifying its row and column numbers, offering flexibility in programmatically navigating a worksheet.
- **Cell address**: the `.Range` property with a specific cell address (e.g., "A1") is a common method for directly accessing a cell's value.
- **Named ranges**: if you have defined named ranges in your workbook, accessing a cell's value via its named range can make your code more readable and easier to manage.

This example provides a solid foundation for retrieving cell values in Excel VBA, demonstrating various methods to suit different programming scenarios. These techniques are fundamental for writing effective VBA code that interacts with worksheet data.

Get current time

Retrieving the current date and time in Excel VBA can be accomplished using the `Now` function. This function returns the current date and time according to the system's settings. Here's an example demonstrating how to get the current time, format it in a specific way, and display it in a message box. Comments within the code provide guidance on each step.

➢ Example: Getting and displaying the current time

```
    Sub GetCurrentTime()
```

```
' This subroutine demonstrates how to retrieve the
current time and display it in a specific format.

' Use the Now function to get the current date and
time.
Dim currentTime As Date
currentTime = Now

' Format the current time as "HH:MM:SS AM/PM".
' The Format function is used to convert the date to a
string in the specified time format.
Dim formattedTime As String
formattedTime = Format(currentTime, "hh:mm:ss AM/PM")

' Display the formatted current time in a message box.
MsgBox "The current time is: " & formattedTime,
vbInformation, "Current Time"
End Sub
```

➤ Key points:

- **Current date and time**: the `Now` function is used to obtain both the current date and time. If you only need the time part, this function still serves well, as it provides the full current timestamp.
- **Formatting time**: the `Format` function allows for custom formatting of date and time values. In this example, the time is formatted using the string `"hh:mm:ss AM/PM"`, which includes hours, minutes, seconds, and the AM/PM indicator.
- **Displaying the time**: the formatted time is then displayed to the user via a `MsgBox`, showcasing the ability to easily present time information in user-friendly applications or macros.

This simple yet practical example illustrates the basics of working with dates and times in VBA, providing a foundation for more complex time-based operations in your Excel macros and applications.

Get current year

Retrieving the current year in Excel VBA can be efficiently done using the `Year` function, which extracts the year from a given date. By applying this function to the current date returned by the `Now` function, you can get the current year. Here's a straightforward example demonstrating this approach, including comments for clarity.

➢ Example: Getting the current year

```
Sub GetCurrentYear()
    ' This subroutine demonstrates how to retrieve the
current year in VBA.

    ' Use the Now function to get the current date and
time.
    Dim currentDate As Date
    currentDate = Now

    ' Use the Year function to extract the year from the
current date.
    Dim currentYear As Integer
    currentYear = Year(currentDate)

    ' Display the current year in a message box.
    MsgBox "The current year is: " & currentYear,
vbInformation, "Current Year"
End Sub
```

➢ Key points:

- **Current date**: the `Now` function returns the current date and time, providing the necessary input for the `Year` function.
- **Extracting the year**: the `Year` function takes a date and returns the year portion as an integer.
- **Displaying the year**: the current year is shown to the user via a `MsgBox`, making this example useful for applications or macros that need to reference the current year dynamically.

This example illustrates a simple yet effective way to work with dates and extract specific components like the year in VBA, serving as a foundation for more complex date-based logic in your Excel projects.

Get date

Retrieving the current date in Excel VBA is straightforward and can be done using the `Date` function, which returns the current system date. This is particularly useful for adding timestamps, performing date calculations, or managing date-based data dynamically. Here's a simple example that demonstrates how to get the current date and display it in a message box with some basic formatting. Comments in the code explain each step.

➢ Example: Getting and displaying the current date

```
Sub GetCurrentDate()
    ' This subroutine demonstrates how to retrieve the
current date and display it with formatting in VBA.

    ' Use the Date function to get the current system
date.
    Dim currentDate As Date
    currentDate = Date

    ' Optionally, format the date. Here, the date is
formatted as "Month Day, Year" (e.g., "January 1, 2024").
    Dim formattedDate As String
    formattedDate = Format(currentDate, "mmmm dd, yyyy")

    ' Display the formatted date in a message box.
    MsgBox "Today's date is: " & formattedDate,
vbInformation, "Current Date"
End Sub
```

➢ Key points:

- **Current date**: the `Date` function returns the current date according to the system's settings.
- **Formatting the date**: the `Format` function is used to convert the date into a more readable string format. The pattern `"mmmm dd, yyyy"` is used here for a full month name, day, and four-digit year, but you can customize this format string to suit your needs.

- **Displaying the date**: the `MsgBox` function shows the current date in the specified format, providing a clear and user-friendly way to present date information within your VBA projects.

This code snippet offers a basic template for working with dates in Excel VBA, illustrating how to retrieve, format, and display the current date, a fundamental capability for many date-driven VBA applications and tasks.

Get file name

Retrieving the name of a file from a full file path in VBA can be accomplished using string manipulation functions. Below is an example demonstrating how to extract the file name from a full path using the `InStrRev` function to find the position of the last backslash ("\") and then the `Mid` function to get the substring that represents the file name. This method works for both Windows file paths. Comments within the code provide additional explanations.

➢Example: Extracting a file name from a full path

```
Sub GetFileNameFromPath()

    ' This subroutine demonstrates how to extract the file
    name from a full file path.

    ' Example full file path. Replace this with your
    actual file path.
    Dim fullPath As String
    fullPath =
"C:\Users\ExampleUser\Documents\SampleFile.txt"

    ' Find the position of the last backslash in the path.
    This marks the beginning of the file name.
    Dim lastBackslash As Integer
    lastBackslash = InStrRev(fullPath, "\")

    ' Extract the file name using the Mid function. Start
    at the character after the last backslash.
    Dim fileName As String
    fileName = Mid(fullPath, lastBackslash + 1)
```

```
' Display the extracted file name in a message box.
MsgBox "The file name is: " & fileName, vbInformation,
"Extracted File Name"
End Sub
```

➢ Key points:

- **Full path input**: the `fullPath` variable holds the complete file path from which the file name is to be extracted.
- **Finding the last separator**: the `InStrRev` function searches the string from its end to find the position of the last backslash, which is common in Windows file paths as a directory separator.
- **Extracting the file name**: the `Mid` function is used to get the substring starting from the character immediately after the last backslash to the end of the string, effectively isolating the file name.
- **Result display**: the extracted file name is then displayed in a message box, confirming the result of the operation.

This example provides a clear method for isolating the file name from a full path, a useful technique for file management tasks, logging operations, or when interacting with the file system in Excel VBA projects.

Get last row

Finding the last used row in an Excel worksheet is crucial for processing data dynamically. Here's a simple and effective example showing how to find the last used row in a specific column using VBA. This approach uses the `End` property combined with `xlUp`, which mimics pressing the "**Ctrl + Up**" arrow keys in Excel, finding the last non-empty cell from the bottom of the worksheet. Comments in the code provide additional explanations.

➢ Example: Finding the last used row in a column

```
Sub FindLastUsedRow()
    ' This subroutine demonstrates how to find the last
used row in a specific column of a worksheet.

    ' Specify the worksheet you're working with.
    Dim ws As Worksheet
    Set ws = ThisWorkbook.Sheets("Sheet1") ' Adjust
"Sheet1" to your actual worksheet name.
```

```
        ' Define the column number you want to check. For
    example, column A is 1, B is 2, etc.
        Dim columnNumber As Long
        columnNumber = 1 ' For column A

        ' Find the last used row in the specified column.
        Dim lastRow As Long
        lastRow = ws.Cells(ws.Rows.Count,
    columnNumber).End(xlUp).Row

        ' Display the last used row number in a message box.
        MsgBox "The last used row in column " & columnNumber &
    " is: " & lastRow, vbInformation, "Last Used Row"
        End Sub
```

➢ Key concepts:

- **Worksheet variable (`ws`)**: this holds the reference to the specific worksheet you're examining. Modify `"Sheet1"` to match the name of your worksheet.
- **Column number (`columnNumber`)**: this indicates the column you're checking. It's set to `1` in this example, which corresponds to column A. Change this number to match the column you're interested in.
- **Finding the last row (`lastRow`)**: the `End(xlUp)` method starts at the bottom of the specified column and moves upward to find the last cell that contains data.
- **Result display**: the last used row number is shown in a message box, providing a clear indication of the extent of data in the specified column.

This code snippet is an effective way to dynamically determine the last used row within a specific column, facilitating tasks like data appending, analysis, or manipulation based on the current dataset's size.

Get length of array

Determining the length (or the total number of elements) of an array in VBA is essential for iterating over the array or for other manipulations. The `UBound` function is commonly used to get the upper boundary of an array, which effectively gives you its size. When working with one-dimensional arrays, the size of the array is `UBound(array) - LBound(array) + 1`, considering that arrays can have a lower boundary different from 1. Here's a simple example demonstrating how to get the length of a one dimensional array:

➤ Example: Getting the length of a one-dimensional array

```
Sub GetLengthOfArray()
    ' This subroutine demonstrates how to determine the
length of a one-dimensional array in VBA.

    ' Declare and initialize a sample array.
    Dim sampleArray() As Integer
    sampleArray = Array(1, 2, 3, 4, 5) ' An example array
with 5 elements.

    ' Calculate the length of the array.
    ' UBound returns the upper boundary of the array, and
LBound returns the lower boundary.
    ' For a 0-based array (default), the length is simply
UBound(sampleArray) + 1.
    ' For arrays that may not start at 0, calculate the
length as shown below to ensure accuracy.
    Dim arrayLength As Integer
    arrayLength = UBound(sampleArray) -
LBound(sampleArray) + 1

    ' Display the length of the array in a message box.
    MsgBox "The length of the array is: " & arrayLength,
vbInformation, "Array Length"
End Sub
```

➤ Key points:

- **Array declaration and initialization**: the example starts by declaring and initializing a one-dimensional array named `sampleArray`.
- **Calculating the length**: the length of the array is calculated using `UBound(sampleArray) - LBound(sampleArray) + 1`. This calculation accounts for arrays that might not start at index 0.
- **Displaying the length**: the calculated length is then displayed in a message box to the user.

This straightforward approach provides a reliable way to determine the size of an array, which is crucial for loops that iterate over array elements or when dynamically managing array data in your VBA projects.

Get month

Extracting the month from a date in Excel VBA can be done using the `Month` function, which returns the month as a number (1 through 12) from a given date. Here's a simple example demonstrating how to use this function to get the month from a specific date, and then optionally converting this number to the month's name using the `MonthName` function. Comments in the code explain each step for clarity.

➢ Example: Getting the month from a date

```vba
Sub GetMonthExample()
    ' This subroutine demonstrates how to get the month
    from a date in VBA.

    ' Define a date variable.
    Dim exampleDate As Date
    exampleDate = #12/31/2023# ' Setting a specific date
    (December 31, 2023).

    ' Use the Month function to extract the month from the
    date.
    Dim monthNumber As Integer
    monthNumber = Month(exampleDate)

    ' Optionally, convert the month number to the month's
    name.
    Dim monthName As String
    monthName = MonthName(monthNumber)

    ' Display the month number and name in a message box.
    MsgBox "The month number is: " & monthNumber & vbCrLf
    & "The month name is: " & monthName, _
            vbInformation, "Month Information"
End Sub
```

➢ Key points:

- **Date variable**: the `exampleDate` variable holds the specific date from which the month will be extracted.
- **Extracting month number**: the `Month` function returns the month as a number from the `exampleDate`.
- **Converting to month name**: the `MonthName` function converts the numeric month to its corresponding name for easier readability.
- **Result display**: a message box shows both the month number and name, providing a clear demonstration of how to work with months in VBA.

This code snippet illustrates the basic usage of date-related functions in VBA, providing a foundation for performing more complex date manipulations and calculations in your Excel macros and applications.

Get month and year from date

Extracting both the month and year from a date in Excel VBA involves using the `Month` and `Year` functions. These functions return the month and year as numbers from a given date. You can further use the `MonthName` function to get the name of the month for more readable output. Here's an example demonstrating how to do this, with comments explaining each step.

➢ Example: Getting month and year from a date

```
Sub GetMonthAndYearFromDate()
    ' This subroutine demonstrates how to extract the
month and year from a specific date.

    ' Define a date variable for demonstration.
    Dim exampleDate As Date
    exampleDate = #11/24/2023# ' Example date: November
24, 2023

    ' Use the Month function to get the month as a number.
    Dim monthNumber As Integer
    monthNumber = Month(exampleDate)

    ' Optionally, get the name of the month for more
readable output.
```

```vba
        Dim monthName As String
        monthName = MonthName(monthNumber)

        ' Use the Year function to get the year.
        Dim yearNumber As Integer
        yearNumber = Year(exampleDate)

        ' Display the extracted month and year in a message
box.
        MsgBox "The date " & Format(exampleDate, "mmmm dd,
yyyy") & " has:" & vbCrLf & _
                "Month: " & monthName & " (" & monthNumber &
")" & vbCrLf & _
                "Year: " & yearNumber, vbInformation, "Month
and Year Information"
        End Sub
```

➤ Key points:

- **Date variable**: `exampleDate` is set to a specific date from which you want to extract the month and year.
- **Month extraction**: the `Month` function gets the month number, and `MonthName` converts this number into the corresponding month name.
- **Year extraction**: the `Year` function retrieves the year from the date.
- **Displaying results**: a message box shows the formatted date, the month (both as a name and number), and the year, providing a complete overview of the date's components.

This example offers a straightforward method for handling dates in VBA, allowing you to separate and utilize individual components of dates, such as the month and year, in your Excel macros and applications.

Get remainder

Calculating the remainder of a division operation in Excel VBA can be accomplished using the `Mod` operator. The `Mod` operator divides two numbers and returns only the remainder. This is particularly useful for determining whether a number is divisible by another or for operations that require cycling through a series of values. Here's a simple example that demonstrates how to use the `Mod` operator to find the remainder of a division. Comments in the code explain each step for clarity.

➢ Example: Using the `Mod` operator to get a remainder

```
Sub GetRemainderExample()
    ' This subroutine demonstrates how to calculate the
remainder of a division operation in VBA.

    ' Declare variables for the dividend and divisor.
    Dim dividend As Integer
    Dim divisor As Integer

    ' Initialize the dividend and divisor.
    dividend = 10 ' Example dividend
    divisor = 3 ' Example divisor

    ' Calculate the remainder using the Mod operator.
    Dim remainder As Integer
    remainder = dividend Mod divisor

    ' Display the result in a message box.
    MsgBox "The remainder of " & dividend & " divided by "
& divisor & " is: " & remainder, _
            vbInformation, "Division Remainder"
End Sub
```

➢ Key Points:

- **Dividend and divisor**: these variables (`dividend` and `divisor`) represent the numbers involved in the division operation.
- `Mod` **operator**: this operator is used to calculate the remainder of dividing `dividend` by `divisor`.
- **Displaying the result**: the result, which is the remainder of the division, is shown in a message box to the user.

This example provides a straightforward demonstration of calculating and utilizing remainders in division operations within VBA, serving as a basic yet essential tool for various programming tasks and logic implementations.

Get sheet name

Retrieving the name of an Excel worksheet using VBA can be very useful, especially when working with multiple sheets or when the script's behavior depends on the specific sheet name. Here's a simple example demonstrating how to get the name of the active worksheet and then how to get the names of all sheets in the workbook. The comments in the code provide guidance for each operation.

➢# Example: Getting sheet names in VBA

```
Sub GetSheetNames()
    ' This subroutine demonstrates how to retrieve the
name of the active worksheet
    ' and the names of all worksheets in the workbook.

    ' Get the name of the active sheet.
    Dim activeSheetName As String
    activeSheetName = ActiveSheet.Name
    MsgBox "The active sheet's name is: " &
activeSheetName, vbInformation, "Active Sheet Name"

    ' Get the names of all sheets in the workbook and
concatenate them into a single string.
    Dim allSheetNames As String
    Dim ws As Worksheet

    ' Initialize the string to collect names.
    allSheetNames = "All sheet names in this workbook:" &
vbCrLf

    ' Loop through each worksheet in the workbook.
    For Each ws In ThisWorkbook.Sheets
        ' Add each sheet's name to the string.
        allSheetNames = allSheetNames & ws.Name & vbCrLf
    Next ws

    ' Display the names of all sheets in a message box.
```

```
        MsgBox allSheetNames, vbInformation, "All Sheet Names"
    End Sub
```

➢ Key points:

- **Active sheet name**: the `ActiveSheet.Name` property is used to get the name of the currently active sheet.
- **All sheets in workbook**: looping through the `ThisWorkbook.Sheets` collection allows you to access each worksheet in the workbook. The `.Name` property of each **Worksheet** object is used to get the sheet's name.
- **Displaying names**: the names are shown in message boxes. The first message box displays the name of the active sheet, and the second message box lists the names of all sheets in the workbook.

This example illustrates basic techniques for working with worksheet names in VBA, providing a foundation for more complex operations that might require dynamically accessing or modifying worksheets based on their names.

Get substring

Extracting a substring from a string in Excel VBA can be done using the `Mid`, `Left`, or `Right` functions, depending on the part of the string you're interested in. Here's an example demonstrating how to use these functions to get substrings from a given string. The comments within the code explain the purpose and usage of each function.

➢ Example: Getting substrings in VBA

```
    Sub GetSubstrings()
        ' This subroutine demonstrates how to extract
    substrings from a given string using VBA functions.

        ' Example string.
        Dim exampleString As String
        exampleString = "Hello, World!"

        ' Using the Mid function to get a substring starting
    at position 8 with a length of 5 characters.
        ' This should return "World".
        Dim midSubstring As String
        midSubstring = Mid(exampleString, 8, 5)
```

```
        Debug.Print "Mid Substring: " & midSubstring


        ' Using the Left function to get the first 5
    characters of the string.
        ' This should return "Hello".
        Dim leftSubstring As String
        leftSubstring = Left(exampleString, 5)
        Debug.Print "Left Substring: " & leftSubstring


        ' Using the Right function to get the last 6
    characters of the string.
        ' This should return "World!".
        Dim rightSubstring As String
        rightSubstring = Right(exampleString, 6)
        Debug.Print "Right Substring: " & rightSubstring


        ' Note: The Debug.Print statements output the results
    to the Immediate Window in the VBA editor.
        End Sub
```

➢ Key points:

- **Mid function**: used to extract a substring from the middle of a string. It requires the starting position and the number of characters to extract.
- **Left function**: retrieves a specified number of characters from the start (left side) of the string.
- **Right function**: retrieves a specified number of characters from the end (right side) of the string.

This example provides a straightforward demonstration of extracting substrings in VBA, showcasing the versatility of string manipulation functions for various programming needs.

Get the value of a cell

Retrieving the value from a specific cell in Excel using VBA is a basic operation that's extremely useful for reading data within macros. Here's a simple example demonstrating how to get the value from a cell by specifying its row and column number. This example also shows how to access a cell using its address (e.g., "A1"). Comments in the code explain each step for clarity.

➢ Example: Getting the value of a cell in VBA

```
Sub GetValueOfACell()
    ' This subroutine demonstrates how to retrieve the
value from a cell in Excel using VBA.

    ' Method 1: Using row and column numbers.
    ' Get the value from the cell in the first row and
first column (A1).
    Dim valueByRowColumn As Variant
    valueByRowColumn =
ThisWorkbook.Sheets("Sheet1").Cells(1, 1).Value
    MsgBox "Value in cell A1 (by row and column): " &
valueByRowColumn

    ' Method 2: Using the cell's address.
    ' Get the value from a specific cell using its
address.
    Dim valueByAddress As Variant
    valueByAddress =
ThisWorkbook.Sheets("Sheet1").Range("A1").Value
    MsgBox "Value in cell A1 (by address): " &
valueByAddress

    ' Note: Replace "Sheet1" with the actual name of your
sheet if different.
End Sub
```

➢ Key points:

- **Access by row and column**: the `.Cells` property is used with row and column numbers to access the value of a specific cell. This method is particularly useful when working with numeric row and column indices.
- **Access by cell address**: the `.Range` property with a cell address provides an alternative way to refer to a cell and retrieve its value.

> This method is convenient when you know the specific address of the cell.
- **Variant data type**: the retrieved cell values are stored in variables declared as `Variant` type, accommodating any type of data contained in the cells.

This code snippet outlines the fundamental approach to accessing cell values in Excel VBA, allowing for the extraction of data for analysis, manipulation, or other processing within your macros.

Get time

Retrieving the current time in Excel VBA can be accomplished using the `Time` function, which returns the current system time. For more detailed operations or formatting, the `Now` function can also be utilized, as it returns both the current date and time, but you can format it to display only the time part. Here's a straightforward example showing how to use these functions to get and display the current time in different formats. Comments in the code provide additional explanations.

➢ Example: Getting and displaying the current time

```
Sub GetCurrentTime()
    ' This subroutine demonstrates how to retrieve and
display the current time in VBA.

    ' Use the Time function to get the current system
time.
    Dim currentTime As Date
    currentTime = Time

    ' Display the current time using the default format.
    MsgBox "Current Time (default format): " &
currentTime, vbInformation, "Current Time"

    ' Alternatively, use the Now function to get both the
current date and time,
    ' then format it to show only the time.
    Dim formattedTime As String
    formattedTime = Format(Now, "hh:mm:ss AM/PM")
```

```
' Display the current time using a custom format.
MsgBox "Current Time (custom format): " &
formattedTime, vbInformation, "Formatted Current Time"
End Sub
```

➢ Key points:

- **Current time with `Time` function**: directly returns the current system time. Displayed in the default time format based on system settings.
- **Custom time formatting with `Now` function**: while `Now` returns both date and time, using the `Format` function allows for custom formatting. In the example, `"hh:mm:ss AM/PM"` is used for a 12-hour format with AM/PM.
- **Displaying time**: the `MsgBox` function presents the time to the user, illustrating two methods to show the current time in VBA.

This example provides a basic understanding of how to work with time in Excel VBA, offering methods to retrieve, format, and display the current time according to your needs, which can be useful in time-tracking applications, timestamps, or scheduling tasks within your VBA projects.

Get today's date

Retrieving today's date in Excel VBA can be efficiently done using the `Date` function, which returns the current system date. This function is invaluable for logging, timestamping, or performing date-sensitive calculations within your macros. Here's a simple example demonstrating how to get today's date and display it in a message box, with comments explaining each step for clarity.

➢ Example: Getting and displaying today's date

```
Sub GetTodaysDate()
    ' This subroutine demonstrates how to retrieve and
    display today's date in VBA.

    ' Use the Date function to get the current system
    date.
    Dim todaysDate As Date
    todaysDate = Date
```

```
        ' Display today's date in a message box.
        ' The Format function is used to convert the date to a
    more readable string format.
        ' Here, the date is formatted as "Month Day, Year"
    (e.g., "March 10, 2024").
        MsgBox "Today's date is: " & Format(todaysDate, "mmmm
    dd, yyyy"), _
                vbInformation, "Today's Date"
    End Sub
```

➢ Key points:

- **Current date**: the `Date` function directly returns today's date, reflecting the current system date.
- **Formatting date**: although not strictly necessary for obtaining the date, the `Format` function enhances readability by converting the date to a specified format, making it more user-friendly.
- **Displaying the date**: the `MsgBox` function is used to show today's date in a message box, providing a simple and effective way to present the information to the user.

This example illustrates a straightforward method for working with dates in Excel VBA, specifically focusing on retrieving and formatting the current date. This capability forms the basis for many date-driven operations in Excel macros and applications.

Get username

Retrieving the username of the person currently logged into the Windows operating system can be done using the `Environ` function in VBA. This function allows access to various environment variables, including the username. Here's how you can use it to get the current user's username and display it in a message box. Comments in the code provide further explanation.

➢ Example: Getting and displaying the username

```
    Sub GetUsername()
        ' This subroutine demonstrates how to retrieve the
    current Windows username using VBA.

        ' Use the Environ function to get the value of the
    USERNAME environment variable.
```

How to do this in VBA?? 202 ready-made macros: Streamline your tasks with proven expert solutions

```
Dim userName As String
userName - Environ("USERNAME")

' Display the username in a message box.
MsgBox "The current user's username is: " & userName,
vbInformation, "Current Username"
End Sub
```

➢ Key points:

- **Environment variable**: the `Environ("USERNAME")` function call retrieves the current user's username as defined in the Windows operating system environment variables.
- **Displaying the username**: the `MsgBox` function is used to show the username in a simple dialog box, making this method useful for personalizing messages, logs, or any functionality that may require identification of the current user.

This straightforward approach to accessing environment variables can be adapted to retrieve other types of system information that might be useful in your Excel VBA projects, enhancing the interaction and personalization of your macros.

Get value from key in dictionary VBA

Using a dictionary in VBA is a powerful way to store and manage pairs of keys and values, similar to associative arrays or maps in other programming languages. The `Scripting.Dictionary` object offers a convenient method to quickly access values by their corresponding keys. Below is an example demonstrating how to create a dictionary, add some key-value pairs to it, and then retrieve a value using its key. Make sure to enable the Microsoft Scripting Runtime to use the dictionary. This can be done by going to **Tools > References** in the VBA editor and checking **"Microsoft Scripting Runtime."**

➢ Example: Retrieving a value by Key from a dictionary

```
Sub GetValueFromDictionary()
    ' This subroutine demonstrates how to get a value from
a key in a Dictionary in VBA.

    ' Declare and create a new instance of the Dictionary
object.
```

```vba
Dim myDictionary As Scripting.Dictionary
Set myDictionary = New Scripting.Dictionary

' Add some key-value pairs to the Dictionary.
myDictionary.Add Key:="A", Item:="Apple"
myDictionary.Add Key:="B", Item:="Banana"
myDictionary.Add Key:="C", Item:="Cherry"

' Specify the key for which you want to retrieve the
value.
Dim keyToFind As String
keyToFind = "B"

' Retrieve the value associated with the specified
key.
Dim valueFound As Variant
If myDictionary.Exists(keyToFind) Then
    valueFound = myDictionary.Item(keyToFind)
    MsgBox "The value for key '" & keyToFind & "' is:
" & valueFound, vbInformation, "Dictionary Value"
Else
    MsgBox "The key '" & keyToFind & "' was not found
in the Dictionary.", vbExclamation, "Key Not Found"
End If
End Sub
```

➤ Key points:

- **Dictionary creation**: a new `Scripting.Dictionary` object is declared and instantiated.
- **Adding key-value pairs**: the `.Add` method is used to populate the dictionary with keys and their corresponding values.
- **Key existence check**: the `.Exists` method checks if a given key is present in the dictionary before attempting to retrieve its value, preventing errors.
- **Retrieving values**: the `.Item` property or simply `myDictionary(keyToFind)` is used to access the value associated with a specific key.

- **Displaying the result**: a message box shows the value associated with the key if it exists, or notifies the user if the key is not found.

This example provides a basic framework for utilizing dictionaries in VBA, demonstrating key operations such as adding items and retrieving values based on keys, which can significantly enhance data handling capabilities in your macros.

Get workbook name

Retrieving the name of the current workbook in Excel VBA is a straightforward task that can be very useful, especially when working with multiple workbooks or when your VBA code needs to reference the workbook in which it is running. Here's an example that demonstrates how to get the name of the workbook and display it in a message box. Comments in the code explain each step for clarity.

➢ Example: Getting and displaying the workbook name

```
Sub GetWorkbookName()
    ' This subroutine demonstrates how to retrieve the
name of the current workbook.

    ' Use the Name property of the ThisWorkbook object to
get the workbook's name.
    Dim workbookName As String
    workbookName = ThisWorkbook.Name

    ' Display the workbook name in a message box.
    MsgBox "The current workbook's name is: " &
workbookName, vbInformation, "Workbook Name"
End Sub
```

➢ Key points:

- **`ThisWorkbook` object**: refers to the workbook where the VBA code is running. This is particularly useful to distinguish it from `ActiveWorkbook`, which refers to the workbook currently active (which might be different if you have multiple workbooks open).
- **Workbook name**: the `.Name` property is used to get the name of the workbook. This name includes the file extension (e.g., "MyWorkbook.xlsx").

- **Displaying the name**: the `MsgBox` function is used to show the workbook name to the user, making this method useful for dynamic file operations, logging, or user notifications within your macros.

This example provides a simple and effective way to access and utilize the workbook name in Excel VBA, serving as a foundation for more complex operations that require workbook identification or manipulation.

Get year

Retrieving the year from a specific date in Excel VBA is straightforward using the `Year` function, which extracts the year portion from a date value. Here's a basic example that demonstrates how to use this function to get the year from a given date. Comments in the code provide additional guidance on each step.

➢ Example: Getting the year from a Date

```vba
Sub GetYearFromDate()
    ' This subroutine demonstrates how to extract the year
    from a specific date in VBA.

    ' Define a date variable for demonstration.
    Dim exampleDate As Date
    exampleDate = #12/31/2023# ' Example date: December
31, 2023

    ' Use the Year function to extract the year from the
date.
    Dim extractedYear As Integer
    extractedYear = Year(exampleDate)

    ' Display the extracted year in a message box.
    MsgBox "The year extracted from the date is: " &
extractedYear, _
            vbInformation, "Extracted Year"
End Sub
```

➢ Key points:

- **Date variable**: `exampleDate` is set to a specific date from which you want to extract the year.

- **Extracting the year**: the `Year` function is applied to `exampleDate` to get the year as an integer.
- **Displaying the result**: a message box shows the year extracted from the provided date, offering a simple way to present this information to the user.

This code snippet demonstrates a fundamental operation involving dates in VBA, providing a base for performing more complex date manipulations and analyses in your Excel macros and applications.

Get yesterday date

Retrieving yesterday's date in Excel VBA is straightforward and can be very useful for date-based calculations, such as generating reports for the previous day. This can be done by subtracting one day from the current date. Here's a simple example demonstrating how to calculate yesterday's date and display it in a message box. Comments within the code provide additional explanations.

➤Example: Getting yesterday's date

```
Sub GetYesterdaysDate()
    ' This subroutine demonstrates how to retrieve
yesterday's date in VBA.

    ' Use the Date function to get the current date and
subtract 1 to get yesterday's date.
    Dim yesterdaysDate As Date
    yesterdaysDate = Date - 1

    ' Optionally, format the date for more readable
output.
    Dim formattedDate As String
    formattedDate = Format(yesterdaysDate, "mmmm dd,
yyyy")

    ' Display yesterday's date in a message box.
    MsgBox "Yesterday's date was: " & formattedDate,
vbInformation, "Yesterday's Date"
End Sub
```

➤Key points:

- **Current date**: the **Date** function returns the current system date.
- **Calculating yesterday**: subtracting **1** from the current date calculates yesterday's date.
- **Formatting the date**: the **Format** function is used to convert the date into a more readable string format, though this step is optional and customizable based on your preferred date format.
- **Displaying the date**: the **MsgBox** function shows yesterday's date in a message box, providing a straightforward way to present this information to the user.

This example illustrates a basic yet practical approach to working with dates in VBA, enabling you to perform date manipulations such as finding the date for "yesterday," which can be applied in various scenarios like logging, reporting, or automated tasks that require date calculations.

Hide columns

Hiding columns in Excel using VBA is a common task that can help manage the visibility of data in your worksheets. Below is a simple example that demonstrates how to hide a specific column as well as a range of columns. This can be very useful for simplifying the view for users or for preparing reports. Comments in the code explain each step for clarity.

➤ Example: Hiding columns in VBA

```
Sub HideColumns()
    ' This subroutine demonstrates how to hide columns in
    an Excel worksheet using VBA.

        ' Hide a single column, Column "B" in this case.
        Columns("B:B").Hidden = True

        ' Hide a range of columns, from Column "D" to Column
    "F".
        Columns("D:F").Hidden = True

        ' If you need to hide columns based on their index
    numbers, you can do it like this:
        ' Columns(2).Hidden = True ' Hides the second column
    (B)
```

How to do this in VBA?? 202 ready-made macros: Streamline your tasks with proven expert solutions

```
        ' Columns("2:6").Hidden = True ' Hides columns from B
    to F


        ' Display a message to indicate completion.
        MsgBox "Specified columns have been hidden.",
    vbInformation, "Hide Columns"
        End Sub
```

➢ Key points:

- **Hiding single column**: use the `Columns("B:B").Hidden = True` syntax to hide a single column by specifying its letter.
- **Hiding multiple columns**: use the `Columns("D:F").Hidden = True` syntax to hide a range of columns by specifying the start and end columns.
- **Using column indexes**: alternatively, columns can be referenced by their index number (e.g., `Columns(2).Hidden = True`) for hiding.
- **Visibility toggle**: the `.Hidden` property is set to `True` to hide the columns. Setting it to `False` would unhide them if needed.

This example provides a straightforward method for controlling column visibility in Excel sheets through VBA, allowing for dynamic adjustments to the user interface of your spreadsheets.

Hide rows

Hiding rows in Excel using VBA is useful for concealing certain data or temporarily removing it from view without deleting any information. Below is an example that demonstrates how to hide a specific row and a range of rows within a worksheet. Comments in the code explain each step to ensure clarity.

➢ Example: Hiding rows in VBA

```
    Sub HideRows()
        ' This subroutine demonstrates how to hide rows in an
    Excel worksheet using VBA.


        ' Hide a single row, row 2 in this case.
        Rows("2:2").Hidden = True


        ' Hide a range of rows, from row 4 to row 6.
        Rows("4:6").Hidden = True
```

```
            ' If you need to work with variable row numbers, you
      can use variables like this:
            Dim startRow As Long, endRow As Long
            startRow = 8
            endRow = 10
            Rows(startRow & ":" & endRow).Hidden = True ' Hides
      rows 8 to 10

            ' Display a message to indicate completion.
            MsgBox "Specified rows have been hidden.",
      vbInformation, "Hide Rows"
            End Sub
```

➢ Key points:

- **Hiding single row**: use the `Rows("2:2").Hidden = True` syntax to hide a single row by specifying its number.
- **Hiding multiple rows**: use the `Rows("4:6").Hidden = True` syntax to hide a range of rows by specifying the start and end row numbers.
- **Using variables**: to dynamically specify the rows to hide, you can use variables (e.g., `startRow` and `endRow`) and concatenate them into the `Rows` method call.
- **Visibility control**: setting the `.Hidden` property to `True` hides the rows. If you need to unhide them later, set this property to `False`.

This example provides a basic but effective method for managing row visibility in Excel through VBA, enhancing the adaptability and user experience of your spreadsheets.

Hide sheet

Hiding a worksheet in Excel using VBA can be an effective way to prevent users from accessing specific data or calculations that you don't want to be immediately visible. Here's a simple example demonstrating how to hide a sheet. Note that Excel provides two methods for hiding sheets: `xlSheetHidden` for regular hiding (where the user can unhide it through the UI) and `xlSheetVeryHidden` (where the sheet can only be made visible through VBA). Comments in the code explain each operation.

➢ Example: Hiding a worksheet

```
Sub HideSheet()
    ' This subroutine demonstrates how to hide a worksheet
    in Excel using VBA.

    ' Hide a sheet by setting its Visible property to
    xlSheetHidden.
    ' The sheet can be unhidden by the user through the
    Excel UI.
    ThisWorkbook.Sheets("Sheet2").Visible = xlSheetHidden

    ' To make a sheet very hidden (cannot be unhidden
    through the Excel UI),
    ' set its Visible property to xlSheetVeryHidden.
    ' ThisWorkbook.Sheets("Sheet3").Visible =
    xlSheetVeryHidden

    ' Replace "Sheet2" and "Sheet3" with the actual names
    of the sheets you want to hide.
    ' Display a message to indicate completion.
    MsgBox "Sheet2 has been hidden. Sheet3 has been made
    very hidden.", vbInformation, "Hide Sheet"
End Sub
```

➢ Key points:

- **Hiding sheets**: the `.Visible` property of a worksheet object is used to control the visibility of the sheet. Setting this property to `xlSheetHidden` hides the sheet in such a way that it can be unhidden by users through the Excel interface.
- **Very hidden sheets**: setting the `.Visible` property to `xlSheetVeryHidden` makes the sheet hidden to the extent that it cannot be made visible again through the Excel user interface; it can only be made visible through VBA code.
- **Customization**: replace `"Sheet2"` and `"Sheet3"` with the names of the sheets you actually intend to hide within your workbook.

This approach allows for dynamic control over sheet visibility, making it suitable for managing access to different parts of your workbook based on user needs or during different phases of your workflow.

Highlight a cell

Highlighting a cell or a range of cells in Excel using VBA is often done to draw attention to specific data points, errors, or important information. This can be achieved by changing the cell's background color using the `.**Interior.Color**` property. Here's a simple example demonstrating how to highlight a single cell and a range of cells in a worksheet. Comments in the code explain each step for clarity.

➢ Example: Highlighting cells in VBA

```
Sub HighlightCells()
    ' This subroutine demonstrates how to highlight a
single cell and a range of cells in Excel using VBA.

    ' Highlight a single cell, B2, by setting its
background color to yellow.
    With
ThisWorkbook.Sheets("Sheet1").Range("B2").Interior
        .Color = RGB(255, 255, 0) ' Yellow color
    End With

    ' Highlight a range of cells, D4:F6, by setting their
background color to light blue.
    With
ThisWorkbook.Sheets("Sheet1").Range("D4:F6").Interior
        .Color = RGB(173, 216, 230) ' Light blue color
    End With

    ' Display a message to indicate completion.
    MsgBox "Cells have been highlighted.", vbInformation,
"Highlight Cells"
End Sub
```

➢ Key points:

- **Cell reference**: use the `.**Range**` property of the `**Sheet**` object to specify the cell or range of cells you want to highlight.

- **Color property**: the `.Interior.Color` property is used to set the background color of the specified cell(s). You can use the `RGB` function to define custom colors.
- **Color selection**: the `RGB` function allows for a wide range of colors by mixing red, green, and blue components. The examples use yellow (`RGB(255, 255, 0)`) for a single cell and light blue (`RGB(173, 216, 230)`) for a range of cells.

This code snippet provides a foundational method for visually distinguishing cells in Excel through color highlighting, facilitating clearer data presentation and analysis within your VBA-driven Excel tasks.

Hyperlink

Adding a hyperlink to a cell in an Excel worksheet using VBA allows you to create direct links to websites, files, email addresses, or even other places within the same workbook. Below is an example demonstrating how to add a hyperlink to a specific cell that directs to a website. The code also shows how to add a hyperlink that opens a new email message. Comments in the code explain each step for clarity.

➤ Example: Adding hyperlinks in VBA

```
Sub AddHyperlinks()
    ' This subroutine demonstrates how to add hyperlinks
    to cells in Excel using VBA.

    ' Reference to the target worksheet.
    Dim ws As Worksheet
    Set ws = ThisWorkbook.Sheets("Sheet1") ' Adjust the
    sheet name as needed.

    ' Add a hyperlink to a website.
    ' This example sets cell A1 to link to the OpenAI
    website.
    ws.Hyperlinks.Add Anchor:=ws.Cells(1, 1), _
                        Address:="https://www.openai.com", _
                        TextToDisplay:="Visit OpenAI"

    ' Add a hyperlink to create an email.
```

```
      ' This example sets cell A2 to open the default mail
client to send an email to a specified address.
      ' Note: Modify the email address and subject as
needed.
      ws.Hyperlinks.Add Anchor:=ws.Cells(2, 1), _

Address:="mailto:example@example.com?subject=Hello", _
                      TextToDisplay:="Send Email to
Example"

      ' Display a message to indicate completion.
      MsgBox "Hyperlinks have been added to the worksheet.",
vbInformation, "Hyperlinks Added"
      End Sub
```

➢ Key points:

- **Worksheet reference**: the `ws` variable holds a reference to the worksheet where the hyperlinks will be added. Adjust `"Sheet1"` to the name of your target worksheet.
- **Adding website hyperlink**: the `.Hyperlinks.Add` method is used to add a hyperlink to a cell, with `Anchor` specifying the cell, `Address` providing the URL, and `TextToDisplay` defining the clickable text.
- **Adding email hyperlink**: a similar approach is used to add an email hyperlink, with the `Address` starting with `"mailto:"` followed by the recipient's email address, and optionally including parameters like `?subject=` to pre-fill the email subject.

This example provides a basic framework for using VBA to enhance Excel worksheets with interactive hyperlinks, facilitating quick access to web resources or simplifying email communication directly from the spreadsheet.

If Else

The `If...Else` statement in VBA is a fundamental control structure that allows you to execute different blocks of code based on certain conditions. It's very useful for decision-making within your macros. Here's an example that demonstrates how to use the `If...Else` statement to compare two numbers and display messages based on their relationship. Comments in the code explain each step.

How to do this in VBA?? 202 ready-made macros: Streamline your tasks with proven expert solutions

➤ Example: Using `If...Else` to compare two numbers

```vba
Sub CompareNumbers()
    ' This subroutine demonstrates how to use the
If...Else statement in VBA
    ' to compare two numbers and display different
messages based on their relationship.

    ' Declare and initialize two numeric variables for
comparison.
    Dim number1 As Integer
    Dim number2 As Integer
    number1 = 10
    number2 = 20

    ' Compare the numbers and display messages
accordingly.
    If number1 > number2 Then
        ' This block executes if number1 is greater than
number2.
        MsgBox "Number 1 is greater than Number 2."
    ElseIf number1 < number2 Then
        ' This block executes if number1 is less than
number2.
        MsgBox "Number 1 is less than Number 2."
    Else
        ' This block executes if neither of the above
conditions are true (i.e., the numbers are equal).
        MsgBox "Number 1 and Number 2 are equal."
    End If
End Sub
```

➤ Key points:

- **Variable declaration and initialization**: the variables `number1` and `number2` are declared and then assigned values for comparison.
- `If...ElseIf...Else` **statement**: this structure evaluates conditions in sequence:

How to do this in VBA?? 202 ready-made macros: Streamline your tasks with proven expert solutions

- The `If` part checks if `number1` is greater than `number2`.
- The `ElseIf` part checks if `number1` is less than `number2`.
- The `Else` part covers the scenario where `number1` and `number2` are equal.
- **Action based on condition**: depending on the result of the condition checks, a different message box is displayed.

This example provides a clear illustration of using the `If...Else` statement in VBA for basic decision-making, enabling you to direct the flow of execution in your macros based on dynamic conditions.

If statement

The `If` statement in VBA is crucial for making decisions and executing code conditionally. Here's a basic example demonstrating how to use an `If` statement to check a condition - in this case, whether a number is positive, negative, or zero. The code includes comments to guide you through each step.

➢ Example: Checking if a number is positive, negative, or zero

```
Sub CheckNumber()
    ' This subroutine uses an If statement to check if a
number is positive, negative, or zero
    ' and displays an appropriate message.

    ' Declare and initialize a variable for the example.
    Dim number As Integer
    number = 0 ' Change this value to test different
scenarios.

    ' Check if the number is positive, negative, or zero
and display a corresponding message.
    If number > 0 Then
        MsgBox "The number is positive."
    ElseIf number < 0 Then
        MsgBox "The number is negative."
    Else
        MsgBox "The number is zero."
    End If
End Sub
```

How to do this in VBA?? 202 ready-made macros: Streamline your tasks with proven expert solutions

➢ Key points:

- **Variable initialization**: the variable `number` is initialized at the start. You can adjust its value to see different outcomes.
- **`If` condition**: the first condition checks if `number` is greater than 0. If true, it executes the code block that follows.
- **`ElseIf` condition**: if the first condition is false, the `ElseIf` condition checks if `number` is less than 0. If this condition is true, it executes its respective code block.
- **`Else` statement**: if none of the previous conditions are met (meaning the number is neither positive nor negative), the `Else` block is executed, indicating the number is zero.

This example provides a simple demonstration of using `If` statements in VBA to perform basic conditional checks and actions, a fundamental concept for creating dynamic and responsive VBA macros.

If Error

Handling errors gracefully in VBA is crucial for creating robust and user-friendly applications. The `If Err.Number <> 0 Then` statement allows you to check if an error has occurred and handle it accordingly. Here's an example that demonstrates how to use this error handling technique to manage an error that might occur during a division operation. This approach uses the `On Error Resume Next` statement to bypass the error and the `Err` object to check the error number. Comments in the code explain each step.

➢ Example: handling a division error

```
Sub DivisionWithErrorHandling()
    ' This subroutine demonstrates how to handle errors in
VBA using the If Err.Number statement.
    ' It attempts to perform a division operation that
might cause a division by zero error.

    Dim numerator As Double
    Dim denominator As Double
    Dim result As Variant

    ' Initialize the numerator and denominator.
    numerator = 10
```

```
        denominator = 0 ' This will potentially cause a
    division by zero error.


        ' Enable error handling to bypass errors.
        On Error Resume Next


        ' Attempt the division operation.
        result = numerator / denominator


        ' Check if an error occurred.
        If Err.Number <> 0 Then
            ' Handle the error. For a division by zero,
    Err.Number will be 11.
            MsgBox "An error occurred: " & Err.Description,
    vbCritical, "Error"
            Err.Clear ' Clear the error so it does not
    persist.
        Else
            ' If no error occurred, display the result.
            MsgBox "The result is: " & result, vbInformation,
    "Result"
        End If


        ' Turn off error bypassing after handling the error.
        On Error GoTo 0
    End Sub
```

➢ Key points:

- **Error handling activation**: `On Error Resume Next` tells VBA to continue execution with the next line of code after an error occurs, instead of breaking.
- **Error checking**: after the operation that might fail, `If Err.Number <> 0 Then` checks whether an error occurred.
- **Error handling**: inside the `If` block, you can handle the error, for example, by showing a message box with `Err.Description`, which contains a description of the error.
- **Clearing the error**: `Err.Clear` is used to reset the error object so that subsequent operations are not affected by the previous error.

- **Reset error handling**: `On Error GoTo 0` disables the error bypassing enabled by `On Error Resume Next`, returning to normal error handling behavior.

This method provides a structured way to handle potential errors in specific parts of your VBA code, enhancing the stability and usability of your macros.

Include quotes in a string

Including quotes within a string in VBA can be done by using double quotation marks ("") inside the string or by using the `Chr` function with the ASCII code for a quotation mark (34). Here are examples demonstrating both methods to include quotes in a string. Comments in the code explain each approach for clarity.

➢ Example: Including quotes in a string

```
Sub IncludeQuotesInString()
    ' This subroutine demonstrates two methods to include
    quotes in a string in VBA.

    ' Method 1: Using double quotation marks ("").
    Dim stringWithQuotes As String
    stringWithQuotes = "She said, ""Hello, world!"""
    ' This will produce: She said, "Hello, world!"

    ' Display the string from Method 1.
    MsgBox stringWithQuotes, vbInformation, "String with
    Quotes (Method 1)"

    ' Method 2: Using the Chr function with the ASCII code
    for a quotation mark (34).
    Dim stringWithQuotesChr As String
    stringWithQuotesChr = "She said, " & Chr(34) & "Hello,
    world!" & Chr(34)
    ' This will also produce: She said, "Hello, world!"

    ' Display the string from Method 2.
```

142

How to do this in VBA?? 202 ready-made macros: Streamline your tasks with proven expert solutions

```
        MsgBox stringWithQuotesChr, vbInformation, "String
    with Quotes (Method 2)"
    End Sub
```

➢ Key points:

- **Double quotation marks**: to include quotes directly in a string, double them up (`""`). VBA interprets this as a single quotation mark in the string output.
- **`Chr` function**: `Chr(34)` returns the quotation mark character (`"`), as 34 is the ASCII code for a double quote. This method is useful when concatenating strings or when you find it clearer than using doubled quotation marks.

Both methods are valid for including quotation marks in strings within VBA code, and you can choose the one that best fits your coding style or the specific needs of your application.

Index

The `Index` function in Excel VBA is versatile, allowing you to retrieve an element from a range or array based on its position. In VBA, this function is typically used in conjunction with arrays. Below is an example demonstrating how to use the `Index` function to access a specific element within a two-dimensional array. This example also illustrates how to create a simple array and retrieve an element based on its row and column indexes. Comments in the code provide clarity on each operation.

➢ Example: Accessing an element in a two-dimensional array with `Index`

```
    Sub UseIndexFunction()
        ' This subroutine demonstrates the use of the Index
    function to access an element
        ' in a two-dimensional array in VBA.

        ' Create a sample two-dimensional array.
        Dim sampleArray(1 To 3, 1 To 2) As Variant ' 3 rows, 2
    columns
        sampleArray(1, 1) = "Row 1, Col 1"
        sampleArray(1, 2) = "Row 1, Col 2"
        sampleArray(2, 1) = "Row 2, Col 1"
        sampleArray(2, 2) = "Row 2, Col 2"
```

143

```vba
sampleArray(3, 1) = "Row 3, Col 1"
sampleArray(3, 2) = "Row 3, Col 2"


' Define the row and column to access.
Dim rowIndex As Integer
Dim columnIndex As Integer
rowIndex = 2
columnIndex = 1


' Access an element using the Application.Index
function.
' Note: Application.Index is more commonly used in
worksheet formulas but can be utilized in VBA.
Dim element As Variant
element = Application.Index(sampleArray, rowIndex,
columnIndex)


' Display the accessed element.
MsgBox "The element at Row " & rowIndex & ", Column "
& columnIndex & " is: " & element, _
        vbInformation, "Element Accessed with Index"
End Sub
```

➢ Key points:

- **Two-dimensional array**: the array `sampleArray` is defined with dimensions to hold a set of sample data.
- **Element access**: the `Application.Index` function is used to retrieve an element from the array based on the specified row and column indexes.
- **Displaying the element**: a message box shows the value of the accessed element, demonstrating how the `Index` function can be used to dynamically access array elements.

This example provides a practical demonstration of using the `Index` function within VBA, a valuable tool for working with arrays and ranges in Excel macros.

Index Match

The combination of `INDEX` and `MATCH` functions is a powerful tool in Excel for looking up values within a range or array, commonly used as an alternative to `VLOOKUP` or `HLOOKUP` with the benefit of more flexibility and efficiency, especially when handling large datasets. In VBA, you can utilize these Excel functions to perform similar lookups within your macros. Below is an example that demonstrates how to use `Application.WorksheetFunction.Index` and `Application.WorksheetFunction.Match` to find and return a value from a table based on a search criterion. Comments in the code provide clarity on each operation.

➢ Example: Using INDEX MATCH in VBA to Look Up a Value

```
Sub UseIndexMatch()
    ' This subroutine demonstrates how to perform a lookup
using the INDEX and MATCH functions in VBA.

    ' Sample data setup. In a real scenario, this would be
your Excel range.
    Dim dataRange As Range
    Set dataRange =
ThisWorkbook.Sheets("Sheet1").Range("A1:B5") ' Assume this
range contains lookup data.
    ' Example data in A1:B5:
    ' A         B
    ' 1 Item    Value
    ' 2 Apple   100
    ' 3 Banana  200
    ' 4 Cherry  300
    ' 5 Date    400

    ' Lookup value.
    Dim lookupValue As String
    lookupValue = "Banana"

    ' Perform the lookup.
    Dim matchIndex As Long
```

```
    matchIndex =
Application.WorksheetFunction.Match(lookupValue,
dataRange.Columns(1), 0)


    ' Use INDEX to retrieve the value from the matched
position in the second column.
    Dim result As Variant
    result =
Application.WorksheetFunction.Index(dataRange.Columns(2),
matchIndex)


    ' Display the result.
    MsgBox "The value for " & lookupValue & " is: " &
result, vbInformation, "Lookup Result"
End Sub
```

➢ Key points:

- **Data range**: the `dataRange` variable represents the range of your data in Excel, which you're looking through. Adjust the range to fit your actual data.
- **Lookup value**: the `lookupValue` is what you're searching for in the first column of your data range.
- **MATCH function**: used to find the position of `lookupValue` within the first column of `dataRange`. The `Match` function returns the row index of the found value.
- **INDEX function**: with the index obtained from `MATCH`, the `Index` function retrieves the value from the corresponding row in the second column of `dataRange`.
- **Error handling**: this basic example does not include error handling for cases where `Match` does not find the lookup value. In production code, consider using `On Error Resume Next` before the `Match` call and check if an error occurred after it.

This example demonstrates how to replicate the functionality of an `INDEX MATCH` combination within VBA, offering a robust method for searching and retrieving data based on specific criteria.

Input

Capturing user input in Excel VBA can be done using the `InputBox` function, which prompts the user to enter information in a dialog box. The information entered by the user can then be used within your macro for various purposes such as filtering data, setting values, or making calculations. Below is an example demonstrating how to use the `InputBox` function to get a user input string, and then display that input back to the user using a message box. Comments in the code explain each step for clarity.

➤ Example: Using `InputBox` to capture user input

```
Sub GetUserInput()
    ' This subroutine demonstrates how to capture user
input using an InputBox and then use that input.

    ' Prompt the user for input using an InputBox.
    ' The first parameter is the prompt message, and the
second parameter is the dialog box title.
    Dim userInput As String
    userInput = InputBox("Please enter your name:", "Name
Entry")

    ' Check if the user clicked Cancel or entered an empty
string.
    If userInput = "" Then
        MsgBox "No input was provided. Exiting
subroutine.", vbExclamation, "No Input"
        Exit Sub ' Exit the subroutine if no input was
provided.
    End If

    ' Display the user input using a message box.
    ' This step is just to confirm that the input was
captured and can be used.
    MsgBox "Hello, " & userInput & "!", vbInformation,
"Greeting"
End Sub
```

➢ Key points:

- **Prompting for input**: the `InputBox` function displays a dialog box where the user can type an input. The function returns the input as a string.
- **Handling empty input**: it's important to check if the user pressed the Cancel button or entered an empty string. This scenario is handled by checking if `userInput` is an empty string and exiting the subroutine if true.
- **Using user input**: after capturing the input, the example demonstrates how to use it by greeting the user with the name they entered.

This simple example provides a foundation for interacting with users in your VBA projects, enabling you to request and utilize input dynamically within your macros.

Insert

Inserting rows, columns, or cells within an Excel worksheet via VBA can significantly automate and speed up data organization tasks. Here's a straightforward example showing how to insert a row, a column, and a single cell. Each operation is detailed with comments for clarity, providing insight into how these basic but essential tasks can be accomplished with VBA.

➢ Example: Inserting rows, columns, and cells in VBA

```
Sub InsertExamples()
    ' This subroutine demonstrates how to insert rows,
columns, and cells in Excel using VBA.

    ' Insert a row above row 5.
    Rows("5:5").Insert Shift:=xlDown,
CopyOrigin:=xlFormatFromLeftOrAbove
    ' This shifts the existing row 5 and below down by one
row.

    ' Insert a column to the left of column C.
    Columns("C:C").Insert Shift:=xlToRight,
CopyOrigin:=xlFormatFromLeftOrAbove
```

```
    ' This shifts the existing column C and to the right,
    to the right by one column.


    ' Insert a cell at position B2, shifting cells down in
    the same column.
    ' This operation inserts a single cell, not an entire
    row or column.
    Range("B2").Insert Shift:=xlDown,
CopyOrigin:=xlFormatFromLeftOrAbove


    ' Notify the user of the insertions.
    MsgBox "A row above row 5, a column left of column C,
    and a cell at B2 have been inserted.", vbInformation,
    "Insertions Completed"
    End Sub
```

➢ Key points:

- **Inserting a row**: the `Rows("5:5").Insert` method inserts a new row above the specified row, in this case, row 5. The `Shift:=xlDown` argument specifies that existing rows should be moved downwards.
- **Inserting a column**: the `Columns("C:C").Insert` method inserts a new column to the left of the specified column, here column C. The `Shift:=xlToRight` argument specifies that existing columns should be moved to the right.
- **Inserting a cell**: the `Range("B2").Insert` method inserts a cell at the specified location, shifting existing cells in the same column downward. This demonstrates how to insert a single cell rather than an entire row or column.
- `CopyOrigin:=xlFormatFromLeftOrAbove`: this optional argument specifies that the formatting for the inserted row, column, or cell should be copied from the left or above the insertion point.

This example provides a practical demonstration of inserting rows, columns, and cells within an Excel worksheet using VBA, a fundamental capability for dynamically managing worksheet layouts in your Excel macros and applications.

Join function

The `Join` function in VBA is used to concatenate (join) an array of strings into a single string, with each element in the array being separated by a specified delimiter. This can be particularly useful when you need to create a string from multiple pieces of data stored in an array. Below is an example demonstrating how to use the `Join` function to combine elements of an array into a single, comma-separated string. Comments in the code explain each step for clarity.

➢Example: Using the `Join` function

```vba
Sub UseJoinFunction()
    ' This subroutine demonstrates how to concatenate an
array of strings into a single string using the Join
function in VBA.

    ' Define an array of strings.
    Dim fruits As Variant
    fruits = Array("Apple", "Banana", "Cherry", "Date")

    ' Use the Join function to concatenate the array
elements into a single string.
    ' The elements will be separated by a comma and a
space.
    Dim allFruits As String
    allFruits = Join(fruits, ", ")

    ' Display the resulting string.
    MsgBox "The concatenated string of fruits is: " &
allFruits, vbInformation, "Joined String"
End Sub
```

➢ Key points:

- **Array of strings**: an array named `fruits` is declared and initialized with several fruit names.
- **Using `Join`**: the `Join` function is called with two arguments: the array to be joined (`fruits`) and the delimiter (`, `), which is a comma followed by a space in this case.

- **Resulting string**: the `allFruits` variable stores the result of the `Join` operation, which is a single string containing all array elements separated by the specified delimiter.
- **Displaying the result**: a message box is used to show the concatenated string, providing a clear example of how the `Join` function simplifies the process of combining array elements into a single string.

This example provides a clear demonstration of the `Join` function's utility in VBA for creating strings from arrays, a handy technique for data presentation, logging, or any situation where array elements need to be outputted in a consolidated format.

Jump

In VBA, creating a "jump" or branching in code typically involves using the `GoTo` statement, which directs the flow of execution to a specified label within a subroutine. This can be useful for error handling or bypassing certain sections of code under specific conditions. However, it's important to use `GoTo` judiciously, as it can make code harder to read and maintain if overused. Below is an example that demonstrates how to use the `GoTo` statement to jump to different parts of a subroutine based on a condition. Comments in the code explain each step.

➤ Example: Using `GoTo` for conditional jumps

```
Sub ConditionalJump()
    ' This subroutine demonstrates how to use the GoTo
statement to conditionally jump to different parts of the
code.

    ' Generate a random number between 1 and 10.
    Dim randomNumber As Integer
    randomNumber = Int((10 * Rnd) + 1)

    ' Check if the random number is odd or even.
    If randomNumber Mod 2 = 0 Then
        ' If the number is even, jump to the EvenNumber
label.
        GoTo EvenNumber
    Else
```

```
                    ' If the number is odd, jump to the OddNumber
label.
            GoTo OddNumber
        End If


    EvenNumber:
        ' Code block executed when the random number is even.
        MsgBox "The number " & randomNumber & " is even.",
    vbInformation, "Even Number"
        GoTo EndSub


    OddNumber:
        ' Code block executed when the random number is odd.
        MsgBox "The number " & randomNumber & " is odd.",
    vbInformation, "Odd Number"
        GoTo EndSub


    EndSub:
        ' This label serves as a common exit point for the
    subroutine to ensure the subroutine cleanly exits after
    executing the relevant block.
        End Sub
```

➢ Key points:

- **Conditional check**: the subroutine starts by checking if a randomly generated number is odd or even using the `Mod` operator.
- `GoTo` **statement**: based on the condition, the `GoTo` statement directs the flow of execution to either the `EvenNumber` or `OddNumber` label.
- **Labels for code blocks**: `EvenNumber` and `OddNumber` serve as labels marking specific sections of code to execute. Execution jumps to these labels based on the earlier condition.
- **Common exit point**: the `EndSub` label acts as a common exit point to ensure that the subroutine exits cleanly, regardless of which condition was met.

This example illustrates the basic use of the `GoTo` statement to control code execution flow in VBA, demonstrating a structured way to handle different execution paths based on conditions.

Jump to a line

In VBA, the `**GoTo**` statement can also be used to jump to a specific line of code, designated by a line label. This is useful for redirecting the flow of execution within a procedure, often in response to specific conditions or errors. Below is an example that demonstrates how to use `**GoTo**` to jump to a specific line in a subroutine. This example will include a basic setup where we simulate a decision-making process, and based on the condition, jump to a labeled line. Comments in the code will guide you through the process.

➢ Example: Jumping to a specific line in VBA

```
Sub JumpToLineExample()
    ' This subroutine demonstrates how to jump to a
specific line in VBA using the GoTo statement.

    ' Generate a random number between 1 and 2 to simulate
a simple decision.
    Dim decision As Integer
    decision = Int((2 * Rnd) + 1)

    ' Decide to jump based on the random number generated.
    If decision = 1 Then
        ' If decision is 1, jump to the Label1 line.
        GoTo Label1
    Else
        ' If decision is 2, jump to the Label2 line.
        GoTo Label2
    End If

Label1:
    ' Code to execute if jumped to Label1.
    MsgBox "Jumped to Label1", vbInformation, "Decision 1"
    GoTo EndSub

Label2:
    ' Code to execute if jumped to Label2.
    MsgBox "Jumped to Label2", vbInformation, "Decision 2"
```

```
EndSub:
    ' This line label acts as a common endpoint to prevent
    fall-through from the above conditions.
    End Sub
```

➢ Key points:

- **Decision making**: a random number (`decision`) is generated to simulate a condition check.
- **`GoTo` statement**: based on the value of `decision`, execution jumps to either `Label1` or `Label2`.
- **Label execution**: each label marks a section of code that executes a specific action—in this case, displaying a message box indicating which label was jumped to.
- **Common endpoint (`EndSub`)**: a final `GoTo EndSub` ensures the subroutine exits cleanly after executing one of the labeled sections, preventing accidental execution of subsequent sections.

This example illustrates how to effectively use `GoTo` for controlling program flow in VBA, guiding execution to specific lines based on runtime conditions or other logic.

Keep leading zeros

Preserving leading zeros in numerical data is essential in various contexts, such as when dealing with ID numbers, ZIP codes, or other data formats where the zeros are significant. Excel automatically removes leading zeros from numbers because it treats them as numerical values by default. However, you can use VBA to format cells to text, ensuring that leading zeros are kept. Here's an example demonstrating how to format a range of cells as text and then set their values, preserving any leading zeros. Comments in the code explain each step for clarity.

➢ Example: Keeping leading zeros in cell values

```
Sub KeepLeadingZeros()
    ' This subroutine demonstrates how to keep leading
    zeros in cell values by formatting cells as text.

    ' Specify the target range you want to format and set
    values for.
```

```
        Dim targetRange As Range
        Set targetRange =
ThisWorkbook.Sheets("Sheet1").Range("A1:A5")


        ' Format the target range as text.
        targetRange.NumberFormat = "@"


        ' Set values in the range. These values will retain
leading zeros because of the text format.
        targetRange.Cells(1, 1).Value = "00123"
        targetRange.Cells(2, 1).Value = "000456"
        targetRange.Cells(3, 1).Value = "0000789"
        targetRange.Cells(4, 1).Value = "00001234"
        targetRange.Cells(5, 1).Value = "12345" ' This value
has no leading zeros but is included for comparison.


        ' Notify the user that the operation is complete.
        MsgBox "Cells have been formatted as text and values
with leading zeros have been set.", vbInformation,
"Operation Complete"
        End Sub
```

➢ Key points:

- **Text format**: setting the `NumberFormat` property of the range to `"@"` formats the cells as text, which is crucial for preserving leading zeros in values.
- **Setting values**: after formatting the range as text, any value you set (including those intended to be numeric) is treated as a text string, thus retaining any leading zeros.
- **Target range**: the example uses a specific range (`A1:A5`) on `Sheet1`. Adjust the `targetRange` variable as necessary to suit your needs.

This method provides a simple and effective way to ensure that leading zeros are kept in Excel cell values, making it suitable for handling data that requires such formatting.

Load user form

Loading and displaying a UserForm in Excel VBA is a common task when creating interactive applications. First, you need to have a UserForm created in the VBA editor. Here's a simple example that demonstrates how to show a UserForm named `**MyUserForm**`. This UserForm should be created beforehand in the VBA editor under the UserForms. You can add controls like text boxes, labels, and command buttons to `**MyUserForm**` as needed. The comments in the code explain each step for clarity.

➢ Step 1: Create the UserForm

1. Open the VBA Editor (ALT + F11).
2. Insert a new UserForm by going to `**Insert > UserForm**`.
3. Optionally, add some controls such as a TextBox or CommandButton.
4. Name the UserForm `**MyUserForm**` in the Properties window.

➢Step 2: Show the UserForm with VBA

```
Sub ShowMyUserForm()
    ' This subroutine demonstrates how to load and show a
UserForm named MyUserForm.

    ' Load the UserForm into memory. This step is optional
as Show method will also load the form.
    ' But it's useful if you need to initialize or set
properties before displaying it.
    Load MyUserForm

    ' Display the UserForm.
    MyUserForm.Show

    ' Note: The Load statement is optional here because
calling Show will automatically load the UserForm if it's
not already loaded.
    ' However, Load can be useful for initializing the
form before it becomes visible.
End Sub
```

➢ Key points:

156

How to do this in VBA?? 202 ready-made macros: Streamline your tasks with proven expert solutions

- **Loading the UserForm**: the `Load` statement initializes the UserForm and loads it into memory but does not display it. This is optional and useful for pre-display initialization.
- **Displaying the UserForm**: the `Show` method makes the UserForm visible to the user.
- **UserForm naming**: ensure that the UserForm name in the code (`MyUserForm`) matches the name given to the actual UserForm in the VBA project.

This example gives a basic overview of how to work with UserForms in VBA, from loading to showing them, providing a foundation for building interactive elements in your Excel applications.

Lock cells

Locking cells in Excel VBA is commonly done to protect specific data or formulas from being altered by users. By default, all cells in a worksheet are locked, but this has no effect until the worksheet is protected. Here's an example that demonstrates how to lock a specific range of cells and then protect the worksheet to enforce the lock. This approach ensures that only the specified cells are locked and that the rest remain editable. Comments in the code explain each step for clarity.

➢ Example: Locking cells and protecting the worksheet

```
Sub LockCells()
    ' This subroutine demonstrates how to lock specific
cells in an Excel worksheet using VBA.

    ' Reference the target worksheet.
    Dim ws As Worksheet
    Set ws = ThisWorkbook.Sheets("Sheet1") ' Adjust the
sheet name as needed.

    ' Unprotect the sheet before making changes to cell
locking.
    ws.Unprotect "YourPassword" ' Replace "YourPassword"
with your sheet's protection password if applicable.

    ' First, ensure that all cells are unlocked.
```

How to do this in VBA?? 202 ready-made macros: Streamline your tasks with proven expert solutions

```
ws.Cells.Locked = False


' Now, specify the range of cells to lock. For
example, lock cells A1 to B2.
    With ws.Range("A1:B2")
        .Locked = True ' Set the Locked property to True
to lock the cells.
    End With


' Protect the worksheet to enforce the locking. Use
the same password as above.
    ws.Protect "YourPassword"


' Notify the user that the cells have been locked.
    MsgBox "Cells A1:B2 have been locked. The worksheet is
now protected.", vbInformation, "Cells Locked"
End Sub
```

➢ Key points:

- **Worksheet reference**: modify the `ws` variable to refer to your target worksheet.
- **Unprotect sheet**: if the worksheet is already protected, you must unprotect it first to change cell properties. Use `ws.Unprotect "YourPassword"` with the actual password.
- **Unlock all cells**: setting `ws.Cells.Locked = False` ensures that all cells are initially unlocked, allowing you to selectively lock only specific cells.
- **Lock specific cells**: the `.Locked = True` property is applied to the target range (`ws.Range("A1:B2")` in this example) to lock those cells.
- **Protect sheet**: re-apply protection to the worksheet with `ws.Protect "YourPassword"` to enforce the cell locking.
- **Password usage**: replace `"YourPassword"` with your actual protection password. If you don't want to use a password, you can omit the password argument or set it as an empty string `""`, but keep in mind that this reduces security.

This method provides a structured way to protect specific parts of your worksheet from unintended modifications, enhancing the integrity of your Excel applications.

Loop

Looping structures in VBA allow you to execute a block of code repeatedly, either a set number of times or until a certain condition is met. One of the most commonly used loops is the `For...Next` loop, which is ideal for iterating over a range of values. Here's an example demonstrating how to use a `For...Next` loop to iterate through a range of numbers, calculate their squares, and output the results to the Immediate Window. Comments in the code explain each step for clarity.

➢ Example: Calculating squares with a `For...Next` Loop

```
Sub CalculateSquares()
    ' This subroutine demonstrates how to use a For...Next
loop to iterate through a range of numbers
    ' and calculate their squares.

    Dim i As Integer ' Loop counter variable
    Dim square As Integer ' Variable to hold the square of
the current number

    ' Define the start and end numbers for the loop.
    Dim startNum As Integer, endNum As Integer
    startNum = 1 ' Starting number
    endNum = 10 ' Ending number

    ' Use the For...Next loop to iterate from startNum to
endNum.
    For i = startNum To endNum
        ' Calculate the square of the current number (i).
        square = i * i

        ' Output the result to the Immediate Window (View
> Immediate Window in the VBA editor).
        Debug.Print "The square of "; i; " is "; square
    Next i ' Move to the next value of i and repeat until
i reaches endNum.
End Sub
```

How to do this in VBA?? 202 ready-made macros: Streamline your tasks with proven expert solutions

➢ Key points:

- **Loop counter (`i`)**: serves as the control variable for the loop, indicating the current iteration.
- **Starting and ending values**: the loop iterates from `startNum` to `endNum`, inclusive.
- **Calculation inside the loop**: for each iteration, the square of the current number (`i`) is calculated and outputted.
- **`Debug.Print`**: outputs the result to the Immediate Window, allowing you to see the loop's progress and the squares of numbers from 1 to 10.

This example showcases the basic structure and functionality of a `For...Next` loop in VBA, illustrating how to use it for repetitive tasks and calculations.

Loop code

A loop is a fundamental concept in programming that allows code to be executed repeatedly based on a condition. One common type of loop in VBA is the `Do While` loop, which continues to run as long as a given condition is true. Here's an example demonstrating how to use a `Do While` loop to iterate through numbers from 1 to 10, doubling each number, and printing the result to the Immediate Window. Comments in the code explain each step.

➢ Example: Doubling numbers with a `Do While` loop

```
Sub DoubleNumbers()
    ' This subroutine demonstrates how to use a Do While
loop to iterate through numbers 1 to 10,
    ' doubling each number and printing the result to the
Immediate Window.

    Dim i As Integer
    i = 1 ' Start from 1

    ' Continue looping as long as i is less than or equal
to 10.
    Do While i <= 10
        ' Double the value of i.
        Dim doubledValue As Integer
        doubledValue = i * 2
```

```
        ' Print the original and doubled values to the
Immediate Window.
        Debug.Print "Original: " & i & ", Doubled: " &
doubledValue

        ' Increment i to move to the next number.
        i = i + 1
    Loop ' End of the Do While loop
End Sub
```

➢ Key points:

- **Initialization**: the variable `i` is initialized to 1, marking the starting point of the loop.
- **Loop condition**: the `Do While` loop continues as long as `i` is less than or equal to 10.
- **Doubling the number**: inside the loop, each number (`i`) is doubled, and both the original and doubled values are printed.
- **Increment**: at the end of each loop iteration, `i` is incremented by 1 to ensure the loop progresses towards its end condition.

This example provides a clear illustration of using the `Do While` loop in VBA for iterative tasks that require condition-based repetition, demonstrating a practical approach to manipulating and displaying a sequence of numbers.

Loop through a column

Looping through a column in Excel VBA is a common task when you need to process or analyze data in each cell of a column sequentially. Below is an example demonstrating how to use a `For` loop to iterate through each cell in a specific column (Column A in this case) of a worksheet from row 1 to the last row with data. This example increments each number found in the column by 1. It showcases basic error handling to skip cells that do not contain numeric values. Comments in the code explain each step for clarity.

➢ Example: Looping through a column and incrementing numeric values

```
Sub IncrementColumnValues()
    ' This subroutine demonstrates how to loop through all
the cells in a specific column (Column A)
    ' and increment each numeric value by 1.
```

```vba
Dim ws As Worksheet
Set ws = ThisWorkbook.Sheets("Sheet1") ' Adjust the
sheet name as needed.

' Determine the last row in Column A with data.
Dim lastRow As Long
lastRow = ws.Cells(ws.Rows.Count, "A").End(xlUp).Row

Dim i As Long ' Loop counter variable
Dim cellValue As Variant ' Variable to hold the cell
value for processing

' Loop through each cell in Column A from row 1 to
lastRow.
For i = 1 To lastRow
    With ws.Cells(i, "A")
        cellValue = .Value ' Get the current cell's
value

        ' Check if the cell contains a numeric value
before trying to increment.
        If IsNumeric(cellValue) Then
            .Value = cellValue + 1 ' Increment the
cell's value by 1
        Else
            ' Optionally handle or skip cells that do
not contain numeric values.
            ' For this example, we'll simply skip
them.
        End If
    End With
Next i

' Notify the user that the operation is complete.
```

```
    MsgBox "All numeric values in Column A have been
    incremented by 1.", vbInformation, "Operation Complete"
    End Sub
```

Attention! This calculation algorithm is not efficient. However, it is great for showing how a loop works.

➤ Key points:

- **Worksheet reference**: modify the `ws` variable to refer to the worksheet you're working with.
- **Finding the last row**: `lastRow` is determined using the `.End(xlUp)` method starting from the bottom of Column A, which finds the last row with data.
- **Looping through cells**: the `For` loop iterates through each row in Column A from the first row to `lastRow`.
- **Incrementing numeric values**: inside the loop, the code checks if the cell contains a numeric value using `IsNumeric` and increments it by 1 if true.

This example provides a practical method for iterating through a column in Excel VBA, processing numeric data in each cell. This approach can be adapted for a wide range of data manipulation and analysis tasks in Excel.

Loop through a range

Looping through a range of cells in Excel VBA allows you to perform actions on each cell within the specified range. This can be particularly useful for data analysis, formatting, or calculation tasks. Below is an example that demonstrates how to use the `For Each` loop to iterate through a specified range and change the background color of each cell to yellow if it contains a numeric value. Comments in the code explain each step for clarity.

➤ Example: Looping through a range and highlighting numeric cells

```
Sub HighlightNumericCells()
    ' This subroutine demonstrates how to loop through a
    specified range of cells,
    ' checking for numeric values and highlighting those
    cells by changing their background color to yellow.

    Dim ws As Worksheet
```

```
Set ws = ThisWorkbook.Sheets("Sheet1") ' Adjust the
sheet name as needed.

' Define the range you want to loop through. In this
case, we'll use A1:C10 on Sheet1.
Dim targetRange As Range
Set targetRange = ws.Range("A1:C10")

Dim cell As Range ' Variable to hold each cell in the
loop.

' Loop through each cell in the specified range.
For Each cell In targetRange
    ' Check if the cell contains a numeric value.
    If IsNumeric(cell.Value) Then
        ' If the cell is numeric, change its
background color to yellow.
        cell.Interior.Color = vbYellow
    End If
Next cell

' Notify the user that the operation is complete.
MsgBox "Numeric cells within the specified range have
been highlighted.", vbInformation, "Highlight Complete"
End Sub
```

➢ Key points:

- **Worksheet reference**: the `ws` variable references the target worksheet. You may need to adjust `"Sheet1"` to the name of your specific worksheet.
- **Specifying the range**: the `targetRange` variable defines the range of cells you intend to loop through. Adjust `"A1:C10"` according to your needs.
- **Looping through each cell**: the `For Each` loop iterates over each cell within `targetRange`. The `cell` variable represents the current cell in the loop.

- **Conditionally formatting cells**: inside the loop, the `If IsNumeric(cell.Value)` statement checks if the cell contains a numeric value. If true, the cell's background color is set to yellow.

This example demonstrates a practical way to use VBA for iterating over a range and applying conditional formatting based on the content of each cell, which can be adapted for various data processing and visualization tasks.

Loop through an array

Looping through an array in Excel VBA is a fundamental technique for processing each element within the array. Here's an example demonstrating how to use the `For Each` loop to iterate through a variant array of fruit names, displaying each fruit name in a message box. Comments in the code explain each step for clarity.

➢ Example: Looping through an array of fruit names

```
Sub LoopThroughArray()
    ' This subroutine demonstrates how to loop through an
array of fruit names and display each name using a message
box.

    ' Declare and initialize an array of fruit names.
    Dim fruits As Variant
    fruits = Array("Apple", "Banana", "Cherry", "Date",
"Elderberry")

    Dim fruit As Variant ' Variable to hold each fruit
name during the loop.

    ' Use the For Each loop to iterate through each
element in the fruits array.
    For Each fruit In fruits
        ' Display the current fruit name in a message box.
        MsgBox "Fruit Name: " & fruit, vbInformation,
"Fruit Loop"
    Next fruit
End Sub
```

➢ Key points:

- **Array initialization**: the `fruits` array is declared and initialized with a list of fruit names. This is a variant array, which is flexible and can hold any type of data.
- **Looping through the array**: the `For Each` loop iterates through each element in the `fruits` array. The `fruit` variable represents the current element being processed.
- Displaying each element: inside the loop, a message box displays the name of the current fruit. This demonstrates how to access and use each element of the array individually.

This example provides a basic demonstration of iterating over an array in VBA, showing how to process or display each element in turn. This approach can be adapted for various purposes, such as performing calculations on array elements, evaluating conditions, or populating worksheet cells.

Loop through rows

Looping through rows in an Excel worksheet using VBA is a common task for processing data row by row. Here's an example demonstrating how to use a `For` loop to iterate through each row in a specified range and check if the value in column A of the current row is greater than a certain value. If so, it highlights the cell in column A. Comments in the code explain each step for clarity.

➢ Example: Looping through rows and highlighting based on condition

```
Sub LoopThroughRowsAndHighlight()
    ' This subroutine demonstrates how to loop through
each row in a specified range
    ' and highlight cells in column A if their value is
greater than 10.

    Dim ws As Worksheet
    Set ws = ThisWorkbook.Sheets("Sheet1") ' Adjust the
sheet name as needed.

    ' Define the start and end row for the loop.
    Dim startRow As Long, endRow As Long
    startRow = 1 ' Start from row 1
```

```vba
    endRow = ws.Cells(ws.Rows.Count, "A").End(xlUp).Row '
Find the last row with data in column A

    Dim row As Long ' Variable for the current row in the
loop

    ' Loop through each row in the specified range.
    For row = startRow To endRow
        ' Check the value in column A of the current row.
        If ws.Cells(row, "A").Value > 10 Then
            ' If the value is greater than 10, highlight
the cell in column A.
            ws.Cells(row, "A").Interior.Color = RGB(255,
255, 0) ' Yellow color
        End If
    Next row

    ' Notify the user that the operation is complete.
    MsgBox "Cells in Column A with values greater than 10
have been highlighted.", vbInformation, "Highlight
Complete"
End Sub
```

➤ Key points:

- **Worksheet reference**: modify the `ws` variable to refer to your target worksheet.
- **Determining the range**: the `startRow` and `endRow` variables define the range of rows to loop through. `endRow` is dynamically calculated to be the last row with data in column A.
- **Looping through rows**: the `For` loop iterates from `startRow` to `endRow`, accessing each row in turn.
- **Conditional highlighting**: inside the loop, an `If` statement checks if the value in column A is greater than 10. If so, the cell's background color is set to yellow.

This example demonstrates a practical way to iterate through rows in an Excel worksheet using VBA, performing conditional checks and applying formatting based on those conditions.

Loop through sheets

Looping through all worksheets in an Excel workbook using VBA allows you to perform actions or apply changes across multiple sheets efficiently. Here's an example demonstrating how to use a `For Each` loop to iterate through each worksheet in the active workbook and rename each sheet by appending " - **Processed**" to its existing name. Comments in the code explain each step for clarity.

➤ Example: Looping through sheets and renaming them

```
Sub LoopThroughSheetsAndRename()
    ' This subroutine demonstrates how to loop through all
worksheets in the active workbook
    ' and append " - Processed" to the name of each sheet.

    Dim ws As Worksheet ' Variable to hold each worksheet
during the loop.

    ' Loop through each worksheet in the active workbook.
    For Each ws In ThisWorkbook.Worksheets
        ' Append " - Processed" to the current worksheet's
name.
        ws.Name = ws.Name & " - Processed"
    Next ws

    ' Notify the user that the operation is complete.
    MsgBox "All sheets have been renamed.", vbInformation,
"Sheets Renamed"
End Sub
```

➤ Key points:

- **Worksheet variable (`ws`)**: serves as a placeholder for each worksheet as the loop iterates through the `Worksheets` collection of `ThisWorkbook`.
- **Renaming sheets**: inside the loop, the name of each worksheet (`ws.Name`) is modified by appending " - **Processed**" to its current name.

- **Workbook scope**: this script affects all worksheets in the workbook where the VBA code resides (`ThisWorkbook`). If you prefer to work with the workbook currently active on the user's screen, you could use `ActiveWorkbook` instead of `ThisWorkbook`.

This example demonstrates a straightforward method for iterating through and renaming worksheets within an Excel workbook using VBA, showcasing the efficiency of processing multiple sheets with a simple loop.

Name a chart

Naming a chart in Excel using VBA is essential for easily identifying and referencing it within your code, especially when working with multiple charts. Below is an example that demonstrates how to create a chart in Excel and then name it using VBA. This example assumes you already have some data to create a chart. If not, please adjust the range `A1:B5` to fit your data structure. Comments in the code explain each step for clarity.

➢ Example: Creating and naming a chart

```
Sub CreateAndNameChart()
    ' This subroutine demonstrates how to create a chart
    and then give it a specific name using VBA.

    Dim chartObj As ChartObject ' Variable to hold the
    newly created chart object.
    Dim ws As Worksheet ' Variable to hold the reference
    to the active worksheet.
    Set ws = ActiveSheet ' Consider using a specific sheet
    name like ThisWorkbook.Sheets("Sheet1").

    ' Add a new chart to the worksheet.
    Set chartObj = ws.ChartObjects.Add(Left:=100,
Width:=375, Top:=50, Height:=225)
    With chartObj
        ' Set the chart data range and chart type.
        .Chart.SetSourceData Source:=ws.Range("A1:B5")
        .Chart.ChartType = xlLine ' Example: Create a line
    chart. Adjust as needed.
```

How to do this in VBA?? 202 ready-made macros: Streamline your tasks with proven expert solutions

```
         ' Name the chart. Ensure the name is unique within
the workbook.
         .Name = "MyNewChart"
     End With


     ' Notify the user that the chart has been created and
named.
     MsgBox "A new chart named '" & chartObj.Name & "' has
been created.", vbInformation, "Chart Created and Named"
     End Sub
```

➤ Key points:

- **Chart object**: a `ChartObject` variable (`chartObj`) is declared to hold the chart created on the worksheet (`ws`).
- **Worksheet reference**: the `ws` variable is set to the active sheet for simplicity. You may specify a particular worksheet if preferred.
- **Creating the chart**: the `ChartObjects.Add` method creates a new chart on the worksheet, with its position and size specified by the `Left`, `Width`, `Top`, and `Height` parameters.
- **Setting data and type**: the chart's data source and type are set using the `.Chart.SetSourceData` method and `.Chart.ChartType` property, respectively.
- **Naming the chart**: the chart is named using the `.Name` property. It's important to use a unique name to avoid conflicts.

This example provides a practical approach to programmatically creating and naming charts in Excel with VBA, facilitating further manipulations or references to the chart in your code.

Name a column

In Excel VBA, you cannot directly assign a name to a column in the same way you can name a range. However, you can name a range that corresponds to an entire column. This approach is often used to make references to the column easier in formulas, VBA code, or for data validation purposes. Here's an example that demonstrates how to name the entire "A" column on the "Sheet1" as "MyColumn". Comments in the code explain each step for clarity.

➤ Example: Naming an entire column as a range

```
Sub NameAColumn()
```

```
' This subroutine demonstrates how to name an entire
column (e.g., Column A) on a worksheet.

Dim ws As Worksheet
Set ws = ThisWorkbook.Sheets("Sheet1") ' Specify the
worksheet by name.

' Create a name for the entire Column A.
' This approach uses the Names collection of the
workbook to add a new name.
ThisWorkbook.Names.Add Name:="MyColumn", RefersTo:="="
& ws.Name & "!A:A"

' Notify the user that the column has been named.
MsgBox "Column A has been named as 'MyColumn'.",
vbInformation, "Column Named"
End Sub
```

➢ Key points:

- **Worksheet reference**: the `ws` variable holds a reference to the specific worksheet, here named "Sheet1". Adjust the name as needed for your workbook.
- **Naming the column**: the `Names.Add` method of the `ThisWorkbook` object is used to create a new named range that refers to the entire column A on "Sheet1". The `Name` parameter is set to the desired name ("MyColumn" in this example), and the `RefersTo` parameter specifies the actual range using Excel's range notation.
- **Workbook scope**: the named range is added to the workbook level (`ThisWorkbook.Names.Add`), making "MyColumn" available across all sheets in the workbook. Ensure that the name you choose is unique within the workbook to avoid conflicts.

This example provides a straightforward method for naming an entire column in Excel through VBA, enhancing the readability and manageability of formulas or code that reference the column.

Name a file

Renaming a file in the file system using VBA involves the `Name` statement, which can rename files or directories. Below is an example demonstrating how to rename a file. This script assumes you have a file named `OldFileName.txt` located in the `C:\Temp\` directory, and you want to rename it to `NewFileName.txt`. Before running this script, ensure the file exists and the path is correct. Also, make sure you have the necessary permissions to modify files in the target directory. Comments in the code explain each step.

➢ Example: Renaming a file with VBA

```
Sub RenameFile()
    ' This subroutine demonstrates how to rename a file
using VBA.

    ' Define the full path of the existing file and the
new file name.
    Dim oldFilePath As String, newFilePath As String
    oldFilePath = "C:\Temp\OldFileName.txt" ' Adjust the
path as necessary.
    newFilePath = "C:\Temp\NewFileName.txt" ' The new file
name and path.

    ' Check if the old file exists to prevent runtime
errors.
    If Dir(oldFilePath) <> "" Then
        ' Use the Name statement to rename the file.
        Name oldFilePath As newFilePath

        ' Notify the user that the file has been renamed.
        MsgBox "File renamed successfully from
OldFileName.txt to NewFileName.txt", vbInformation, "File
Renamed"
    Else
        ' Notify the user if the original file was not
found.
```

How to do this in VBA?? 202 ready-made macros: Streamline your tasks with proven expert solutions

```
        MsgBox "The original file was not found.",
    vbCritical, "File Not Found"
        End If
    End Sub
```

➤ Key points:

- **File paths**: `oldFilePath` and **newFilePath** are strings that store the full paths of the old and new filenames, respectively. Ensure these paths are correctly set to reflect the actual locations on your system.
- **Existence check**: the `Dir` function checks if the old file exists before attempting to rename it. This is a crucial step to avoid errors.
- **Renaming the file**: the `Name` statement performs the actual renaming of the file.
- **Error handling**: basic error handling is implemented with an `If` statement to ensure the file exists. For more complex operations, consider implementing more comprehensive error handling to catch and respond to potential issues (e.g., permission issues, file locks).

This example provides a basic template for file renaming operations within VBA, demonstrating the importance of verifying file existence and correctly specifying file paths.

Name a new workbook

Creating and naming a new workbook in Excel VBA involves generating a new instance of a Workbook object and then saving it with a specified name. Below is an example demonstrating how to create a new workbook and save it with a given name to a specified path. Please adjust the file path (`"C:\Temp\MyNewWorkbook.xlsx"`) as necessary to match your system's directory structure and naming preferences. Comments in the code explain each step for clarity.

➤ Example: Creating and naming a new workbook

```
    Sub CreateAndNameNewWorkbook()
        ' This subroutine demonstrates how to create a new
    workbook and save it with a specific name.

        ' Create a new workbook. A reference to the new
    workbook is stored in the wb variable.
        Dim wb As Workbook
```

```vba
Set wb = Workbooks.Add


    ' Define the full path and name of the new workbook.
    ' Ensure you have write permission in the target
directory.
    ' Change the path and file name as needed.
    Dim filePath As String
    filePath = "C:\Temp\MyNewWorkbook.xlsx"


    ' Save the new workbook with the specified name and
path.
    ' If a file with the same name already exists, it will
be overwritten without warning.
    ' To avoid accidental overwrites, you can use the Dir
function to check if the file already exists.
    If Dir(filePath) = "" Then ' Check if the file does
not already exist.
        wb.SaveAs Filename:=filePath
        MsgBox "New workbook has been created and saved
as: " & filePath, vbInformation, "Workbook Created"
    Else
        MsgBox "A file with the same name already exists.
Please choose a different name or path.", vbExclamation,
"File Exists"
    End If


    ' Optionally, you can close the new workbook after
saving.
    ' wb.Close SaveChanges:=False
End Sub
```

➤ Key points:

- **Creating a new workbook**: the `Workbooks.Add` method creates a new workbook, and a reference to this workbook is stored in the `wb` variable.
- **Specifying the file path**: the `filePath` variable should be adjusted to the desired location and name of the new workbook.

- **Saving the workbook**: the `SaveAs` method is used to save the new workbook with the specified file path and name.
- **Avoiding overwrites**: the script checks if a file with the intended name already exists at the specified location. If so, it alerts the user rather than overwriting the existing file.
- **Closing the new workbook**: the new workbook remains open after saving. If desired, you can close it using `wb.Close SaveChanges:=False`.

This example provides a basic framework for creating, naming, and saving new workbooks using VBA, including simple error handling to avoid overwriting existing files.

Name a range

Naming a range in Excel VBA allows you to easily reference a specific set of cells within your macros and formulas. Below is an example demonstrating how to name a range programmatically. This script names a range consisting of cells A1 through A5 on "Sheet1" as "MyNamedRange". Comments in the code explain each step for clarity.

➢ Example: Naming a range in VBA

```
Sub NameARange()
    ' This subroutine demonstrates how to programmatically
name a range in Excel using VBA.

    Dim ws As Worksheet
    Set ws = ThisWorkbook.Sheets("Sheet1") ' Specify the
worksheet by name.

    ' Define the range you want to name.
    ' In this example, we're naming the range A1:A5 on
Sheet1.
    Dim targetRange As Range
    Set targetRange = ws.Range("A1:A5")

    ' Create a named range. Replace "MyNamedRange" with
the desired name.
```

```
    ' This name will be workbook-wide (unique across the
workbook).
    ThisWorkbook.Names.Add Name:="MyNamedRange",
RefersTo:=targetRange

    ' Notify the user that the range has been named.
    MsgBox "Range " & targetRange.Address & " has been
named 'MyNamedRange'.", vbInformation, "Range Named"
    End Sub
```

➢ Key points:

- **Worksheet reference**: the `ws` variable is set to the specific worksheet ("Sheet1" in this example) where the range is located. Adjust this to the name of your worksheet.
- **Specifying the range**: the `targetRange` variable is set to the range that you intend to name, in this example, `A1:A5` on "Sheet1".
- **Naming the range**: the `ThisWorkbook.Names.Add` method creates a new named range. The `Name` parameter is set to "MyNamedRange", and `RefersTo` is set to the `targetRange`. Ensure that the name you choose is unique within the workbook to avoid conflicts.
- **Notification**: a message box confirms the operation, showing the address of the range and the name it has been given.

This example provides a basic template for naming ranges in Excel using VBA, enhancing your ability to work with specific subsets of data programmatically.

Name a shape

Naming a shape in Excel using VBA allows you to easily reference and manipulate the shape within your macros. This can be particularly useful for dynamic reports or interactive dashboards. Below is an example demonstrating how to add a shape to a worksheet and then give it a specific name. This script assumes you're adding a rectangle, but Excel VBA supports various shape types. Comments in the code explain each step for clarity.

➢ Example: Adding and naming a shape

```
Sub AddAndNameShape()
    ' This subroutine demonstrates how to add a shape to a
worksheet and give it a specific name using VBA.
```

```vba
Dim ws As Worksheet
Set ws = ThisWorkbook.Sheets("Sheet1") ' Specify the
worksheet by name.


' Add a rectangle shape to the worksheet. Adjust the
left, top, width, and height values as needed.
Dim shp As Shape
Set shp = ws.Shapes.AddShape(msoShapeRectangle, 10,
10, 100, 50) ' msoShapeRectangle is the type of the shape.


' Name the shape. Replace "MyRectangle" with your
desired shape name.
' Ensure the name is unique within the worksheet to
avoid conflicts.
shp.Name = "MyRectangle"


' Notify the user that the shape has been added and
named.
MsgBox "A rectangle named 'MyRectangle' has been added
to " & ws.Name, vbInformation, "Shape Added and Named"
End Sub
```

➢ Key points:

- **Worksheet reference**: the `ws` variable holds a reference to the target worksheet. Adjust `"Sheet1"` to the name of your specific worksheet.
- **Adding the shape**: the `ws.Shapes.AddShape` method is used to add a new shape to the worksheet. This example uses `msoShapeRectangle` for a rectangle, along with its position and size parameters (left, top, width, height).
- **Naming the shape**: after creation, the shape's `Name` property is set to `"MyRectangle"`. It's important to use a unique name to easily reference the shape later in your code.
- **Feedback to user**: a message box confirms the addition and naming of the shape on the specified worksheet.

How to do this in VBA?? 202 ready-made macros: Streamline your tasks with proven expert solutions

This example provides a straightforward method for adding and naming shapes in Excel through VBA, enhancing the interactive and visual aspects of your spreadsheets.

Name a sheet

Renaming a sheet in an Excel workbook using VBA is straightforward and allows you to dynamically adjust your workbook structure. Below is an example demonstrating how to rename a specific sheet to a new name. This script assumes you want to rename "Sheet1" to "MyNewSheetName". Before running this code, ensure that "Sheet1" exists in your workbook and that there isn't already a sheet named "MyNewSheetName". Comments in the code explain each step for clarity.

➢ Example: Renaming a worksheet

```
Sub RenameSheet()
    ' This subroutine demonstrates how to rename a
specific sheet in an Excel workbook using VBA.

    ' Specify the current name of the sheet you want to
rename.
    Dim currentSheetName As String
    currentSheetName = "Sheet1"

    ' Specify the new name you want to give to the sheet.
    Dim newSheetName As String
    newSheetName = "MyNewSheetName"

    ' Check if a sheet with the new name already exists to
avoid duplication errors.
    Dim sheetExists As Boolean
    sheetExists = False
    Dim ws As Worksheet
    For Each ws In ThisWorkbook.Sheets
        If ws.Name = newSheetName Then
            sheetExists = True
            Exit For
        End If
```

```
      Next ws


      ' Rename the sheet if the new name is not already in
use.
      If Not sheetExists Then
          ThisWorkbook.Sheets(currentSheetName).Name =
newSheetName
          MsgBox "Sheet has been renamed to '" &
newSheetName & "'.", vbInformation, "Sheet Renamed"
      Else
          MsgBox "A sheet with the name '" & newSheetName &
"' already exists. Please choose a different name.",
vbExclamation, "Name In Use"
      End If
End Sub
```

➢ Key points:

- **Current and new sheet names**: variables `currentSheetName` and `newSheetName` hold the current name of the sheet you wish to rename and the new name you want to assign, respectively.
- **Checking for duplicate names**: the script iterates through all sheets in the workbook to check if the new name is already in use, preventing errors due to name duplication.
- **Renaming the sheet**: if no sheet with the new name exists, the specified sheet is renamed using the `.Name` property.
- **User feedback**: message boxes inform the user whether the renaming was successful or if the chosen new name is already in use.

This example provides a practical method for renaming sheets within an Excel workbook using VBA, incorporating checks to ensure the new name is unique within the workbook.

Name a workbook

Renaming a workbook in Excel using VBA involves saving the workbook with a new name. This operation is akin to performing a "Save As" action. It's important to note that after renaming (saving) the workbook under a new name, the workbook will continue to be open under this new name, and the original file will remain unchanged unless deleted separately. Below is an example that demonstrates how to save the active workbook with a new name. Make sure to adjust the file path ("C:\Temp\MyNewWorkbookName.xlsx"`) to a suitable location on your system. Comments in the code explain each step for clarity.

➢ Example: Saving the active workbook with a new name

```
Sub SaveWorkbookWithNewName()
    ' This subroutine demonstrates how to save the active
workbook with a new name, effectively renaming it.


    ' Define the full path and new name for the workbook.
    ' Change the path and file name as needed to match
your requirements.
    Dim newFilePath As String
    newFilePath = "C:\Temp\MyNewWorkbookName.xlsx"


    ' Use the SaveAs method to save the workbook with the
new name.
    ' IMPORTANT: Performing this action will change the
name of the workbook as it is open in Excel.
    ' The original workbook file will remain on disk
unchanged unless you delete it.
    ActiveWorkbook.SaveAs Filename:=newFilePath


    ' Notify the user that the workbook has been saved
with the new name.
    MsgBox "The workbook has been saved with the new name:
" & newFilePath, vbInformation, "Workbook Renamed"
End Sub
```

➢ Key points:

- **Path and filename**: the `newFilePath` variable should be carefully set to reflect the desired full path and name of the workbook after it is saved.
- `SaveAs` **method**: this method saves the currently active workbook with a new name and path. After execution, the Excel workbook open in the application will have this new name.
- **Original file**: the original workbook file remains unchanged and present at its location. If you want to remove the original file, you

would need to perform additional file operations using VBA or manually.

- **Permissions and safety**: ensure you have write permissions to the directory specified in `newFilePath` and that you are aware of overwriting any existing files with the same name.

This example provides a straightforward method for renaming (or saving a copy of) an Excel workbook using VBA, allowing for dynamic file management within Excel projects.

Name active workbook

Naming or rather saving the active workbook with a new name in Excel using VBA can be done using the `SaveAs` method. This action is equivalent to performing a "Save As" in Excel, which creates a new file with the provided name while keeping the workbook open under this new name. Below is a concise example that saves the active workbook with a new name. Adjust the file path (`"C:\Temp\MyActiveWorkbook.xlsx"`) to a suitable location on your system. Ensure the directory exists and you have the necessary permissions to write to it. Comments in the code explain each step.

➢ Example: Saving the active workbook with a new name

```
Sub SaveActiveWorkbookWithNewName()
    ' This subroutine demonstrates how to save the active
    workbook with a new name.


    ' Define the full path and name for the new workbook.
    ' Adjust the path to a suitable location on your
    system.
    Dim newFilePath As String
    newFilePath = "C:\Temp\MyActiveWorkbook.xlsx"


    ' Save the active workbook with the new name using the
    SaveAs method.
    ' This will not overwrite the existing workbook but
    create a new one with the specified name.
    ActiveWorkbook.SaveAs Filename:=newFilePath
```

```
' Notify the user that the workbook has been saved
under a new name.
    MsgBox "The active workbook has been saved with the
new name: " & newFilePath, vbInformation, "Workbook Named"
End Sub
```

➤ Key points:

- **Path and filename**: the `newFilePath` variable specifies the full path and name where you want to save the active workbook. Ensure this path is accessible and the filename is appropriate for your needs.
- **Using `SaveAs`**: the `SaveAs` method saves the active workbook with the specified name and path. If a file with the same name already exists at the location, it will be overwritten without warning, so you may want to add checks to prevent accidental data loss.
- **Active workbook**: this script operates on the `ActiveWorkbook`, which is the workbook currently in focus. If you have multiple workbooks open, ensure the correct one is active before running the script.

This example provides a practical method for dynamically renaming or creating a copy of the active Excel workbook using VBA, facilitating file management tasks directly from within your Excel projects.

Number value excel VBA

Converting a string to a numeric value in Excel VBA is a common task, especially when dealing with data input that comes in as text. VBA provides several ways to perform this conversion, and one straightforward method is using the `Val` function. The `Val` function converts the numbers contained in a string to a numeric data type. Here's an example demonstrating how to use `Val` to convert a string to a number and then perform a simple arithmetic operation with the result. Comments in the code explain each step for clarity.

➤ Example: Converting string to number and adding

```
Sub ConvertStringToNumberAndAdd()
    ' This subroutine demonstrates how to convert a string
to a number using the Val function
    ' and then adds a value to the numeric result.

    ' Example string that starts with numeric characters.
```

```
Dim numericString As String
numericString = "12345.67 and some text"


' Convert the string to a number using the Val
function.
Dim numberValue As Double
numberValue = Val(numericString)


' Perform an arithmetic operation on the number (e.g.,
adding 100).
Dim result As Double
result = numberValue + 100


' Display the original string, the converted number,
and the result of the addition.
MsgBox "Original String: " & numericString & vbCrLf &

_

        "Converted Number: " & numberValue & vbCrLf & _
        "Result after adding 100: " & result,
vbInformation, "String to Number Conversion"
End Sub
```

➢ Key points:

- **String with numeric content**: the `numericString` variable is initialized with a value that starts with numeric characters. The `Val` function will stop reading the string at the first character it doesn't recognize as part of a number.
- **Using `Val` function**: `Val(numericString)` converts the numeric part of `numericString` to a `Double`. It ignores any trailing characters that cannot be converted to a number.
- **Arithmetic operation**: after conversion, the example adds 100 to the numeric value to demonstrate that you can perform arithmetic operations on the result.
- **Result display**: a message box shows the original string, the converted number, and the final result to illustrate the conversion and calculation process.

This example illustrates a basic but effective method for handling numeric data contained in strings, enabling you to perform calculations or data manipulations within your VBA-powered Excel applications.

Offset a range

Using the `Offset` property in Excel VBA allows you to reference a range that is a specific number of rows and columns away from a defined starting range. This is particularly useful for dynamically navigating through a worksheet based on variable conditions. Below is an example demonstrating how to use `Offset` to select a range that is 2 rows down and 1 column to the right of the range `A1`. Comments in the code explain each step for clarity.

➢ Example: Using offset to reference a new range

```
Sub UseOffset()
    ' This subroutine demonstrates how to use the Offset
property to reference a range
    ' that is a specific number of rows and columns away
from a starting range.

    Dim ws As Worksheet
    Set ws = ThisWorkbook.Sheets("Sheet1") ' Adjust the
sheet name as needed.

    ' Define the starting range.
    Dim startRange As Range
    Set startRange = ws.Range("A1")

    ' Use the Offset property to reference a new range
that is 2 rows down and 1 column to the right of A1.
    ' Offset(Rows, Columns)
    Dim newRange As Range
    Set newRange = startRange.Offset(2, 1)

    ' Select the new range.
    ' Note: Selecting a range is just for demonstration
and typically not recommended to use in actual programs
```

How to do this in VBA?? 202 ready-made macros: Streamline your tasks with proven expert solutions

```
    ' for performance reasons and because it requires the
workbook to be active.
    newRange.Select

    ' Optionally, you might want to do something with the
newRange, like setting a value or formatting.
    ' For demonstration, we'll set the value of the new
range.
    newRange.Value = "Offset Example"

    ' Notify the user where the new range is located.
    MsgBox "The new range is located at: " &
newRange.Address, vbInformation, "Offset Range Selected"
End Sub
```

➢ Key points:

- **Worksheet reference**: the `ws` variable is set to reference the specific worksheet you're working with. Adjust `"Sheet1"` to the name of your target worksheet.
- **Starting range**: `startRange` is defined as the starting point for the offset, in this case, cell `A1`.
- **Using `Offset`**: the `Offset` method is applied to `startRange` to get a new range that is 2 rows down and 1 column to the right. `Offset` takes two arguments: the number of rows to move down (positive) or up (negative) and the number of columns to move right (positive) or left (negative).
- **Selecting the new range**: for demonstration purposes, `newRange.Select` visually selects the cell in Excel. In practical applications, direct manipulation of the range (`newRange.Value = "Offset Example"`) without selecting it is preferred for efficiency.

This example illustrates a basic application of the `Offset` property to navigate and manipulate cells relative to a specific starting point in VBA, enhancing the dynamism of Excel macros.

Offset active cell

Utilizing the `Offset` property with the active cell in Excel VBA allows you to reference or manipulate a cell that is a specific number of rows and columns away from the active (currently selected) cell. This can be particularly useful for

185

dynamic cell operations based on user selection or action. Below is an example demonstrating how to use `Offset` to select a cell that is 1 row down and 1 column to the right of the active cell. Comments in the code explain each step for clarity.

➢ Example: Selecting a cell using offset from the active cell

```
Sub SelectCellUsingOffsetFromActiveCell()
    ' This subroutine demonstrates how to use the Offset
property with the active cell
    ' to reference and select a cell that is offset by a
specific number of rows and columns.

    ' Check if there is a cell actively selected to
prevent runtime errors.
    If Not ActiveCell Is Nothing Then
        ' Use Offset to reference a cell that is 1 row
down and 1 column to the right of the active cell.
        ' Then, select this cell.
        ' Note: This action changes the active cell to the
newly selected cell.
        ActiveCell.Offset(1, 1).Select
    Else
        ' If no cell is actively selected, display a
message to the user.
        MsgBox "There is no active cell selected.",
vbCritical, "No Active Cell"
    End If
End Sub
```

➢ Key points:

- **Active cell check**: the subroutine starts by checking if there is an active cell to avoid errors in case there's no active selection.
- **Using `Offset`**: the `Offset` method is applied to the `ActiveCell` to reference a new cell. The parameters `(1, 1)` indicate moving 1 row down and 1 column to the right from the active cell.
- **Selecting the new cell**: the `Select` method is called on the cell returned by `Offset`, making it the new active cell. This demonstrates

 how to programmatically change the selection based on the current active cell's position.
- **Error handling**: a basic check for `ActiveCell` being `Nothing` provides simple error handling to ensure there's a selection before attempting to use `Offset`.

This example illustrates a simple yet powerful way to navigate and manipulate worksheet cells relative to the current active cell using VBA, enhancing the interactivity of Excel macros based on user selections.

Open a csv file

Opening a CSV (Comma Separated Values) file in Excel using VBA is a common task, especially for automating data importation and processing workflows. Below is an example that demonstrates how to open a CSV file located at a specific path. This script assumes you have a CSV file named `Example.csv` located in the `C:\Temp\` directory. Adjust the file path and name as necessary to match your file's location. Comments in the code explain each step for clarity.

➢ Example: Opening a CSV file in Excel VBA

```
Sub OpenCSVFile()
    ' This subroutine demonstrates how to open a CSV file
in Excel using VBA.

    ' Define the full path to the CSV file.
    Dim csvFilePath As String
    csvFilePath = "C:\Temp\Example.csv" ' Adjust the path
and filename as necessary.

    ' Use the Workbooks.Open method to open the CSV file.
    Workbooks.Open Filename:=csvFilePath

    ' Notify the user that the file has been opened.
    MsgBox "CSV file opened successfully.", vbInformation,
"File Opened"
    End Sub
```

➢ Key points:

- **File path specification**: the `csvFilePath` variable stores the full path to the CSV file you wish to open. Ensure this path accurately reflects the location of your file.
- **Opening the CSV file**: the `Workbooks.Open` method is used to open the specified CSV file in Excel. Excel will automatically parse the CSV based on its default settings or those specified in the regional settings of your system.
- **User notification**: a message box confirms the successful opening of the CSV file, providing immediate feedback that the operation has completed.

This example provides a straightforward method for opening CSV files using VBA, making it easier to automate the process of working with external data within Excel.

Open a folder

To open a folder from Excel using VBA, you can utilize the `Shell` function along with the `Explorer.exe` command. This approach allows you to open any specified folder in the Windows File Explorer. Below is an example demonstrating how to open the `C:\Temp\` directory. Adjust the folder path as necessary to match the directory you wish to open. Comments in the code explain each step for clarity.

➤ Example: Opening a folder using VBA

```
Sub OpenFolder()
    ' This subroutine demonstrates how to open a folder
using VBA by calling the Windows Shell command.


    ' Define the path to the folder you want to open.
    Dim folderPath As String
    folderPath = "C:\Temp\" ' Adjust the folder path as
needed.


    ' Use the Shell function to open the specified folder
in Windows File Explorer.
    Shell "explorer.exe " & folderPath, vbNormalFocus


    ' No message box is needed since the action of opening
the folder is visible to the user.
```

```
        End Sub
```
➢ Key points:

- **Folder path specification**: the `folderPath` variable holds the path to the directory you intend to open. Make sure this path is correctly specified to the desired folder.
- **Using `Shell` function**: the `Shell` function executes the `explorer.exe` command with the specified folder path, which opens the folder in Windows File Explorer.
- **Visibility and focus**: the `vbNormalFocus` argument ensures that the opened folder window receives normal focus, making it immediately visible and usable by the user.

This example provides a practical method for programmatically opening folders directly from Excel VBA, enhancing the interactivity and efficiency of your Excel applications by integrating them with the operating system's file management capabilities.

Open a new workbook

Opening a new workbook in Excel using VBA is straightforward and can be useful for various tasks, including data processing, reporting, or simply starting a new file programmatically. Below is an example that demonstrates how to create a new workbook and then activates it to allow for immediate use. Comments in the code explain each step for clarity.

➢ Example: Creating and activating a new workbook

```
Sub OpenNewWorkbook()
    ' This subroutine demonstrates how to open a new
workbook using VBA.


    ' Create a new workbook. The new workbook becomes the
active workbook.
    Workbooks.Add


    ' Optional: Store a reference to the new workbook in a
variable, if you need to manipulate it further.
    Dim newWorkbook As Workbook
    Set newWorkbook = ActiveWorkbook
```

```
        ' Optional: You can give the new workbook a temporary
    name by saving it. Adjust the file path as needed.
        ' newWorkbook.SaveAs "C:\Temp\MyNewWorkbook.xlsx"


        ' Notify the user that the new workbook has been
    created and activated.
        MsgBox "A new workbook has been created and is now
    active.", vbInformation, "New Workbook Opened"
    End Sub
```

➢ Key points:

- **Creating the workbook**: the `Workbooks.Add` method creates a new workbook. By default, this new workbook becomes the active workbook in Excel.
- **Reference to the new workbook**: although not strictly necessary for simply opening a new workbook, storing a reference to the new workbook in a variable (`newWorkbook`) is useful for further manipulation, such as adding data or formatting.
- **Optional saving**: if you want to immediately save the new workbook with a specific filename and location, you can use the `SaveAs` method. Be sure to adjust the file path according to your needs. This step is commented out because it may not be necessary for all use cases and requires specifying a valid file path.
- **User feedback**: a message box confirms that the new workbook has been created and is now active, providing clear feedback on the action taken.

This example provides a basic yet effective method for creating new workbooks using VBA, demonstrating the flexibility of Excel VBA for programmatically managing workbooks.

Open a text file in Excel

Opening and reading a text file in Excel VBA can be done using the `Open` statement in combination with file input functions such as `Input` or `Line Input`. This allows you to process or read the file line by line or in other specific ways depending on your needs. Below is an example demonstrating how to open a text file for reading, read its contents line by line, and output the text to the Immediate Window. Adjust the file path (`"C:\Temp\Example.txt"`) to match the location of your text file. Comments in the code explain each step for clarity.

How to do this in VBA?? 202 ready-made macros: Streamline your tasks with proven expert solutions

➢ Example: Opening and reading a text file

```vba
Sub OpenAndReadTextFile()
    ' This subroutine demonstrates how to open a text file
    and read its contents line by line in VBA.

    ' Define the path to the text file.
    Dim filePath As String
    filePath = "C:\Temp\Example.txt" ' Adjust the file
    path as needed.

    ' Variable for storing a line of text read from the
    file.
    Dim fileLine As String

    ' Open the text file for reading. Assign it to file
    number 1.
    Open filePath For Input As #1

    ' Read the file line by line until the end of the file
    is reached.
    Do Until EOF(1) ' EOF(1) checks if the end of the file
    (file number 1) has been reached.
        Line Input #1, fileLine ' Read a line of text into
    the variable fileLine.
        ' Output the read line to the Immediate Window
    (press Ctrl+G in VBA editor to view).
        Debug.Print fileLine
    Loop

    ' Close the file after reading its contents.
    Close #1

    ' Notify the user that the file has been read and
    output to the Immediate Window.
```

```
     MsgBox "Text file has been read. Check the Immediate
     Window for output.", vbInformation, "File Read"
     End Sub
```

➤ Key points:

- **File path specification**: the `filePath` variable stores the full path to the text file you intend to open and read. Make sure this path correctly points to your file.
- **Opening the file**: the `Open` statement with the `For Input As #1` option opens the file for reading and associates it with file number 1.
- **Reading line by line**: the `Do Until EOF(1)` loop reads the file line by line using `Line Input #1, fileLine`. The `EOF` function is used to check if the end of the file has been reached.
- **Outputting the text**: each line read from the file is output to the Immediate Window using `Debug.Print`. This can be replaced or supplemented with other actions, such as writing the text to a worksheet.
- **Closing the file**: it's important to close the file with `Close #1` after finishing reading to free up system resources.

This example illustrates a basic method for opening and reading a text file using VBA, providing a foundation for more complex text processing or data import tasks.

Open a user form

Opening a UserForm in Excel VBA is a straightforward task that involves simply calling the `Show` method on the UserForm object. This example assumes you have a UserForm named `MyUserForm`. If you haven't already created the UserForm, you can do so by following these steps in the VBA editor:

1. Go to the "Insert" menu and select "UserForm".
2. In the Properties window (usually on the left side of the VBA editor), set the `Name` property to `MyUserForm`.
3. You can add controls (like buttons, text boxes, etc.) to the UserForm as needed by using the Toolbox.

Once your UserForm is ready, use the following VBA code to show it.

➤ Example: Showing a UserForm

```
     Sub ShowMyUserForm()
```

```
        ' This subroutine demonstrates how to open or show a
     UserForm named MyUserForm.


        ' Show the UserForm.
     MyUserForm.Show


        ' Note: The UserForm will be displayed modally by
     default, meaning that you cannot interact with
        ' other parts of Excel until you close the UserForm.
     If you need the UserForm to be non-modal,
        ' you can use MyUserForm.Show vbModeless.
     End Sub
```

➢ Key points:

- **Showing the userform**: the `Show` method displays the UserForm. By default, UserForms are shown modally, which means you must close the UserForm before you can interact with Excel again.
- **Modal vs. modeless**: if you want the UserForm to be modeless (allowing interaction with Excel while the UserForm is open), use `MyUserForm.Show    vbModeless`   instead   of   just `MyUserForm.Show`.

This code snippet is a basic demonstration of opening a UserForm in Excel VBA, providing a simple way to interact with users, gather inputs, or display information.

Open a Word document

To open a Word document from Excel VBA, you can use the Word Application object. This example demonstrates how to open an existing Word document using Excel VBA with late binding, which doesn't require setting a reference to the Word Object Library. If you prefer early binding, which offers more detailed IntelliSense in the VBA editor, you would need to set a reference to the Microsoft Word Object Library via Tools > References in the VBA editor. For the purpose of broad compatibility and simplicity, this example uses late binding.

➢ Example: Opening a Word document using Excel VBA (Late Binding)

Sub OpenWordDocument()

```vba
    ' This subroutine demonstrates how to open an existing
Word document using Excel VBA with late binding.

    ' Define the full path to the Word document.
    Dim docPath As String
    docPath = "C:\Temp\MyDocument.docx" ' Adjust the path
to your document's location.

    ' Create a new instance of the Word application.
    Dim wordApp As Object
    Set wordApp = CreateObject("Word.Application")

    ' Make the Word application visible.
    wordApp.Visible = True

    ' Open the specified document.
    wordApp.Documents.Open docPath

    ' Optionally, you can hold the opened document in a
variable for further manipulation.
    Dim wordDoc As Object
    Set wordDoc = wordApp.ActiveDocument

    ' Notify the user that the document has been opened.
    MsgBox "Word document opened successfully: " &
docPath, vbInformation, "Document Opened"
End Sub
```

➢ Key points:

- **Late binding**: this method uses `CreateObject("Word.Application")` to create a Word application instance without needing a direct reference to the Word Object Library. This approach enhances compatibility across different versions of Office but sacrifices compile-time type checking and IntelliSense.
- **Document path**: ensure that `docPath` is correctly set to the full path of the Word document you wish to open.
- **Visibility**: setting `wordApp.Visible = True` ensures that the Word application is visible to the user once it's launched.

194

- **Opening the document**: the `Documents.Open` method is used to open the document specified by `docPath`.
- **Active document**: after opening, the document becomes the active document in the Word application instance. You can interact with it using the `wordDoc` variable for further automation tasks.

This example provides a practical method for opening Word documents programmatically from Excel VBA, facilitating cross-application automation and data processing tasks.

Open a workbook

Opening an Excel workbook using VBA is a common task that can help automate the process of working with multiple files. Below is an example demonstrating how to open an existing workbook. This script assumes you have a workbook named `ExampleWorkbook.xlsx` located in the `C:\Temp\` directory. Adjust the file path as necessary to match the location of your workbook. Comments in the code explain each step for clarity.

➤ Example: Opening an existing workbook

```
Sub OpenExistingWorkbook()
    ' This subroutine demonstrates how to open an existing
Excel workbook using VBA.

    ' Define the full path to the workbook you want to
open.
    Dim workbookPath As String
    workbookPath = "C:\Temp\ExampleWorkbook.xlsx" ' Adjust
the file path as needed.

    ' Use the Workbooks.Open method to open the specified
workbook.
    Workbooks.Open Filename:=workbookPath

    ' Notify the user that the workbook has been opened.
    MsgBox "Workbook opened successfully: " &
workbookPath, vbInformation, "Workbook Opened"
    End Sub
```

➤ Key points:

How to do this in VBA?? 202 ready-made macros: Streamline your tasks with proven expert solutions

- **File path specification**: the `workbookPath` variable stores the full path to the workbook you intend to open. Ensure this path correctly points to your file.
- **Opening the workbook**: the `Workbooks.Open` method is used with the `Filename` parameter set to `workbookPath`. This opens the specified workbook in Excel.
- **User notification**: a message box confirms the successful opening of the workbook, providing clear feedback on the action taken.

This example provides a straightforward method for opening workbooks using VBA, making it easier to automate workflows that involve multiple Excel files.

Open Excel

Opening a new instance of Excel from within another application, such as Word or Access, can be done using VBA through the automation of Excel Application object. This process is known as creating an automation object or using late binding to interact with Excel. Here's how you can do it, demonstrated with VBA code intended to be run from an application outside of Excel, like Word or Access:

➢ Example: Opening a new instance of Excel from another application

```
Sub OpenNewExcelInstance()
    ' This subroutine demonstrates how to open a new
instance of Excel using VBA from another application.

    ' Declare an object variable to hold the Excel
Application instance.
    Dim excelApp As Object

    ' Create a new instance of the Excel Application.
    ' The CreateObject function is used here for late
binding, which does not require a reference to the Excel
object library.
    Set excelApp = CreateObject("Excel.Application")

    ' Make the Excel Application visible.
    excelApp.Visible = True
```

196

```
    ' Optionally, create a new workbook in the new
instance of Excel.
    excelApp.Workbooks.Add


    ' Notify the user that a new instance of Excel has
been opened with a new workbook.
    MsgBox "A new instance of Excel has been opened with a
new workbook.", vbInformation, "Excel Opened"
End Sub
```

➢ Key points:

- **Late binding**: this method uses `CreateObject("Excel.Application")` to create a new Excel application object without needing a reference set to the Excel object library. This approach ensures compatibility across different versions of Office but sacrifices compile-time type checking and IntelliSense.
- **Visibility**: making the Excel application visible (`excelApp.Visible = True`) is crucial, as Excel starts invisibly when instantiated via automation.
- **New workbook**: the `Workbooks.Add` method creates a new workbook within the new Excel instance. This step is optional depending on your needs.
- **Notification**: a message box at the end informs the user that a new Excel instance has been opened. This is also optional and can be tailored to the specific requirements of your automation task.

This example provides a basic template for opening a new instance of Excel and optionally a new workbook from an external VBA host application, demonstrating how VBA can be used for cross-application automation.

Open hyperlink

To open a hyperlink using VBA, you can utilize the `FollowHyperlink` method of the Application object. This method allows you to navigate to a URL or a file path from within your VBA code. Here's a straightforward example that demonstrates how to open a hyperlink to a website. You can adjust the URL to any web address or file path you need to open. Comments in the code explain each step for clarity.

➢Example: Opening a hyperlink to a website

```
Sub OpenHyperlink()
```

```
' This subroutine demonstrates how to open a hyperlink
using VBA.

' Define the URL you want to open.
Dim urlString As String
urlString = "https://www.example.com" ' Replace with
your desired URL

' Use the FollowHyperlink method to open the URL in
the default web browser.
Application.FollowHyperlink Address:=urlString,
NewWindow:=True

' Notify the user that the hyperlink has been opened.
' Note: In many cases, the browser will open almost
instantly, and this message will appear after.
MsgBox "The hyperlink to " & urlString & " has been
opened in your default browser.", vbInformation,
"Hyperlink Opened"
End Sub
```

Key points:

- **URL specification**: the `urlString` variable holds the URL to the website you wish to open. This can be replaced with any valid URL or a file path.
- Using `FollowHyperlink`: The `Application.FollowHyperlink` method is used to navigate to the specified URL. The `NewWindow` parameter is set to `True` to open the hyperlink in a new browser window or tab, depending on the browser's settings and behavior.
- User notification: a message box confirms the action taken. This is particularly useful for confirming that the macro has completed its action, especially in cases where the browser might take a moment to launch or if the URL leads to a file download rather than opening a webpage.

This example illustrates a basic application of the `FollowHyperlink` method in VBA to open webpages or files, demonstrating how VBA can interact with other applications and resources outside of Excel.

Open xlsx file

Opening an `.xlsx` file in Excel using VBA is a common task that helps automate workflows involving multiple Excel files. Below is an example demonstrating how to open an existing `.xlsx` workbook. This script assumes you have a workbook named `ExampleWorkbook.xlsx` located in the `C:\Temp\` directory. Adjust the file path as necessary to match the location of your `.xlsx` file. Comments in the code explain each step for clarity.

➤ Example: Opening an `.xlsx` workbook

```
Sub OpenXLSXFile()
    ' This subroutine demonstrates how to open an existing
    .xlsx workbook using VBA.

    ' Define the full path to the workbook you want to
    open.
    Dim workbookPath As String
    workbookPath = "C:\Temp\ExampleWorkbook.xlsx" ' Adjust
    the file path as needed.

    ' Use the Workbooks.Open method to open the specified
    workbook.
    Workbooks.Open Filename:=workbookPath

    ' Notify the user that the workbook has been opened.
    MsgBox "Workbook opened successfully: " &
    workbookPath, vbInformation, "Workbook Opened"
End Sub
```

➤ Key points:

- File path specification: the `workbookPath` variable stores the full path to the `.xlsx` workbook you intend to open. Ensure this path correctly points to your file.
- Opening the workbook: the `Workbooks.Open` method is used with the `Filename` parameter set to `workbookPath`. This opens the specified workbook in Excel.
- User notification: a message box confirms the successful opening of the workbook, providing clear feedback on the action taken.

How to do this in VBA?? 202 ready-made macros: Streamline your tasks with proven expert solutions

This example provides a straightforward method for opening `.xlsx` workbooks using VBA, making it easier to automate workflows that involve multiple Excel files.

Parse Json

Parsing JSON in Excel VBA requires a bit of setup since VBA doesn't natively support JSON parsing. However, you can use the `ScriptControl` object to evaluate JSON as a JavaScript Object, which VBA can then work with. Note that `ScriptControl` is only available in 32-bit versions of Office and might not work in 64-bit versions due to security updates in newer versions of Office. As an alternative for 64-bit or for more robust JSON parsing, you might consider using a third-party JSON parser like VBA-JSON.

Here's a simple example using `ScriptControl` to parse a JSON string. This example assumes a very basic JSON structure for demonstration purposes:

```
{
  "name": "John",
  "age": 30,
  "city": "New York"
}
```

➢ VBA Code to parse JSON (32-bit Office)

```
Sub ParseJSONUsingScriptControl()
    ' This subroutine demonstrates parsing a simple JSON
string using ScriptControl.
    ' Note: ScriptControl works only in 32-bit versions of
Office.

    ' JSON string to parse
    Dim jsonString As String
    jsonString = "{""name"": ""John"", ""age"": 30,
""city"": ""New York""}"

    ' Create an instance of ScriptControl
    Dim sc As Object
    Set sc = CreateObject("ScriptControl")
    sc.Language = "JScript"
```

```vba
' Evaluate the JSON string as a JavaScript object
Dim jsObject As Object
Set jsObject = sc.Eval("(" & jsonString & ")")

' Extract values from the JavaScript object
Dim name As String, age As Long, city As String
name = jsObject.name
age = jsObject.age
city = jsObject.city

' Display the extracted values
MsgBox "Name: " & name & vbCrLf & "Age: " & age &
vbCrLf & "City: " & city, vbInformation, "Parsed JSON"
End Sub
```

➢ Important notes:

- **Compatibility**: this method is compatible only with 32-bit versions of Microsoft Office.
- **Security settings**: `ScriptControl` might be disabled on your system due to security settings.
- **Alternative for 64-bit Office**: for 64-bit versions of Office or to work with more complex JSON, consider using a library like VBA-JSON. This requires downloading and importing the library into your project. You can find VBA-JSON on GitHub.

This approach allows basic interaction with JSON data within the constraints of VBA's capabilities and your Office version's limitations. For complex JSON data or 64-bit Office versions, using a dedicated JSON parsing library will provide more flexibility and functionality.

Parse XML

Parsing XML in Excel VBA can be efficiently handled using the `MSXML2.DOMDocument` object. This method allows you to load and parse XML content, and then navigate through its elements and attributes. Below is an example demonstrating how to parse a simple XML string. This XML contains information about a book, including its title, author, and publication year. Comments in the code explain each step for clarity.

➢ Sample XML

How to do this in VBA?? 202 ready-made macros: Streamline your tasks with proven expert solutions

```
<?xml version="1.0"?>
<book>
    <title>Learning XML</title>
    <author>John Doe</author>
    <year>2021</year>
</book>
```

➢ VBA Code to parse XML

```vba
Sub ParseXML()
    ' This subroutine demonstrates how to parse XML using
VBA.

    ' XML string to parse
    Dim xmlString As String
    xmlString = "<?xml version='1.0'?>" & _
                "<book>" & _
                    "<title>Learning XML</title>" & _
                    "<author>John Doe</author>" & _
                    "<year>2021</year>" & _
                "</book>"

    ' Create an instance of the DOMDocument object.
    Dim xmlDoc As Object
    Set xmlDoc = CreateObject("MSXML2.DOMDocument")

    ' Load the XML string into the DOMDocument object.
    xmlDoc.LoadXML xmlString

    ' Verify that the XML document is loaded.
    If xmlDoc.parseError.ErrorCode <> 0 Then
        MsgBox "Error in XML: " & xmlDoc.parseError.reason
        Exit Sub
    End If

    ' Extract elements by their tag name.
    Dim title As String, author As String, year As String
```

```
            title = xmlDoc.getElementsByTagName("title")(0).Text
            author = xmlDoc.getElementsByTagName("author")(0).Text
            year = xmlDoc.getElementsByTagName("year")(0).Text

            ' Display the extracted information.
            MsgBox "Title: " & title & vbCrLf & _
                   "Author: " & author & vbCrLf & _
                   "Year: " & year, vbInformation, "Parsed XML
        Content"
        End Sub
```

➢ Key points:

- **Creating the DOMDocument object**: the `MSXML2.DOMDocument` object is used to load and parse the XML string.
- **Loading XML**: the `LoadXML` method of the `DOMDocument` object parses the XML string.
- **Error checking**: the `parseError` property checks for errors in the XML parsing process. It's a good practice to include error handling to catch and respond to parsing errors.
- **Extracting elements**: the `getElementsByTagName` method is used to access elements within the XML by their tag names. Since this method returns a collection of nodes, `(0)` is used to access the first (and in this case, only) item for each element.
- **Displaying information**: the extracted data is displayed using a message box.

This example provides a basic demonstration of how to parse and extract information from an XML document using VBA, which can be adapted for more complex XML structures or incorporated into larger data processing tasks.

Paste range

Pasting content in Excel using VBA can involve various scenarios, such as pasting from the clipboard, pasting values, formats, or both. Here's a basic example that demonstrates how to copy a range from one location and paste it into another location within the same worksheet. This script will copy the range "A1:A5" and paste it into the starting cell "B1". Comments in the code explain each step for clarity.

➢ Example: Copy and paste a range in Excel VBA

```
        Sub CopyAndPasteRange()
```

```vba
' This subroutine demonstrates how to copy and paste a
range in Excel using VBA.

Dim sourceRange As Range
Dim destinationRange As Range
Dim ws As Worksheet

' Set a reference to the worksheet where the operation
will take place
' Adjust "Sheet1" to the name of your target worksheet
Set ws = ThisWorkbook.Sheets("Sheet1")

' Define the source range you want to copy
Set sourceRange = ws.Range("A1:A5")

' Define the destination range where you want to paste
the copied data
' Here, we're starting the paste operation at cell
"B1"
Set destinationRange = ws.Range("B1")

' Perform the copy operation
sourceRange.Copy

' Perform the paste operation
' Paste the copied data into the destination range
destinationRange.PasteSpecial Paste:=xlPasteAll,
Operation:=xlNone, SkipBlanks:=False, Transpose:=False

' Optionally, you can clear the clipboard after the
paste operation
Application.CutCopyMode = False

' Notify the user that the operation is complete
MsgBox "Range copied and pasted successfully.",
vbInformation, "Paste Complete"
```

```
        End Sub
```

➤ Key points:

- Worksheet reference: the variable `ws` is set to reference the worksheet where the copy and paste operation will occur. Adjust `"Sheet1"` to the name of your target worksheet.
- Source and destination ranges: the `sourceRange` variable defines the range to copy, and the `destinationRange` variable specifies where to paste the copied content.
- **Copy and paste operation**: the `Copy` method is called on `sourceRange` to copy its content. The `PasteSpecial` method is then used on `destinationRange` to paste the copied content. The `PasteSpecial` method offers flexibility, allowing you to specify exactly what part of the copied content (formulas, values, formats, etc.) you want to paste.
- **Clearing the clipboard**: setting `Application.CutCopyMode = False` clears Excel's clipboard, which prevents the marquee around the copied range and potentially minimizes memory usage.
- **User notification**: a message box informs the user once the operation is complete.

This example provides a foundational approach to copying and pasting ranges within an Excel workbook using VBA, demonstrating how to manipulate worksheet data programmatically.

Paste special

Using the `PasteSpecial` method in Excel VBA allows you to paste clipboard contents into a worksheet with specific options, such as pasting only the values, formulas, formats, or making operations like addition or subtraction on the pasted values. Here's an example that demonstrates how to copy a range and then use `PasteSpecial` to paste only the values and number formats into a different range. This example assumes that the source range "A1:A5" contains some data you want to copy to "B1:B5". Comments in the code explain each step for clarity.

➤ Example: Using PasteSpecial to paste values and number formats

```
        Sub UsePasteSpecial()
            ' This subroutine demonstrates how to use PasteSpecial
        to paste only the values and number formats.
```

How to do this in VBA?? 202 ready-made macros: Streamline your tasks with proven expert solutions

```vba
Dim ws As Worksheet
' Set a reference to the active worksheet.
' You can change this to a specific worksheet e.g.,
Set ws = ThisWorkbook.Sheets("Sheet1")
Set ws = ActiveSheet

' Copy the source range.
ws.Range("A1:A5").Copy

' Use PasteSpecial to paste only the values and number
formats into the destination range.
' Note: The destination cell is the top-left cell of
the range where you want to paste the values.
ws.Range("B1").PasteSpecial
Paste:=xlPasteValuesAndNumberFormats

' Clear the clipboard to remove the moving dashed
border from the copied range.
Application.CutCopyMode = False

' Notify the user.
MsgBox "Values and number formats have been pasted
successfully from A1:A5 to B1:B5.", vbInformation, "Paste
Special Completed"
End Sub
```

➤ Key points:

- **Worksheet reference**: the script starts by setting a reference to the worksheet where the operation will take place. This example uses the `ActiveSheet` for simplicity.
- **Copying data**: the `Copy` method is called on the source range (`"A1:A5"`) to copy its contents.
- **PasteSpecial method**: the `PasteSpecial` method is used with the `Paste:=xlPasteValuesAndNumberFormats` argument to paste only the values and number formats from the copied range to the destination starting at `"B1"`.

- **Clearing the clipboard**: `Application.CutCopyMode = False` is used after pasting to clear the clipboard and remove the moving dashed border around the copied range.
- **Notification**: a message box informs the user that the operation has been completed successfully.

This example provides a basic demonstration of how to use the `PasteSpecial` method for more controlled pasting actions within Excel workbooks using VBA, allowing for precise data manipulation and presentation.

Paste values

Pasting only the values of a copied range into another range in Excel using VBA is a common task, especially when you want to preserve the raw data without carrying over formulas, formatting, or comments. Here's an example demonstrating how to copy a range from one location and paste only its values into another location within the same worksheet. This script will copy the range "A1:A5" and paste only its values starting from cell "B1". Comments in the code explain each step for clarity.

➤ Example: Copying and pasting only values

```
Sub CopyAndPasteValues()
    ' This subroutine demonstrates how to copy a range and
then paste only its values into another range using VBA.

    Dim ws As Worksheet
    ' Set a reference to the active worksheet.
    ' You can specify a particular sheet by name using:
Set ws = ThisWorkbook.Sheets("Sheet1")
    Set ws = ActiveSheet

    ' Copy the source range.
    ws.Range("A1:A5").Copy

    ' Use PasteSpecial to paste only the values into the
destination range.
    ' The destination range is specified by the top-left
cell of where you want to paste the values ("B1" in this
case).
```

How to do this in VBA?? 202 ready-made macros: Streamline your tasks with proven expert solutions

```vba
ws.Range("B1").PasteSpecial Paste:=xlPasteValues


    ' Clear the clipboard to remove the moving dashed
    border around the copied range.
    Application.CutCopyMode = False


    ' Inform the user that the operation has completed.
    MsgBox "Values have been successfully pasted from
    A1:A5 to B1:B5.", vbInformation, "Paste Values Completed"
    End Sub
```

➤ Key points:

- **Worksheet reference**: the variable `ws` is set to reference the active worksheet. You can adjust this to target a specific worksheet by name if needed.
- **Copying the range**: the `Copy` method is called on the source range (`"A1:A5"`) to copy its contents.
- **Pasting only values**: the `PasteSpecial` method with the `Paste:=xlPasteValues` argument is used to paste only the values from the copied range to the specified destination starting at `"B1"`.
- **Clearing the clipboard**: using `Application.CutCopyMode = False` clears Excel's clipboard, which prevents the marquee (moving dashed border) around the copied range and minimizes memory usage.
- **User notification**: a message box confirms the successful completion of the operation, providing clear feedback to the user.

This example illustrates a basic yet effective method for copying a range and pasting only its values into another location within an Excel workbook using VBA, demonstrating how to manipulate data programmatically while preserving its integrity.

Pause

Introducing a pause or delay in VBA code execution can be useful for various reasons, such as waiting for a process to complete or simply slowing down the execution for demonstration purposes. VBA does not have a built-in `Pause` or `Sleep` function like some other programming languages, but you can use the `Application.Wait` method or call the Windows Sleep API function for this purpose.

Here are two examples showing how to introduce a pause in your VBA code:

How to do this in VBA?? 202 ready-made macros: Streamline your tasks with proven expert solutions

➢ Example 1: Using `**Application.Wait**`

```
Sub PauseUsingApplicationWait()
    ' This subroutine demonstrates pausing code execution
using Application.Wait

    Dim dtmWaitUntil As Date

    ' Calculate the time for 5 seconds from now
    dtmWaitUntil = Now + TimeValue("00:00:05")

    ' Display a message before pausing
    MsgBox "Pausing for 5 seconds", vbInformation, "Pause
Started"

    ' Wait until the specified future time
    Application.Wait dtmWaitUntil

    ' Display a message after pausing
    MsgBox "Pause completed", vbInformation, "Resume
Execution"
End Sub
```

➢ Example 2: Using the windows sleep API

First, declare the Sleep function at the beginning of your module:

```
#If VBA7 Then
    Declare PtrSafe Sub Sleep Lib "kernel32" (ByVal
dwMilliseconds As LongPtr)
#Else
    Declare Sub Sleep Lib "kernel32" (ByVal dwMilliseconds
as Long)
#End If
```

Then, use the Sleep function in your subroutine:

```
Sub PauseUsingSleep()
    ' This subroutine demonstrates pausing code execution
using the Sleep API
```

```vba
    ' Display a message before pausing
    MsgBox "Pausing for 5 seconds", vbInformation, "Pause
Started"

    ' Pause execution for 5000 milliseconds (5 seconds)
    Sleep 5000

    ' Display a message after pausing
    MsgBox "Pause completed", vbInformation, "Resume
Execution"
End Sub
```

➤ Key points:

- **Application.Wait**: this method is simple to use but pauses the entire application, which might not be desirable in all situations.
- **Windows Sleep API**: provides more flexibility and does not freeze the application, but requires declaring the external function. The use of `PtrSafe` and `LongPtr` is necessary for compatibility with 64-bit versions of Office (`VBA7`).

Both methods allow you to introduce a delay in your VBA code execution, but they do so in slightly different ways. Choose the one that best suits your needs based on the behavior you want during the pause.

Press Enter key

Simulating a key press, such as the Enter key, in Excel VBA can be done using the `SendKeys` method. This method allows you to send keystrokes to the active application. For example, to simulate pressing the Enter key, you would use `SendKeys "~"`, as the tilde (`~`) character represents the Enter key in the syntax understood by `SendKeys`.

Here's a simple example that demonstrates how to use `SendKeys` to simulate pressing the Enter key. This might be useful in various automation scenarios where you need to confirm a dialog box, submit a form, or simply move to the next line in a control that accepts text input.

➤ Example: Simulating the Enter key press

```vba
Sub SimulateEnterKeyPress()
```

```
    ' This subroutine demonstrates how to simulate
pressing the Enter key using VBA.

    ' Inform the user about what's going to happen
    MsgBox "After you click OK, the Enter key will be
simulated.", vbInformation, "Prepare for Enter Key
Simulation"

    ' Simulate pressing the Enter key.
    SendKeys "~", True

    ' Optionally, add a slight delay to ensure the
keystroke is processed.
    Application.Wait (Now + TimeValue("0:00:01"))

    ' Notify the user that the simulated key press has
occurred.
    ' Depending on your specific use case, this message
box may interfere with the automation,
    ' so it might be necessary to adjust or remove this
notification.
    MsgBox "The Enter key was simulated.", vbInformation,
"Enter Key Pressed"
End Sub
```

➤ Key points and considerations:

- **Use of `SendKeys`**: the `SendKeys` method is powerful but should be used cautiously, as it sends keystrokes to the active window. This means that if the user changes the active window or application focus while the script is running, the keystrokes might not go to the intended target.
- Timing: the effectiveness of `SendKeys` can depend on the timing of the key press relative to other actions being performed by your application or script. The optional delay introduced by `Application.Wait` is one way to manage timing, but the optimal approach will depend on your specific context.
- User notification: while informative message boxes are included in this example for clarity and confirmation, they may not be

appropriate for all automation tasks, especially those requiring unattended execution.

This example provides a basic template for simulating key presses in VBA. However, because `SendKeys` interacts with the active window and can be affected by user actions or system focus changes, it's important to carefully consider its use in your scripts, particularly for tasks requiring precise control or reliability.

Print

Printing a range or worksheet in Excel using VBA is a common task that can help automate reporting and documentation processes. Below is an example that demonstrates how to print a specific range from a worksheet. Additionally, I'll show you how to print the entire worksheet. Comments in the code explain each step for clarity.

➤ Example 1: Printing a specific range

```
Sub PrintSpecificRange()
    ' This subroutine demonstrates how to print a specific
range from a worksheet in Excel using VBA.

    Dim ws As Worksheet
    ' Set a reference to the worksheet. Adjust "Sheet1" to
your target worksheet's name.
    Set ws = ThisWorkbook.Sheets("Sheet1")

    ' Define the specific range you want to print.
    Dim printRange As Range
    Set printRange = ws.Range("A1:D20")

    ' Print the defined range.
    printRange.PrintOut Copies:=1, Collate:=True,
IgnorePrintAreas:=False

    ' Notify the user that the print command has been
executed.
    MsgBox "The specified range has been sent to the
printer.", vbInformation, "Print Command Sent"
```

How to do this in VBA?? 202 ready-made macros: Streamline your tasks with proven expert solutions

```
End Sub
```

➤ Example 2: Printing the entire worksheet

```
Sub PrintEntireWorksheet()
    ' This subroutine demonstrates how to print the entire
worksheet in Excel using VBA.

    Dim ws As Worksheet
    ' Set a reference to the worksheet. Adjust "Sheet1" to
your target worksheet's name.
    Set ws = ThisWorkbook.Sheets("Sheet1")

    ' Print the entire worksheet.
    ws.PrintOut Copies:=1, Collate:=True

    ' Notify the user that the print command has been
executed.
    MsgBox "The entire worksheet has been sent to the
printer.", vbInformation, "Print Command Sent"
End Sub
```

➤ Key points:

- **Worksheet reference**: modify the `ws` variable to refer to the specific worksheet you want to print.
- Specifying the range: in the first example, the `printRange` variable is used to define the range that you intend to print. Adjust the range as needed for your data.
- **PrintOut method**: the `PrintOut` method is used to send the print job to the default printer. It allows specifying several parameters such as the number of copies (`Copies`), whether to collate multiple copies (`Collate`), and whether to ignore print areas set on the worksheet (`IgnorePrintAreas`) for the range print example.
- User notification: a message box confirms the print command has been sent. This is useful for scripts where immediate feedback to the user is necessary.

These examples illustrate basic approaches to printing ranges and entire worksheets using VBA, enabling you to integrate printing capabilities into your Excel automation scripts effectively.

213

Print a variable

Printing the value of a variable to the Immediate Window in the VBA Editor is a fundamental debugging technique that helps you monitor the flow of your code and the state of your data. To "print" a variable's value, you can use the `Debug.Print` statement. This outputs the variable's value to the Immediate Window, which you can view by pressing `Ctrl+G` in the VBA Editor.

Here's a simple example demonstrating how to use `Debug.Print` to print the value of a variable:

➢ Example: Printing the value of a variable

```
Sub PrintVariableValue()
    ' This subroutine demonstrates how to print the value
of a variable to the Immediate Window using VBA.

    ' Define a sample variable and assign it a value
    Dim sampleVariable As String
    sampleVariable = "Hello, World!"

    ' Print the value of the variable to the Immediate
Window
    Debug.Print "The value of sampleVariable is: " &
sampleVariable

    ' Additionally, to show how you can print numeric
variables
    Dim numericVariable As Integer
    numericVariable = 42

    ' Print the numeric variable
    Debug.Print "The value of numericVariable is: " &
numericVariable
End Sub
```

➢ Key points:

- **Immediate window**: ensure the Immediate Window is open (`Ctrl+G` in the VBA Editor) to see the output of `Debug.Print`.

- **String concatenation**: the ampersand (`&`) is used to concatenate (join) strings, allowing you to combine text with variable values in the output.
- **Variable types**: this example shows printing both a `String` variable and an `Integer` variable, demonstrating that `Debug.Print` can handle different data types seamlessly.

Using `Debug.Print` is invaluable for debugging and understanding how data flows through your VBA scripts, making it easier to diagnose and fix issues.

Print an array

Printing the contents of an array to the Immediate Window in the VBA Editor can be achieved by looping through the array and using the `Debug.Print` statement for each element. This method is useful for debugging purposes or when you need to inspect the values stored in an array during code execution.

Here's a simple example that demonstrates how to print all elements of a one-dimensional array:

➢ Example: Printing a one-dimensional array

```
Sub PrintArrayContents()
    ' This subroutine demonstrates how to print the
    contents of a one-dimensional array to the Immediate
    Window.

    ' Define and initialize an array of sample data.
    Dim sampleArray() As Variant
    sampleArray = Array("Apple", "Banana", "Cherry",
    "Date")

    ' Variable to store the current index in the loop.
    Dim i As Integer

    ' Loop through each element of the array and print its
    value.
    For i = LBound(sampleArray) To UBound(sampleArray)
        Debug.Print "Element at index " & i & ": " &
    sampleArray(i)
```

```
Next i

    ' Notify the user that the array contents have been
printed.
    MsgBox "The contents of the array have been printed to
the Immediate Window.", vbInformation, "Array Printed"
    End Sub
```

➢ Key points:

- **Immediate window**: make sure the Immediate Window is visible (`Ctrl+G` in the VBA Editor) to see the output of `Debug.Print`.
- Looping through the array: the `For` loop, together with `LBound` (lower bound) and `UBound` (upper bound) functions, ensures that every element of the array is accessed and printed. This works regardless of the array's size.
- `Debug.Print`: this statement outputs the text to the Immediate Window, allowing you to inspect the values within the array.
- **User notification**: a message box at the end of the subroutine provides feedback that the operation has completed, which can be especially useful if the Immediate Window is not immediately visible or if you are running multiple subroutines consecutively.

This example provides a straightforward method for examining the values stored within an array during the execution of VBA code, which is a common requirement when debugging or validating data processing logic.

Quit Excel application

Closing the Excel application programmatically using VBA involves calling the `Quit` method on the Excel Application object. This action will close Excel entirely, so it's important to ensure that all necessary work is saved and that no unsaved work will be lost. Here's a simple example of how to quit the Excel application using VBA. Please use this code cautiously, as it will close Excel and all open workbooks:

➢ Example: Quitting the Excel application

```
Sub QuitExcelApplication()
    ' This subroutine demonstrates how to quit the Excel
application using VBA.
```

How to do this in VBA?? 202 ready-made macros: Streamline your tasks with proven expert solutions

```vba
    ' Prompt the user to save their work before quitting
Excel.
    Dim response As Integer
    response = MsgBox("Are you sure you want to close
Excel? Make sure all your work is saved.", vbYesNo +
vbExclamation, "Close Excel")

    If response = vbYes Then
        ' If the user clicks "Yes", quit the Excel
application.
        Application.Quit
    Else
        ' If the user clicks "No", do nothing and let them
return to their work.
        MsgBox "Operation cancelled. Returning to Excel.",
vbInformation, "Operation Cancelled"
    End If
End Sub
```

➢ Key points:

- **User confirmation**: given the potential impact of closing Excel, the code starts with a message box asking the user to confirm their intention. This helps prevent accidentally closing Excel and losing unsaved work.
- `Application.Quit`: this method quits Excel. Before using it, ensure that all workbooks are saved if needed, as unsaved changes will be lost unless you implement additional code to handle unsaved workbooks.
- **Cancel operation**: if the user decides not to quit Excel (clicks "No"), a message box informs them that the operation has been cancelled, allowing them to return to their work without closing Excel.

This example provides a basic approach to quitting Excel through VBA while incorporating a user confirmation step to prevent accidental closure of the application.

Reading data from a cell

Reading data from a cell in Excel using VBA involves accessing the `Value` property of a `Range` or `Cells` object. This basic operation is essential for various tasks, such as data analysis, reporting, or dynamic content generation based on spreadsheet data. Here's how to read data from a specific cell:

➢ Example: Reading data from a cell

```
Sub ReadDataFromCell()
    ' This subroutine demonstrates how to read data from a
    specific cell in an Excel worksheet using VBA.

    Dim ws As Worksheet
    Dim cellData As Variant

    ' Set the worksheet object to the sheet that contains
    the data you want to read.
    ' Adjust "Sheet1" to the name of your target
    worksheet.
    Set ws = ThisWorkbook.Sheets("Sheet1")

    ' Read data from a specific cell.
    ' This example reads the value from cell A1.
    cellData = ws.Cells(1, 1).Value

    ' Alternatively, you can reference the cell directly.
    cellData = ws.Range("A1").Value

    ' Display the read data in a message box.
    MsgBox "The data in cell A1 is: " & cellData,
    vbInformation, "Data Read"
End Sub
```

➢ Key points:

- **Worksheet object**: the `ws` variable is assigned to the specific worksheet from which you intend to read data. Ensure the worksheet name matches your actual worksheet.

- **Reading data**: the `.Value` property is used to access the content of a cell, either by specifying its row and column numbers with `Cells(row, column)` or directly with its address using `Range("A1")`.
- **Data storage**: the read data is stored in the `cellData` variable, which can then be used within your VBA code for further processing or displayed directly to the user, as shown in this example.

This example provides a simple yet effective illustration of how to read data from a cell in an Excel workbook using VBA, laying the groundwork for more advanced data manipulation and analysis tasks.

Read text file

Reading a text file line by line in Excel VBA can be accomplished using the `Open` statement along with the `Input #` or `Line Input #` commands for reading the file contents. Below is an example that demonstrates how to open a text file, read its contents line by line, and output the text to the Immediate Window. This script assumes you have a text file named `Example.txt` located in the `C:\Temp\` directory. Adjust the file path as necessary to match the location of your text file. Comments in the code explain each step for clarity.

➤ Example: Reading a text file line by line

```
Sub ReadTextFile()
    ' This subroutine demonstrates how to read a text file
line by line in VBA.

    ' Define the path to the text file.
    Dim filePath As String
    filePath = "C:\Temp\Example.txt" ' Adjust the file
path as needed.

    ' Variable to store a line of text read from the file.
    Dim fileLine As String

    ' Open the text file for reading. Assign it to file
number 1.
    Open filePath For Input As #1
```

```
    ' Read the file line by line until the end of the file
is reached.
    Do Until EOF(1) ' EOF(1) checks if the end of the file
(file number 1) has been reached.
        Line Input #1, fileLine ' Read a line of text into
the variable fileLine.
        ' Output the read line to the Immediate Window
(press Ctrl+G in VBA editor to view).
        Debug.Print fileLine
    Loop


    ' Close the file after reading its contents.
    Close #1


    ' Notify the user that the file contents have been
output to the Immediate Window.
    MsgBox "Text file has been read. Check the Immediate
Window for output.", vbInformation, "File Read"
    End Sub
```

➢ Key points:

- **File path specification**: the `filePath` variable stores the full path to the text file you intend to open and read. Make sure this path correctly points to your file.
- **Opening the file**: the `Open` statement with the `For Input As #1` option opens the file for reading and associates it with file number 1.
- **Reading line by line**: the `Do Until EOF(1)` loop reads the file line by line using `Line Input #1, fileLine`. The `EOF` function is used to check if the end of the file has been reached.
- **Outputting the text**: each line read from the file is output to the Immediate Window using `Debug.Print`. This can be replaced or supplemented with other actions, such as writing the text to a worksheet.
- **Closing the file**: it's important to close the file with `Close #1` after finishing reading to free up system resources.

This example provides a basic method for opening, reading, and processing a text file line by line using VBA, demonstrating a key technique for handling external text data within Excel projects.

Read XML file in excel VBA

Reading and parsing an XML file in Excel VBA can be efficiently done using the `MSXML2.DOMDocument` object, which provides methods and properties for navigating and processing XML documents. This example demonstrates how to load an XML file from disk, parse it, and then extract specific pieces of information from the XML structure. The example assumes an XML file named `Example.xml` located in the `C:\Temp\` directory, with the following simple content for demonstration purposes:

```xml
<?xml version="1.0"?>
<catalog>
    <book id="bk1001">
        <author> Nguyen, Klemens </author>
        <title> 22 VBA scripts to increase Excel and Word security
</title>
        <genre>Computer</genre>
        <price>7.33</price>
        <publish_date> 2024 March 5
</publish_date>
        <description> In the digital age, the security of your Excel and Word documents is not just an option; it's a necessity.</description>
    </book>
    <!-- Add more <book> elements as needed -->
</catalog>
```

➤ VBA code to read and parse XML file

```vba
Sub ReadAndParseXMLFile()
    ' This subroutine demonstrates how to read and parse
an XML file in Excel VBA.

    Dim xmlDoc As Object
    Set xmlDoc = CreateObject("MSXML2.DOMDocument")

    ' Specify the path to your XML file.
```

```vba
Dim xmlFilePath As String
xmlFilePath = "C:\Temp\Example.xml"

' Load the XML file.
xmlDoc.Async = False
xmlDoc.Load xmlFilePath

' Check to ensure the XML file was loaded
successfully.
If xmlDoc.parseError.ErrorCode <> 0 Then
    MsgBox "Error loading XML file: " &
xmlDoc.parseError.reason, vbCritical, "XML Error"
    Exit Sub
End If

' Extract and display information from the XML.
' For demonstration, extract details of the first
book.
Dim bookNode As Object
Set bookNode = xmlDoc.SelectSingleNode("//book")

If Not bookNode Is Nothing Then
    Dim author As String
    Dim title As String
    Dim price As String

    author = bookNode.SelectSingleNode("author").Text
    title = bookNode.SelectSingleNode("title").Text
    price = bookNode.SelectSingleNode("price").Text

    MsgBox "Book Details:" & vbCrLf & _
            "Author: " & author & vbCrLf & _
            "Title: " & title & vbCrLf & _
            "Price: $" & price, vbInformation, "XML
Book Details"
    Else
```

```
            MsgBox "No book element found.", vbExclamation,
    "XML Parsing"
        End If
    End Sub
```

➢ Key points:

- **DOMDocument object**: used for loading and parsing the XML document. This object is part of the Microsoft XML, v6.0 library (MSXML2), but here we're using late binding with `CreateObject` to avoid the need for setting a reference.
- **Loading the XML file**: the `.Load` method of the `DOMDocument` object is used to load the XML file from the specified path.
- **Error checking**: it's important to check for errors after attempting to load the XML file to ensure the parsing process can proceed without issues.
- **Navigating the XML**: the `.SelectSingleNode` method is used to find the first `<book>` element in the XML. This method and others like `.SelectNodes` can be used to navigate and extract data from the XML document.
- **Extracting data**: once the relevant node(s) are selected, their `.Text` property can be used to get the actual data contained within an element.

This example provides a foundational approach to working with XML files in Excel VBA, demonstrating how to load, parse, and extract data from XML for further processing or analysis.

Redim an array

Resizing an array dynamically in VBA can be achieved using the `ReDim` statement. This is particularly useful when you don't know the exact size of the array upfront. You can declare an array without specifying its size and then resize it later using `ReDim`. It's also possible to preserve the contents of the array when resizing by using `ReDim Preserve`.

Here's an example that demonstrates how to dynamically resize an array using `ReDim`, both with and without preserving the array's contents:

➢ Example: Dynamically resizing an array with ReDim

```
    Sub DynamicArrayResizing()
        ' Declare an array without initially specifying its
    size
```

```vba
Dim dynamicArray() As Integer

' Dynamically resize the array to hold 5 elements
ReDim dynamicArray(4) ' Arrays are zero-based; hence,
4 represents the 5th element.

' Assign values to the array
Dim i As Integer
For i = LBound(dynamicArray) To UBound(dynamicArray)
    dynamicArray(i) = i * 2 ' Example: fill the array
with even numbers
Next i

' Display the current contents of the array
Debug.Print "Initial array contents:"
For i = LBound(dynamicArray) To UBound(dynamicArray)
    Debug.Print dynamicArray(i)
Next i

' Resize the array while preserving its contents to
hold 10 elements
ReDim Preserve dynamicArray(9) ' Resize the array to
10 elements, preserving existing contents

' Fill the newly added elements with values
For i = 5 To UBound(dynamicArray)
    dynamicArray(i) = i * 2 ' Continue filling the
array with even numbers
Next i

' Display the new contents of the array after resizing
Debug.Print "Array contents after resizing:"
For i = LBound(dynamicArray) To UBound(dynamicArray)
    Debug.Print dynamicArray(i)
Next i
```

```
        ' Note: Using 'ReDim Preserve' can only resize the
    last dimension of a multi-dimensional array
    End Sub
```

➢ Key points:

- **Initial resizing**: `ReDim dynamicArray(4)` initially resizes the array to hold 5 elements.
- **Assigning values**: the first `For` loop fills the array with values.
- **Preserving contents**: `ReDim Preserve dynamicArray(9)` resizes the array to 10 elements while preserving the existing contents.
- **Filling additional elements**: the second `For` loop assigns values to the newly added elements in the array.
- **Limitation**: when using `ReDim Preserve`, you can only resize the last dimension of a multi-dimensional array, and you cannot change the number of dimensions.

This example demonstrates a fundamental technique for working with dynamically sized arrays in VBA, allowing for flexible data storage and manipulation within your macros.

Refresh all queries Excel

Refreshing all queries in an Excel workbook can be a crucial step in ensuring that your data is up-to-date, especially when dealing with external data sources like databases, web services, or other data files. Excel's VBA provides a straightforward method to programmatically refresh all queries. Below is an example demonstrating how to use VBA to refresh all queries in the active workbook.

➢ Example: Refreshing all queries in an Excel Workbook

```
    Sub RefreshAllQueries()
        ' This subroutine demonstrates how to refresh all
    queries in the active Excel workbook.


        ' Check if there are any queries to refresh
        If Not ActiveWorkbook.Queries.Count > 0 Then
            MsgBox "There are no queries to refresh.",
    vbInformation, "No Queries"
            Exit Sub
        End If
```

```vba
    ' Display a message to let the user know the process
has started
    MsgBox "Refreshing all queries. Please wait...",
vbInformation, "Refresh Started"

    ' Refresh all connections in the workbook
    ActiveWorkbook.RefreshAll

    ' Optionally, wait for all refreshes to complete
before proceeding.
    ' This ensures that subsequent code only runs after
all data is refreshed.
    Do While Application.BackgroundQueryRunning
        DoEvents ' Yield execution so that the Excel
interface remains responsive.
    Loop

    ' Notify the user that all queries have been
refreshed.
    MsgBox "All queries have been refreshed.",
vbInformation, "Refresh Complete"
End Sub
```

➢ Key points:

- **Checking for queries**: before attempting to refresh, it checks if there are any queries in the workbook to avoid unnecessary operations or errors.
- **User notifications**: message boxes inform the user when the refresh process starts and completes. This can be particularly useful for queries that take a long time to refresh.
- `RefreshAll` method: the `ActiveWorkbook.RefreshAll` method is used to refresh all data connections in the workbook, including queries, pivot tables, and other data tables linked to external sources.
- **Background queries**: the loop with `Application.BackgroundQueryRunning` checks if there are any

queries still being refreshed in the background. The `DoEvents` function keeps the application responsive during this wait.

This example provides a comprehensive approach to refreshing all queries in an Excel workbook using VBA, enhancing the automation of data management tasks.

Refresh Pivot Table

Refreshing a PivotTable in Excel using VBA is a straightforward task that ensures your PivotTable displays the most up-to-date data available in its source. Below is an example demonstrating how to refresh a specific PivotTable on a specific worksheet. This script assumes you have a PivotTable named "PivotTable1" on a worksheet named "Sheet1". Adjust the worksheet name and PivotTable name as necessary to match your workbook's setup. Comments in the code explain each step for clarity.

➢ Example: Refreshing a specific PivotTable

```
Sub RefreshSpecificPivotTable()
    ' This subroutine demonstrates how to refresh a
    specific PivotTable in Excel using VBA.

    Dim ws As Worksheet
    ' Set a reference to the worksheet containing the
    PivotTable.
    ' Adjust "Sheet1" to the name of your target
    worksheet.
    Set ws = ThisWorkbook.Sheets("Sheet1")

    Dim pt As PivotTable
    ' Set a reference to the specific PivotTable you want
    to refresh.
    ' Adjust "PivotTable1" to the name of your target
    PivotTable.
    Set pt = ws.PivotTables("PivotTable1")

    ' Refresh the PivotTable.
    pt.RefreshTable
```

```
        ' Notify the user that the PivotTable has been
    refreshed,
        MsgBox "PivotTable '" & pt.Name & "' has been
    refreshed.", vbInformation, "PivotTable Refreshed"
        End Sub
```

➢ Key points:

- **Worksheet and PivotTable references**: the script begins by setting references to the specific worksheet (`ws`) and PivotTable (`pt`) that you want to refresh. This ensures that the refresh action is applied correctly to the intended PivotTable.
- **Refreshing the PivotTable**: the `RefreshTable` method is used to refresh the PivotTable, updating its data based on the current contents of its source data range or table.
- **User notification**: a message box confirms the successful completion of the refresh operation. This feedback is especially useful in automated processes where the user may not see immediate visual confirmation of the refresh in the Excel interface.

This example provides a basic template for refreshing a PivotTable using VBA, which can be easily adapted for use with multiple PivotTables or incorporated into larger data processing and reporting macros.

Refresh power query

Refreshing Power Query queries (also known as Get & Transform) in Excel using VBA involves interacting with the `WorkbookQuery` objects within the `Workbook.Queries` collection. To refresh all Power Query connections, you can use the `Workbook.RefreshAll` method, but if you want to refresh a specific query by name, you need to work with the `QueryTable` object associated with the query.

Below is an example demonstrating how to refresh a specific Power Query by name. This is useful when you have multiple queries and only need to update one without refreshing the entire workbook's data connections.

➢ Example: refreshing a specific Power Query

```
    Sub RefreshSpecificPowerQuery()
        ' This subroutine demonstrates how to refresh a
    specific Power Query in Excel using VBA.
```

How to do this in VBA?? 202 ready-made macros: Streamline your tasks with proven expert solutions

```vba
    Dim queryName As String
    ' Specify the name of the query you want to refresh.
    queryName = "YourQueryName" ' Replace with your actual
query name

    Dim isFound As Boolean
    isFound = False

    ' Loop through all Workbook connections
    Dim conn As WorkbookConnection
    For Each conn In ThisWorkbook.Connections
        ' Check if the connection's name matches the query
you're looking for
        If conn.Name = queryName Then
            ' Refresh the Power Query connection
            conn.Refresh

            isFound = True
            Exit For
        End If
    Next conn

    ' Notify the user whether the specified query was
found and refreshed
    If isFound Then
        MsgBox "Query '" & queryName & "' has been
refreshed.", vbInformation, "Query Refreshed"
    Else
        MsgBox "Query '" & queryName & "' was not found.",
vbExclamation, "Query Not Found"
    End If
End Sub
```

➤ Key points:

- **Query identification**: the script starts by specifying the name of the Power Query you wish to refresh. You must replace

> `'"YourQueryName"'` with the actual name of the query in your workbook.
- **Searching for the query**: the `For Each` loop checks each connection in `ThisWorkbook.Connections` to find a match for the specified query name.
- **Refreshing the query**: when a match is found, the `conn.Refresh` method is called to refresh the query. The loop then exits to avoid unnecessary iterations.
- **Feedback to user**: the script provides feedback via a message box indicating whether the query was successfully found and refreshed, or if the query name provided did not match any existing queries in the workbook.

This example provides a targeted approach to refreshing specific Power Query queries using VBA, which can be particularly useful in workbooks with multiple data connections where refreshing all connections might be inefficient or disruptive.

Refresh query table

Refreshing a QueryTable in Excel using VBA involves targeting a specific query table by its name or index in a worksheet and then calling the `Refresh` method on that query table object. This is particularly useful when you have data connected to external sources such as databases, web services, or text files, and you need to update the data in Excel to reflect any changes in the external source.

Here's an example demonstrating how to refresh a specific QueryTable in a worksheet. This example assumes you have a QueryTable on a worksheet named "Sheet1". Adjust the worksheet name and the QueryTable name/index as necessary to match your setup.

➢ Example: Refreshing a specific QueryTable

```
Sub RefreshSpecificQueryTable()
    ' This subroutine demonstrates how to refresh a
specific QueryTable in Excel using VBA.

    Dim ws As Worksheet
    ' Set a reference to the worksheet containing the
QueryTable.
```

```
    ' Adjust "Sheet1" to the name of your target
worksheet.
    Set ws = ThisWorkbook.Sheets("Sheet1")

    Dim qt As QueryTable
    ' Assuming we know the name or index of the
QueryTable, we'll reference it directly.
    ' If you're using the QueryTable's name, replace 1
with "YourQueryTableName".
    ' Example: Set qt =
ws.QueryTables("YourQueryTableName")
    Set qt = ws.QueryTables(1)

    ' Refresh the QueryTable.
    qt.Refresh BackgroundQuery:=False

    ' Notify the user that the QueryTable has been
refreshed.
    MsgBox "QueryTable has been refreshed.",
vbInformation, "Refresh Complete"
    End Sub
```

➢ Key points:

- **Worksheet reference**: the script starts by setting a reference to the specific worksheet (`ws`) containing the QueryTable.
- **QueryTable reference**: the QueryTable is then referenced directly either by its index (e.g., `ws.QueryTables(1)`) or by its name if known (e.g., `ws.QueryTables("YourQueryTableName")`). Adjust this part according to your actual QueryTable identifier.
- Refreshing the QueryTable: the `Refresh` method is called on the `QueryTable` object with `BackgroundQuery:=False` to refresh the data synchronously. Setting `BackgroundQuery` to `False` ensures that the macro waits until the refresh is complete before moving on to the next line of code.
- User notification: a message box informs the user that the QueryTable refresh operation has completed.

How to do this in VBA?? 202 ready-made macros: Streamline your tasks with proven expert solutions

This example demonstrates how to programmatically refresh a specific QueryTable in Excel using VBA, which can be adapted to refresh multiple QueryTables or integrated into larger data processing and analysis macros.

Remove double quotes from string

Removing double quotes from a string in Excel VBA can be achieved using the `Replace` function. This function searches for a specified substring within a string and replaces it with another substring. To remove double quotes, you would search for the double quote character (`"`) and replace it with an empty string (`""`).

Here's an example demonstrating how to remove double quotes from a string:

Example: Removing double quotes from a string

```
Sub RemoveDoubleQuotes()
    ' This subroutine demonstrates how to remove double
quotes from a string in VBA.

    ' Example string with double quotes
    Dim originalString As String
    originalString = "This is a ""sample"" string with
""double quotes""."

    ' Remove double quotes from the string
    ' The Replace function is used here to replace double
quotes (Chr(34)) with an empty string
    Dim stringWithoutQuotes As String
    stringWithoutQuotes = Replace(originalString, Chr(34),
"")

    ' Display the original and modified strings
    MsgBox "Original string: " & originalString & vbCrLf &
_

            "String without double quotes: " &
stringWithoutQuotes, _
            vbInformation, "Remove Double Quotes"
End Sub
```

➢ Key points:

- **Original string**: `originalString` contains the initial string value with double quotes. Note that in VBA, to include a double quote inside a string, you must use two double quote characters (`""`) as an escape sequence.
- Using `Replace` function: the `Replace` function is called with `Chr(34)` as the substring to find, where `Chr(34)` represents the double quote character. The function replaces all occurrences of this character with an empty string, effectively removing them from the original string.
- **Displaying results**: a message box shows both the original string and the modified string without double quotes, allowing you to compare the before and after results.

This example provides a straightforward method for removing double quotes from strings in VBA, which can be particularly useful when processing text data that may include unwanted quotation marks.

Remove duplicates

Removing duplicates from a range or table in Excel using VBA is a common task that can help clean up data sets. Excel VBA offers the `RemoveDuplicates` method, which can be applied to a range or table to remove duplicate rows based on specified column(s).

Here's an example demonstrating how to remove duplicates from a specific range in a worksheet, considering all columns in the determination of duplicates. This script assumes you have data in columns A to D from row 1 (which includes headers) onwards on a worksheet named "Sheet1". Adjust the range and worksheet as necessary for your data.

➢ Example: Removing duplicates from a range

```
Sub RemoveDuplicatesFromRange()
    ' This subroutine demonstrates how to remove duplicate
rows from a specific range in Excel using VBA.

    Dim ws As Worksheet
    ' Set a reference to the worksheet containing the
data.
    Set ws = ThisWorkbook.Sheets("Sheet1")
```

```
Dim dataRange As Range
' Set a reference to the range from which you want to
remove duplicates.
' Adjust the range according to your data. Here, it's
assumed data is in columns A to D.
Set dataRange = ws.Range("A1:D" &
ws.Cells(ws.Rows.Count, "A").End(xlUp).Row)


' Remove duplicates from the range.
' The Columns array parameter specifies the columns to
consider for duplicates.
' Here, an array with 1 to 4 indicates that duplicates
will be identified based on all four columns.
dataRange.RemoveDuplicates Columns:=Array(1, 2, 3, 4),
Header:=xlYes


' Notify the user that duplicates have been removed.
MsgBox "Duplicates have been removed based on columns
A to D.", vbInformation, "Remove Duplicates Completed"
End Sub
```

➢ Key points:

- **Worksheet** reference: adjust `ThisWorkbook.Sheets("Sheet1")` to target the correct worksheet.
- **Range reference**: the `dataRange` is set to encompass the columns A to D up to the last row with data in column A. This may need adjustment based on your actual data layout.
- `RemoveDuplicates` **method**: this method is called on `dataRange` to remove duplicate rows. The `Columns` parameter specifies which columns to consider when determining duplicates. In this example, all four columns (A to D) are considered by passing `Array(1, 2, 3, 4)`. Adjust this array if you want to consider a different set of columns.
- **Header parameter**: the `Header:=xlYes` argument specifies that the first row of the range contains headers and should not be considered as data for duplicate checks.

This example provides a basic approach to removing duplicates from a specified range in Excel using VBA, enhancing data integrity and consistency for analysis or reporting.

Remove filter

Removing filters from a worksheet in Excel using VBA can be necessary to reset the view of a data set or prepare a sheet for a new analysis. Here's a simple example demonstrating how to remove filters from a specific worksheet. If filters are applied, this code will remove them; if no filters are applied, the code will not affect the worksheet.

➤ Example: Removing filters from a worksheet

```
Sub RemoveFilters()
    ' This subroutine demonstrates how to remove filters
from a worksheet in Excel using VBA.

    Dim ws As Worksheet
    ' Set a reference to the target worksheet.
    ' Adjust "Sheet1" to the name of your worksheet.
    Set ws = ThisWorkbook.Sheets("Sheet1")

    ' Check if the worksheet has filters applied.
    If ws.AutoFilterMode Then
        ' Remove the filters.
        ws.AutoFilterMode = False
    End If

    ' Notify the user that filters have been removed, if
they were applied.
    MsgBox "All filters have been removed from '" &
ws.Name & "'.", vbInformation, "Filters Removed"
End Sub
```

➤ Key points:

- **Worksheet reference**: the variable `ws` is set to reference the worksheet from which you want to remove the filters. You need to adjust `"Sheet1"` to the name of your target worksheet.

- **Checking and removing filters**: the `AutoFilterMode` property of the worksheet object is used to determine if filters are currently applied (`True` if filters are applied). Setting `AutoFilterMode` to `False` removes the filters from the worksheet.
- **User notification**: after removing the filters, a message box informs the user that the operation is complete. This confirmation is helpful, especially when working with macros that perform multiple operations on worksheets.

This example provides a straightforward method for removing filters from a worksheet, which can be easily adapted to work across multiple sheets or integrated into larger data processing routines in Excel using VBA.

Rename a file

Renaming a file in Excel VBA can be achieved using the `Name` statement. This statement allows you to change the name or move a file, but in this example, we'll focus on renaming. It's important to ensure the new file name does not already exist in the target directory, as the `Name` statement will overwrite an existing file without warning.

Here's a simple example that demonstrates how to rename a file. This script assumes you have a file named `OldFileName.txt` in the `C:\Temp\` directory that you want to rename to `NewFileName.txt`. Adjust the file paths as necessary to match your scenario.

➢ Example: Renaming a file

```
Sub RenameFile()
    ' This subroutine demonstrates how to rename a file
    using VBA.


    ' Define the full path of the existing file.
    Dim oldFilePath As String
    oldFilePath = "C:\Temp\OldFileName.txt" ' Adjust the
    path and file name as necessary.


    ' Define the full path of the new file name.
    Dim newFilePath As String
    newFilePath = "C:\Temp\NewFileName.txt" ' Adjust the
    path and new file name as necessary.
```

```
        ' Check if the old file exists to prevent runtime
    errors.
        If Dir(oldFilePath) <> "" Then
            ' Use the Name statement to rename the file.
            Name oldFilePath As newFilePath

            ' Notify the user that the file has been renamed.
            MsgBox "File has been renamed to '" & newFilePath
    & "'.", vbInformation, "File Renamed"
        Else
            ' Notify the user that the old file was not found.
            MsgBox "The file '" & oldFilePath & "' was not
    found.", vbExclamation, "File Not Found"
        End If
    End Sub
```

➤ Key points:

- **Old and new file paths**: `oldFilePath` and `newFilePath` variables store the full paths of the old and new file names, respectively. Make sure these paths are correctly set to reflect your actual files.
- **File existence check**: the `Dir` function checks if the old file exists before attempting the rename operation. This prevents the `Name` statement from throwing an error if the old file does not exist.
- **Using `Name` statement**: the `Name` statement is straightforward for renaming files but does not provide error handling directly. It's wrapped in an `If` statement checking for the file's existence for basic error handling.
- **User notification**: message boxes inform the user whether the file was successfully renamed or if the original file was not found.

This example provides a basic approach to file renaming in Excel VBA, demonstrating essential file manipulation techniques within VBA scripts.

Rename a sheet

Renaming a worksheet in Excel using VBA is a straightforward task that can significantly improve the clarity and organization of your workbook. Here's an example demonstrating how to rename a specific sheet. This script assumes you have a sheet named "OldSheetName" that you want to rename to

237

"NewSheetName". Make sure to adjust the sheet names as necessary to match your workbook's setup.

➤ Example: Renaming a worksheet

```vba
Sub RenameSheet()
    ' This subroutine demonstrates how to rename a
specific worksheet in Excel using VBA.

    ' Define the current (old) and new names for the
worksheet.
    Dim oldSheetName As String
    Dim newSheetName As String
    oldSheetName = "OldSheetName" ' Adjust this to your
current sheet name.
    newSheetName = "NewSheetName" ' Adjust this to the
desired new sheet name.

    ' Check if the sheet with the old name exists to
prevent runtime errors.
    Dim ws As Worksheet
    On Error Resume Next ' Ignore errors in the next
statement.
    Set ws = ThisWorkbook.Sheets(oldSheetName)
    On Error GoTo 0 ' Turn back on regular error handling.

    ' If the worksheet exists, rename it.
    If Not ws Is Nothing Then
        ws.Name = newSheetName
        MsgBox "Sheet renamed to '" & newSheetName & "'.",
vbInformation, "Sheet Renamed Successfully"
    Else
        MsgBox "Sheet '" & oldSheetName & "' not found.",
vbExclamation, "Error"
    End If
End Sub
```

➤ Key points:

How to do this in VBA?? 202 ready-made macros: Streamline your tasks with proven expert solutions

- **Sheet names**: variables `oldSheetName` and `newSheetName` are used to store the names of the sheet you want to rename and what you want to rename it to, respectively.
- **Error handling**: `On Error Resume Next` is used before attempting to set the `ws` worksheet object to handle the case where the specified old sheet name does not exist. This prevents the macro from stopping due to a runtime error. `On Error GoTo 0` is used immediately afterward to revert to normal error handling.
- **Renaming the sheet**: if the worksheet object `ws` is successfully set (i.e., the sheet exists), its `Name` property is updated to `newSheetName`, effectively renaming the sheet.
- **User feedback**: message boxes provide feedback to the user about the outcome of the operation, indicating either successful renaming or that the specified sheet could not be found.

This example provides a basic yet effective method for renaming worksheets in Excel via VBA, enhancing the automation of workbook organization tasks.

Return a value from a function

Creating a function in VBA that returns a value involves defining the function with a specific return type and using the function name within the procedure to assign the value you wish to return. Below is a simple example demonstrating how to create and use a function that calculates the area of a rectangle and returns the result. This example clearly shows how to define a function, pass arguments, and return a value.

➢ Example: Calculating and returning the area of a rectangle

```
Function CalculateArea(length As Double, width As Double)
As Double
    ' This function calculates the area of a rectangle
given its length and width.

    ' Calculate the area.
    CalculateArea = length * width

    ' The value of the function is automatically returned
to the caller.
End Function
```

How to do this in VBA?? 202 ready-made macros: Streamline your tasks with proven expert solutions

To use this function and display the returned value, you can call it from a subroutine like so:

```
Sub ShowRectangleArea()
    ' This subroutine demonstrates how to use the
CalculateArea function and display the result.

    Dim rectLength As Double
    Dim rectWidth As Double
    Dim area As Double

    ' Example values for length and width
    rectLength = 10
    rectWidth = 5

    ' Call the CalculateArea function and store the
returned value in the 'area' variable.
    area = CalculateArea(rectLength, rectWidth)

    ' Display the calculated area.
    MsgBox "The area of the rectangle is: " & area,
vbInformation, "Rectangle Area"
End Sub
```

➢ Key points:

- **Function definition**: the `CalculateArea` function is defined to take two `Double` arguments (`length` and `width`) and return a `Double` value, which is the area of the rectangle.
- **Returning a value**: the function returns a value by assigning the calculated area to `CalculateArea`, which is the name of the function itself. In VBA, this syntax is used to specify the return value.
- **Using the function**: the `ShowRectangleArea` subroutine demonstrates how to call the `CalculateArea` function, pass arguments to it, and use the returned value. In this example, the returned area is displayed in a message box.

This example illustrates the basic structure and syntax for creating and using functions in VBA that return values, allowing for modular, reusable code that can perform calculations, process data, and more.

Round up

Rounding numbers up in VBA can be achieved using the `WorksheetFunction.RoundUp` method or the `Ceiling` function. Both approaches allow you to specify the number of digits to which you want to round up. The `RoundUp` function is more straightforward for most rounding needs, while `Ceiling` can be useful for more complex rounding scenarios, like rounding to the nearest multiple of a specified value.

Here's an example using both methods to round a number up to the nearest whole number and to a specified number of decimal places.

➢Example 1: Using `RoundUp` to round a number up

```
Sub RoundNumberUp()
    ' This subroutine demonstrates how to round a number
up to the nearest whole number and decimal place.

    Dim originalNumber As Double
    originalNumber = 3.14159 ' Example number

    ' Round the number up to the nearest whole number.
    Dim roundedUpWhole As Double
    roundedUpWhole =
Application.WorksheetFunction.RoundUp(originalNumber, 0)

    ' Round the number up to two decimal places.
    Dim roundedUpTwoDecimals As Double
    roundedUpTwoDecimals =
Application.WorksheetFunction.RoundUp(originalNumber, 2)

    ' Display the results.
    MsgBox "Original Number: " & originalNumber & vbCrLf &
_
            "Rounded Up to Nearest Whole Number: " &
roundedUpWhole & vbCrLf & _
            "Rounded Up to Two Decimal Places: " &
roundedUpTwoDecimals, vbInformation, "Round Up Results"
End Sub
```

➢ Example 2: Using `**Ceiling**` for advanced rounding

```
Sub RoundNumberUsingCeiling()
    ' This subroutine demonstrates how to round a number
up to the nearest multiple of a specified value using
Ceiling.

    Dim originalNumber As Double
    originalNumber = 3.14159 ' Example number

    ' Round the number up to the nearest 0.05.
    Dim roundedUpNearestFiveCents As Double
    roundedUpNearestFiveCents =
Application.WorksheetFunction.Ceiling(originalNumber,
0.05)

    ' Display the results.
    MsgBox "Original Number: " & originalNumber & vbCrLf &
_

        "Rounded Up to Nearest 0.05: " &
roundedUpNearestFiveCents, vbInformation, "Ceiling
Results"
End Sub
```

➢ Key points:

- `**RoundUp**` **method**: rounds a number up away from zero to a specified number of digits. In the example, it's used to round to the nearest whole number and to two decimal places.
- `**Ceiling**` **function**: rounds a number up, away from zero, to the nearest multiple of the specified significance. The example demonstrates rounding to the nearest 0.05, which can be particularly useful for financial calculations.
- **Displaying results**: both examples use a message box to display the original number and the rounded results, allowing you to see the effect of each rounding method clearly.

These examples showcase basic and advanced rounding techniques in VBA, enabling precise control over how numbers are rounded in your Excel applications.

Run a query in Access VBA

Running a query in Access using VBA can be done in several ways depending on the type of query and its purpose. Here's a simple example demonstrating how to execute a SELECT query and process the results. This script assumes you have an Access database with a table named `MyTable` and you want to retrieve data from it.

➢ Example: Running a SELECT query and processing results

```vba
Sub RunSelectQuery()
    ' This subroutine demonstrates how to run a SELECT
query and process the results in Access VBA.

    ' Declare database and recordset objects
    Dim db As DAO.Database
    Dim rs As DAO.Recordset
    Dim strSQL As String

    ' SQL query to execute
    strSQL = "SELECT * FROM MyTable WHERE ConditionField =
'SomeValue'"

    ' Get the current database
    Set db = CurrentDb

    ' Execute the query and get the recordset
    Set rs = db.OpenRecordset(strSQL, dbOpenDynaset)

    ' Check if the recordset is empty
    If Not (rs.BOF And rs.EOF) Then
        ' Move to the first record if not empty
        rs.MoveFirst

        ' Loop through the recordset
        Do Until rs.EOF
            ' Process each record. For example, print the
value of the first field
```

```
                    Debug.Print rs.Fields(0).Value
                    ' Move to the next record
                    rs.MoveNext
               Loop
          Else
               MsgBox "No records found.", vbInformation
          End If

          ' Clean up
          rs.Close
          Set rs = Nothing
          Set db = Nothing
     End Sub
```

➢ Key Points:

- **DAO recordset**: this example uses the Data Access Objects (DAO) library to execute the query and retrieve the results. Ensure your Access project references the Microsoft DAO Object Library.
- **SQL query**: the SQL string (`strSQL`) contains the actual SQL command to be executed. Adjust this query to match your database schema and data retrieval needs.
- **Processing results**: the example checks if the recordset is empty (`BOF` and `EOF` properties) and then loops through the records, printing the value of the first field of each record to the Immediate Window (`Debug.Print` statement). Modify this part to suit how you need to process or display the data.
- **Clean up**: always close the recordset and set the object variables to `Nothing` after you're done to free up resources.

This example demonstrates a basic approach to executing SELECT queries and handling their results in Access VBA, providing a foundation for developing more complex data retrieval and processing functionalities within your Access applications.

Run JavaScript

Running JavaScript directly from Excel VBA isn't supported in a straightforward manner because VBA is designed to interact within the Microsoft Office environment, and JavaScript is typically executed within a web browser context or a Node.js environment. However, you can use VBA to interact with Internet

How to do this in VBA?? 202 ready-made macros: Streamline your tasks with proven expert solutions

Explorer, allowing you to execute JavaScript within the context of a web page loaded in the browser. This method is less common and generally recommended only for specific automation tasks that require interaction with web pages.

Below is an example that demonstrates how to open Internet Explorer, navigate to a web page, and then run a simple JavaScript code snippet on that page. This example assumes you're trying to execute JavaScript that changes the document's background color, a basic operation to illustrate the process.

➢ Example: Running JavaScript in Internet Explorer via VBA

```vba
Sub RunJavaScriptInIE()
    ' Create an Internet Explorer application object
    Dim ie As Object
    Set ie = CreateObject("InternetExplorer.Application")

    ' Make the Internet Explorer application visible
    ie.Visible = True

    ' Navigate to a webpage, for example, Google
    ie.Navigate "https://www.google.com"

    ' Wait for the page to fully load
    Do While ie.Busy Or ie.readyState <> 4
        DoEvents
    Loop

    ' Run a JavaScript code snippet to change the
background color of the page
    ie.document.parentWindow.execScript
"document.body.style.backgroundColor = 'yellow';",
"JavaScript"

    ' Optionally, close Internet Explorer
    ' ie.Quit

    ' Clean up
    Set ie = Nothing
```

245

```
    End Sub
```

➤ Key points:

- **Internet explorer object**: the script starts by creating an Internet Explorer application object. This object is used to control Internet Explorer programmatically.
- **Page navigation**: the `Navigate` method loads a specified URL. Replace `"https://www.google.com"` with the actual URL where you need to run your JavaScript.
- **Wait for page load**: it's crucial to wait until the page is fully loaded before attempting to run JavaScript to ensure that the DOM is fully available.
- **Executing JavaScript**: the `execScript` method is used to execute JavaScript code on the loaded page. The example changes the page's background color to yellow.
- **Closing IE**: you can optionally close Internet Explorer programmatically by calling `ie.Quit`. Be cautious with this if you plan to execute further operations or inspections.

This method is somewhat deprecated and should be used with understanding of its limitations and security implications. Modern web automation tasks are often better handled with more current tools and technologies, such as Selenium WebDriver, which offers bindings for various programming languages including Python and can interact with modern web browsers like Chrome and Firefox.

Run SQL query

Running an SQL query from Excel VBA can be achieved by establishing a connection to a database using ActiveX Data Objects (ADO). This allows you to execute SQL queries and retrieve data directly into Excel. Below is a basic example demonstrating how to connect to a database, run a SELECT SQL query, and output the results to the Immediate Window. This example uses a connection to a Microsoft Access database, but the concept can be adapted for other database systems by changing the connection string.

➤ Example: Running an SQL query and outputting results

```
    Sub RunSQLQuery()
        ' This subroutine demonstrates how to run an SQL query
    from Excel VBA using ADO.
```

How to do this in VBA?? 202 ready-made macros: Streamline your tasks with proven expert solutions

```vba
    ' Add a reference to the Microsoft ActiveX Data
Objects Library
    ' by going to Tools -> References in the VBA editor

    Dim conn As ADODB.Connection
    Dim rs As ADODB.Recordset
    Dim sql As String

    ' Initialize the connection and recordset objects
    Set conn = New ADODB.Connection
    Set rs = New ADODB.Recordset

    ' Define the connection string (example for Access
database)
    ' Adjust the path to your database file
    Dim connString As String
    connString = "Provider=Microsoft.ACE.OLEDB.12.0;" & _
                "Data
Source=C:\Path\To\YourDatabase.accdb;"

    ' Open the connection
    conn.Open connString

    ' Define the SQL query
    ' Adjust the SQL query to suit your data schema
    sql = "SELECT * FROM YourTableName WHERE SomeCondition
= 'Value'"

    ' Execute the query and get the results
    Set rs = conn.Execute(sql)

    ' Check if there are records
    If Not rs.EOF Then
        ' Move to the first record
        rs.MoveFirst
```

```vba
    ' Loop through the recordset and print the results
    Do Until rs.EOF
        Debug.Print rs.Fields("YourFieldName").Value
        rs.MoveNext
    Loop
Else
    Debug.Print "No records found."
End If


' Clean up
rs.Close
conn.Close
Set rs = Nothing
Set conn = Nothing
End Sub
```

➤ Key points:

- **ADO library reference**: ensure you have added a reference to the Microsoft ActiveX Data Objects Library in the VBA editor under Tools -> References. This is necessary for the `ADODB.Connection` and `ADODB.Recordset` objects to work.
- **Connection string**: the `connString` variable holds the connection string to the database. This example uses a Microsoft Access database. For other databases like SQL Server, MySQL, or Oracle, the connection string format will differ.
- **SQL query**: the `sql` variable should contain your SQL query. This example selects all records from `YourTableName` where `SomeCondition` equals `'Value'`. Adjust this to fit your actual SQL query needs.
- **Outputting results**: this example uses `Debug.Print` to output the results to the Immediate Window in the VBA editor. For real-world applications, you might want to output the data to an Excel worksheet instead.
- **Cleaning up**: closing the recordset and connection and setting the objects to `Nothing` is important for freeing up resources.

This example provides a basic framework for executing SQL queries from Excel VBA and can be adapted for use with various databases by changing the connection string and SQL query as needed.

Run update query in Access VBA

Executing an UPDATE SQL query in Access using VBA involves using the `DoCmd.RunSQL` method or the `CurrentDb.Execute` method. Both approaches can run an SQL statement that updates records in your database. For actions that change data, `CurrentDb.Execute` is often preferred because it doesn't display warning messages by default, unlike `DoCmd.RunSQL`, which requires setting `DoCmd.SetWarnings` to disable/enable warning messages temporarily.

Here's an example using `CurrentDb.Execute` to run an UPDATE SQL query, which updates records in a table named `YourTableName`. This example changes the value of a field named `YourFieldName` to a new value where another field, `ConditionField`, meets a certain condition.

➢ Example: Running an UPDATE SQL query in Access VBA

```
Sub RunUpdateQuery()
    ' This subroutine demonstrates how to execute an
UPDATE SQL query in Access VBA.

    ' SQL statement to update records
    Dim sql As String
    sql = "UPDATE YourTableName SET YourFieldName =
'NewValue' WHERE ConditionField = 'SomeCondition'"

    ' Use CurrentDb.Execute to run the query without
displaying warning messages
    CurrentDb.Execute sql, dbFailOnError

    ' Check for errors (optional)
    If CurrentDb.RecordsAffected > 0 Then
        MsgBox CurrentDb.RecordsAffected & " record(s)
were updated.", vbInformation, "Update Successful"
    Else
        MsgBox "No records were updated.", vbInformation,
"Update Info"
    End If
End Sub
```

How to do this in VBA?? 202 ready-made macros: Streamline your tasks with proven expert solutions

➢ Key points:

- **SQL query**: adjust the `sql` string to reflect your actual UPDATE statement. Ensure the table name (`YourTableName`), field names (`YourFieldName`, `ConditionField`), and criteria (`'NewValue'`, `'SomeCondition'`) match your database schema.
- **Executing the query**: `CurrentDb.Execute` runs the SQL query. The `dbFailOnError` option is specified to ensure that Access raises an error if the query fails, which is useful for debugging.
- **Handling warnings**: unlike `DoCmd.RunSQL`, using `CurrentDb.Execute` does not display warning messages about updating records, making it a cleaner option for programmatic database updates.
- **Feedback on the operation**: after running the update query, a message box shows how many records were affected by the update. This provides immediate feedback about the operation's success.

This example offers a straightforward method to programmatically execute UPDATE SQL queries within an Access database, facilitating data manipulation and management through VBA.

Save as

Saving a workbook under a new name in Excel using VBA can be accomplished using the `SaveAs` method of the Workbook object. This method allows you to specify the new file name, location, and optionally the file format. Below is an example demonstrating how to use the `SaveAs` method to save the active workbook with a new name and in a specific format.

➢ Example: Saving the active workbook with a new name and format

```
Sub SaveWorkbookAsNewFile()
    ' This subroutine demonstrates how to save the active
workbook under a new name and format using VBA.

    ' Define the full path and name of the new file
    Dim newFilePath As String
    newFilePath = "C:\Temp\NewWorkbook.xlsx" ' Change the
path and file name as needed

    ' Specify the file format. For example,
xlOpenXMLWorkbook for .xlsx format
```

How to do this in VBA?? 202 ready-made macros: Streamline your tasks with proven expert solutions

```
    ' For different formats, you can use constants like
xlCSV, xlExcel8 (for .xls), etc.
    Dim fileFormat As Long
    fileFormat = xlOpenXMLWorkbook

    ' Save the active workbook with the new name and
format
    ' Ensure you do not overwrite important files by
confirming the file path before saving
    ActiveWorkbook.SaveAs Filename:=newFilePath,
FileFormat:=fileFormat

    ' Notify the user that the workbook has been saved
successfully
    MsgBox "Workbook has been saved as " & newFilePath,
vbInformation, "Save As Completed"
    End Sub
```

➤ Key points:

- **New file path and name**: the `newFilePath` variable should be updated to reflect the desired location and name of the new workbook. Ensure the directory exists and you have write permissions.
- **File format**: the `fileFormat` variable specifies the format in which the workbook is to be saved. `xlOpenXMLWorkbook` corresponds to the `.xlsx` format. Adjust this based on your requirements. Refer to Excel VBA documentation for a full list of `XlFileFormat` constants.
- **SaveAs method**: the `ActiveWorkbook.SaveAs` method is used to save the workbook. This action saves all changes to the new file and the active workbook now points to the newly saved file.
- **Avoiding overwrites**: be cautious with the file path and name to avoid overwriting existing files unless intended.

This example provides a foundational approach to programmatically saving workbooks under new names and formats, enhancing automation capabilities in Excel projects.

Save file

Saving the current workbook in Excel using VBA is a straightforward task that can be accomplished using the `Save` method. This method saves the workbook with its current name and format. If the workbook is being saved for the first time, the `SaveAs` method should be used instead, which allows you to specify a file name and location.

Here's a simple example demonstrating how to save the current workbook:

➢ Example: Saving the current workbook

```
Sub SaveCurrentWorkbook()
    ' This subroutine demonstrates how to save the current
workbook using VBA.

    ' Check if the workbook has been saved previously
    If Not ThisWorkbook.Saved Then
        ' If the workbook hasn't been saved, use SaveAs
with a specified path and name
        ' Change "C:\Temp\MyWorkbook.xlsx" to your desired
path and file name
        ThisWorkbook.SaveAs "C:\Temp\MyWorkbook.xlsx"
    Else
        ' If the workbook has already been saved, just
save the changes
        ThisWorkbook.Save
    End If

    ' Notify the user that the workbook has been saved
    MsgBox "Workbook has been saved.", vbInformation,
"Saved Successfully"
End Sub
```

➢ Key points:

• **Checking if saved**: before saving, the code checks if the workbook has been saved previously using `ThisWorkbook.Saved`. This property returns `True` if no changes have been made to the workbook since the last save.

- **First save**: if the workbook hasn't been saved before (`ThisWorkbook.Saved` is `False`), it uses `SaveAs` to specify a new file path and name. You'll need to adjust the path `"C:\Temp\MyWorkbook.xlsx"` to your requirements.
- **Subsequent saves**: if the workbook has already been saved, it simply calls `ThisWorkbook.Save` to save the latest changes.
- **User notification**: a message box notifies the user after the workbook is saved, providing clear feedback that the operation has completed.

This example provides a basic yet effective method for saving changes to the current workbook in Excel via VBA, suitable for both newly created and previously saved workbooks.

Save workbook

Saving a workbook in Excel using VBA is a fundamental task that can be performed using either the `Save` method, to save changes to the current workbook, or the `SaveAs` method, to save the workbook with a new name or to a new location. Here's how you can use both methods effectively:

➢ Example 1: Saving the current workbook

```
Sub SaveActiveWorkbook()
    ' Check if the workbook has a filename (has been saved
before)
    If Len(ThisWorkbook.FullName) > 0 Then
        ' Save the workbook
        ThisWorkbook.Save
        MsgBox "Workbook saved.", vbInformation, "Success"
    Else
        MsgBox "Workbook has not been saved before. Please
save using Save As.", vbExclamation, "Save Required"
    End If
End Sub
```

➢ Example 2: Saving the workbook with a new name or to a new location

This example shows how to use the `SaveAs` method to save the active workbook to a specified path. This is particularly useful for creating backups or saving versions of a workbook under different names.

```
Sub SaveWorkbookAsNewFile()
```

```
      ' Define the full path and filename for the new
workbook
      Dim newFilePath As String
      newFilePath = "C:\Temp\MyNewWorkbook.xlsx" ' Adjust
this path as needed

      ' Save the workbook with the new name
      ThisWorkbook.SaveAs Filename:=newFilePath

      MsgBox "Workbook saved as " & newFilePath,
vbInformation, "Success"
      End Sub
```

➢ Key points:

- **Checking if saved**: in the first example, `ThisWorkbook.FullName` is used to check if the workbook has been saved before. An unsaved workbook doesn't have a full path and filename.
- `Save` **method**: saves changes to the workbook. If the workbook hasn't been saved before, it won't automatically prompt for a filename and location; you'll need to handle this scenario in your code.
- `SaveAs` **method**: allows you to save the workbook with a new name or to a new location. It's useful for creating backups, saving new versions, or initially saving unsaved workbooks.
- **Specifying path and filename**: when using `SaveAs`, you must specify the full path and filename for the new workbook. Adjust `newFilePath` to your desired location and filename.

These examples cover basic scenarios for saving workbooks in Excel using VBA, from simple saves to saving with new names or locations, enhancing automation capabilities within Excel projects.

Save XLSM file

Saving a workbook as an `.xlsm` (Excel Macro-Enabled Workbook) file in Excel using VBA is straightforward with the `SaveAs` method, which allows specifying the file format. The `.xlsm` format is essential when your workbook contains macros and you want to retain and enable these macros in the saved file.

➢ Example: Saving the active workbook as an XLSM file

```vba
Sub SaveWorkbookAsXLSM()
    ' Define the full path and filename where you want to
save the workbook
    ' Ensure the directory exists and adjust the path and
file name as needed
    Dim filePath As String
    filePath = "C:\Temp\MyWorkbook.xlsm"

    ' Save the active workbook as an XLSM file
    ' xlOpenXMLWorkbookMacroEnabled is the file format for
.xlsm files
    ActiveWorkbook.SaveAs Filename:=filePath,
FileFormat:=xlOpenXMLWorkbookMacroEnabled

    ' Notify the user that the workbook has been saved
    MsgBox "Workbook has been saved as " & filePath,
vbInformation, "Save As XLSM Completed"
End Sub
```

➢ Key points:

- **File path**: the `filePath` variable should be updated to reflect the desired save location and filename for your workbook. Ensure the path exists on your system.
- **FileFormat**   **parameter**:   the `FileFormat:=xlOpenXMLWorkbookMacroEnabled` argument in the `SaveAs` method specifies that the workbook should be saved as a macro-enabled workbook (`.xlsm`). This is crucial for preserving and enabling macros contained in the workbook.
- **User notification**: a message box confirms the successful saving of the workbook, providing immediate feedback about the operation's completion.

This example illustrates a fundamental approach to programmatically saving Excel workbooks as macro-enabled files, ensuring that any embedded VBA macros are retained and can be executed in the saved workbook.

Save XLSM file as XLSX

Saving a `.xlsm` (Excel Macro-Enabled Workbook) file as a `.xlsx` (Excel Workbook) using VBA involves using the `SaveAs` method with the `FileFormat` parameter set to `xlOpenXMLWorkbook`. This conversion is useful for distributing a non-macro version of your workbook or for environments where macros are not permitted.

➢ Example: Saving a XLSM file as XLSX

```
Sub SaveXLSMasXLSX()
    ' Define the full path and filename for the new XLSX
file
    ' Ensure the directory exists and adjust the path and
file name as needed
    Dim filePath As String
    filePath = "C:\Temp\MyWorkbook.xlsx"

    ' Save the active workbook as an XLSX file
    ' xlOpenXMLWorkbook is the file format for .xlsx
files, which do not enable macros
    ActiveWorkbook.SaveAs Filename:=filePath,
FileFormat:=xlOpenXMLWorkbook

    ' Notify the user that the workbook has been saved in
the new format
    MsgBox "Workbook has been saved as " & filePath,
vbInformation, "Save As XLSX Completed"
End Sub
```

➢ Key points:

- **File path adjustment**: change `filePath` to your desired save location and filename. The path must exist on your system.
- **FileFormat parameter**: by specifying `FileFormat:=xlOpenXMLWorkbook`, the `SaveAs` method saves the workbook in the `.xlsx` format. This format does not support macros, so any existing VBA code will not be saved or executable in the new file.

How to do this in VBA?? 202 ready-made macros: Streamline your tasks with proven expert solutions

- **User notification**: a message box confirms that the operation has completed successfully, providing clear feedback about the file conversion.

This code snippet demonstrates how to programmatically convert and save an Excel workbook from a macro-enabled format to a non-macro format, ensuring compatibility with environments where macros are restricted or unnecessary.

Save XLSX file

Saving an Excel workbook as an `.xlsx` file using VBA is done with the `SaveAs` method of the Workbook object. When saving a workbook in the `.xlsx` format, it's crucial to specify the `FileFormat` parameter to ensure that Excel saves the file in the correct format. The `.xlsx` format is the default for Excel 2007 and later versions and is used for workbooks that do not contain macros.

➢ Example: Saving the active workbook as an XLSX file

```
Sub SaveWorkbookAsXLSX()
    ' Define the full path and filename where you want to
save the workbook.
    ' Ensure the directory exists and adjust the path and
file name as needed.
    Dim filePath As String
    filePath = "C:\Temp\MyNewWorkbook.xlsx"

    ' Save the active workbook as an XLSX file.
    ' xlOpenXMLWorkbook is the file format for .xlsx files
(without macros).
    ActiveWorkbook.SaveAs Filename:=filePath,
FileFormat:=xlOpenXMLWorkbook

    ' Notify the user that the workbook has been saved.
    MsgBox "Workbook has been saved as " & filePath,
vbInformation, "Save As XLSX Completed"
End Sub
```

➢ Key points:

- **File path**: update the `filePath` variable to reflect the desired save location and file name for your workbook. Ensure the specified path exists on your system to prevent any errors during the save operation.

- **FileFormat parameter**: the `FileFormat:=xlOpenXMLWorkbook` argument specifies that the workbook should be saved in the `.xlsx` format, suitable for workbooks that do not include macros or Excel 4.0 macro sheets.
- **User notification**: a message box is displayed upon successful saving of the workbook, providing immediate feedback about the operation's completion.

This example illustrates the fundamental approach to programmatically saving Excel workbooks in the `.xlsx` format using VBA, facilitating automation and file management within Excel projects.

Select a cell

Selecting a cell in Excel using VBA is a basic operation that can be easily accomplished by specifying the cell's address and using the `Select` method. Here's a simple example that demonstrates how to select a specific cell within a worksheet.

➢ Example: Selecting a specific cell

```
Sub SelectSpecificCell()
    ' This subroutine demonstrates how to select a
specific cell in Excel using VBA.

    ' Specify the worksheet name where the cell is
located.
    ' Adjust "Sheet1" to the name of your target
worksheet.
    Dim ws As Worksheet
    Set ws = ThisWorkbook.Sheets("Sheet1")

    ' Activate the worksheet before selecting a cell.
    ws.Activate

    ' Select a specific cell. In this example, cell B2 is
selected.
    ' Adjust "B2" to the address of your target cell.
```

```
ws.Range("B2").Select

        ' Notify the user that the cell has been selected.
        MsgBox "Cell B2 has been selected.", vbInformation,
    "Cell Selected"
    End Sub
```

➢ Key points:

- **Worksheet reference**: the variable `ws` is set to reference the specific worksheet you're targeting. Make sure to adjust `"Sheet1"` to the actual name of your worksheet.
- **Activating the worksheet**: it's important to activate the worksheet (`ws.Activate`) before attempting to select a cell within it. This ensures that the correct worksheet is in focus.
- **Selecting the cell**: the `ws.Range("B2").Select` statement selects the specified cell. You can change `"B2"` to any cell address that you need to select.
- **User notification**: a message box confirms that the specified cell has been selected. This step is optional but useful for demonstration or debugging purposes.

This example provides a straightforward method for selecting a specific cell within an Excel worksheet using VBA, which is a fundamental operation for numerous automation and data manipulation tasks.

Select a sheet

Selecting a worksheet in Excel using VBA is a fundamental task that can be easily achieved with a simple command. This is particularly useful when you want to perform operations on a specific sheet within a workbook. Here's how to select a sheet by name:

➢ Example: Selecting a worksheet by name

```
Sub SelectWorksheetByName()
    ' This subroutine demonstrates how to select a
worksheet by its name using VBA.

    ' Specify the name of the worksheet you want to
select.
```

```
    ' Adjust "MySheetName" to the actual name of your
target worksheet.
    Dim sheetName As String
    sheetName = "MySheetName"

    ' Check if the worksheet exists before attempting to
select it.
    Dim ws As Worksheet
    On Error Resume Next ' Ignore errors temporarily.
    Set ws = ThisWorkbook.Sheets(sheetName)
    On Error GoTo 0 ' Revert to default error handling.

    ' If the worksheet exists, select it.
    If Not ws Is Nothing Then
        ws.Select
        MsgBox "Worksheet '" & sheetName & "' has been
selected.", vbInformation, "Sheet Selected"
    Else
        MsgBox "Worksheet '" & sheetName & "' does not
exist.", vbCritical, "Error"
    End If
End Sub
```

➤ Key points:

- **Worksheet name**: the `sheetName` variable holds the name of the worksheet you want to select. Make sure to replace `"MySheetName"` with the actual name of your worksheet.
- **Error handling**: the script uses basic error handling (`On Error Resume Next` and `On Error GoTo 0`) to gracefully handle cases where the specified worksheet does not exist. This prevents the macro from crashing and provides a user-friendly error message instead.
- **Selecting the worksheet**: the `ws.Select` statement is used to select the worksheet if it exists. This makes the specified worksheet the active sheet in the Excel interface.
- **User feedback**: the macro provides feedback to the user through message boxes, indicating whether the worksheet was successfully selected or if the specified worksheet does not exist.

How to do this in VBA?? 202 ready-made macros: Streamline your tasks with proven expert solutions

This example provides a clear method for selecting a specific worksheet within an Excel workbook using VBA, enhancing navigation and data manipulation capabilities within your macros and applications.

Sendkeys VBA

Using `SendKeys` in VBA allows you to send keystrokes to the active application. This can be useful for automating interactions with software interfaces that do not provide direct methods for control via VBA. However, caution is advised when using `SendKeys` because it sends keystrokes to whichever application is active, which may not always be the one you intend. Here's an example that demonstrates how to use `SendKeys` to interact with Notepad, a simple text editor available in Windows.

➢ Example: Opening Notepad and using `SendKeys`

```
Sub UseSendKeysWithNotepad()
    ' This subroutine demonstrates how to open Notepad and
    use SendKeys to write text.

    ' Start Notepad
    Shell "notepad.exe", vbNormalFocus
    Application.Wait Now + TimeValue("00:00:02") ' Wait 2
    seconds for Notepad to open

    ' Write text in Notepad
    SendKeys "Hello, this is text written by VBA using
    SendKeys.", True
    Application.Wait Now + TimeValue("00:00:01") ' Wait 1
    second

    ' Optionally, you can simulate pressing Enter
    SendKeys "{ENTER}", True
    Application.Wait Now + TimeValue("00:00:01") ' Wait 1
    second

    ' Continue writing text
    SendKeys "This is the second line.", True
End Sub
```

How to do this in VBA?? 202 ready-made macros: Streamline your tasks with proven expert solutions

➤ Key points:

- **Opening an application**: the `Shell` function is used to open Notepad (`"notepad.exe"`). The `vbNormalFocus` argument ensures that Notepad opens and is ready to receive input.
- **Waiting**: `Application.Wait` is used to pause the execution of the VBA script for a few seconds, ensuring that Notepad has time to open and become the active window before sending keystrokes.
- **Sending keystrokes**: `SendKeys` is used to simulate typing text into Notepad. Each call to `SendKeys` includes the text to be typed and a `True` parameter to wait for the keystrokes to be processed before continuing.
- **Simulating special keys**: special keys (like Enter) are represented in `SendKeys` by enclosing the key code in braces (`{}`). For example, `{ENTER}` simulates pressing the Enter key.

➤Caution:

- **Active window dependency**: `SendKeys` sends keystrokes to the active window. If the user changes focus to another window while the code is running, `SendKeys` will send keystrokes to that window instead.
- **Security and stability**: `SendKeys` can lead to unpredictable results and should be used with caution, especially in environments where stability is crucial.

This example demonstrates a basic use of `SendKeys` in VBA to automate simple tasks in other applications, such as typing text in Notepad.

Set a cell value

Setting the value of a cell in Excel using VBA is one of the most fundamental operations. You can specify a cell by its address and assign a value to it. Here's a straightforward example that demonstrates how to set the value of a specific cell in a worksheet.

➤Example: Setting the value of a cell

```
Sub SetCellValue()
    ' This subroutine demonstrates how to set the value of
a specific cell in Excel using VBA.
```

```
        ' Specify the worksheet name where the cell is
    located.
        ' Adjust "Sheet1" to the name of your target
    worksheet.
        Dim ws As Worksheet
        Set ws = ThisWorkbook.Sheets("Sheet1")

        ' Set the value of cell A1 to "Hello, World!"
        ws.Range("A1").Value = "Hello, World!"

        ' Another way to reference a cell directly
        ws.Cells(1, 1).Value = "Hello, World!"

        ' Notify the user that the cell value has been set.
        MsgBox "The value of cell A1 has been set to 'Hello,
    World!'", vbInformation, "Cell Value Set"
        End Sub
```

➢ Key points:

- **Worksheet reference**: the `ws` variable is set to reference the specific worksheet by its name. Ensure `"Sheet1"` matches the name of your worksheet.
- **Setting the cell value**: the `Value` property of the `Range` object is used to set the value of cell A1. The `Range("A1").Value` method is straightforward for referencing cells by their Excel address. Alternatively, `Cells(1, 1).Value` references the cell at the first row and first column, which is another way to access cell A1.
- **User feedback**: a message box confirms that the operation is complete, providing immediate feedback to the user.

This example illustrates a basic yet essential technique for manipulating cell values in Excel through VBA, suitable for a wide range of data processing and automation tasks.

Set a range

Setting a range in Excel VBA involves specifying a group of cells that you want to work with. You can define a range using the `Range` object, and then perform various operations on it, such as setting values, formatting cells, or applying formulas. Here's a simple example that demonstrates how to define a range and set the same value for all cells within that range.

➤ Example: Setting values in a specified range

```vba
Sub SetRangeValue()
    ' This subroutine demonstrates how to define a range
    and set values for all cells within that range in Excel
    using VBA.

    ' Specify the worksheet name where the range is
    located.
    ' Adjust "Sheet1" to the name of your target
    worksheet.
    Dim ws As Worksheet
    Set ws = ThisWorkbook.Sheets("Sheet1")

    ' Define the range you want to work with.
    ' In this example, we'll work with cells from A1 to
    C3.
    Dim targetRange As Range
    Set targetRange = ws.Range("A1:C3")

    ' Alternatively, you can use the Cells property to
    define the range.
    ' Set targetRange = ws.Range(ws.Cells(1, 1),
    ws.Cells(3, 3))

    ' Set the same value for all cells in the defined
    range.
    targetRange.Value = "Hello, World!"

    ' Notify the user that the operation has been
    completed.
    MsgBox "The range A1:C3 has been set to 'Hello,
    World!'", vbInformation, "Range Set"
End Sub
```

How to do this in VBA?? 202 ready-made macros: Streamline your tasks with proven expert solutions

➢ Key points:

- **Worksheet reference**: the variable `ws` is set to reference the specific worksheet by its name. Ensure that `"Sheet1"` is adjusted to match the name of your worksheet.
- **Defining the range**: the `Range` object is used to define the target range, `targetRange`, by specifying the start and end cells as a string (`"A1:C3"`). This can be adjusted to any range you need to work with.
- **Setting the range value**: the `Value` property of the `targetRange` object is used to set the value for all cells within the range to "Hello, World!".
- **Alternative range definition**: the commented-out line shows an alternative way to define the range using the `Cells` property, which is useful when you need to define ranges dynamically.

This example illustrates a fundamental method for defining and manipulating ranges in Excel via VBA, enabling efficient data manipulation and automation within your Excel workbooks.

Set row height in Excel VBA

Adjusting the row height in Excel using VBA is a straightforward task that can significantly improve the readability and presentation of your spreadsheets. Here's an example demonstrating how to set the height of a specific row in a worksheet.

➢ Example: Setting the height of a specific row

```
Sub SetRowHeight()
    ' This subroutine demonstrates how to set the height
of a specific row in Excel using VBA.

    ' Specify the worksheet you're working with.
    ' Adjust "Sheet1" to the name of your target
worksheet.
    Dim ws As Worksheet
    Set ws = ThisWorkbook.Sheets("Sheet1")

    ' Specify the row number you want to adjust.
    ' In this example, we're adjusting row 5.
    Dim targetRow As Long
```

```
targetRow = 5


' Specify the new height you want for the row.
' In this example, we're setting the row height to 25
points.
Dim newRowHeight As Double
newRowHeight = 25


' Set the height of the specified row.
ws.Rows(targetRow).RowHeight = newRowHeight


' Notify the user that the row height has been
adjusted.
MsgBox "The height of row " & targetRow & " has been
set to " & newRowHeight & " points.", vbInformation, "Row
Height Set"
End Sub
```

➤ Key points:

- **Worksheet reference**: the `ws` variable is used to reference the specific worksheet by its name. Make sure `"Sheet1"` matches the actual name of your worksheet.
- **Target row**: the `targetRow` variable specifies the row number whose height you want to adjust. This can be modified to target any row in the worksheet.
- **New row height**: the `newRowHeight` variable holds the new height (in points) that you want to set for the row. Adjust this value according to your needs.
- **Setting the row height**: the `RowHeight` property of the `Rows` object is used to set the height of the specified row to the new value.
- **User feedback**: a message box confirms the successful adjustment of the row height, providing immediate feedback about the operation's completion.

This example illustrates a basic method for setting the height of a specific row in an Excel worksheet using VBA, which can be easily adapted to adjust multiple rows or incorporate into larger data formatting routines.

Sgn

The `Sgn` function in VBA (Visual Basic for Applications) is used to determine the sign of a number. It returns -1 if the number is negative, 0 if the number is zero, and 1 if the number is positive. This function can be quite useful in financial calculations, data analysis, and scenarios where the sign of a value influences decision-making or further calculations.

Here's a simple example demonstrating how to use the `Sgn` function with different types of numerical inputs:

➢ Example: Using the Sgn function

```
Sub UseSgnFunction()
    ' This subroutine demonstrates the use of the Sgn
function in VBA.

    Dim testValue1 As Double
    Dim testValue2 As Double
    Dim testValue3 As Double

    testValue1 = -123.45 ' Negative value
    testValue2 = 0        ' Zero
    testValue3 = 678.9    ' Positive value

    ' Determine the sign of each test value
    Dim result1 As Integer
    Dim result2 As Integer
    Dim result3 As Integer

    result1 = Sgn(testValue1) ' Expected to return -1
    result2 = Sgn(testValue2) ' Expected to return 0
    result3 = Sgn(testValue3) ' Expected to return 1

    ' Display the results
    MsgBox "Sign of " & testValue1 & ": " & result1 &
vbCrLf & _
```

How to do this in VBA?? 202 ready-made macros: Streamline your tasks with proven expert solutions

```
                "Sign of " & testValue2 & ": " & result2 &
        vbCrLf & _
                "Sign of " & testValue3 & ": " & result3,
        vbInformation, "Sgn Function Results"
        End Sub
```

➢ Key points:

- **Test values**: the subroutine initializes three variables (`testValue1`, `testValue2`, and `testValue3`) with a negative number, zero, and a positive number, respectively.
- **Using Sgn**: the `Sgn` function is called with each test value as an argument to determine its sign.
- **Results**: the sign of each number is stored in corresponding result variables (`result1`, `result2`, and `result3`) and then displayed in a message box to the user.

This example illustrates the basic usage of the `Sgn` function in VBA, showcasing how to determine the sign of various numbers, a technique applicable in numerous programming scenarios.

Split a string

Splitting a string into an array based on a delimiter is a common task in Excel VBA, enabling the processing of each substring individually. The `Split` function in VBA makes this task straightforward. It takes a string and a delimiter as inputs and returns an array containing the substrings.

➢ Example: Splitting a string into substrings

```
        Sub SplitStringExample()
            ' This subroutine demonstrates how to split a string
        into substrings based on a delimiter in VBA.

            ' The original string to be split
            Dim originalString As String
            originalString = "apple,banana,cherry,grape"

            ' The delimiter used to split the string
            Dim delimiter As String
            delimiter = ","
```

How to do this in VBA?? 202 ready-made macros: Streamline your tasks with proven expert solutions

```
' Split the string into an array of substrings
Dim substrings() As String
substrings = Split(originalString, delimiter)


' Display each substring in the Immediate Window (Ctrl
+ G to view)
Dim i As Integer
For i = LBound(substrings) To UBound(substrings)
    Debug.Print substrings(i)
Next i
End Sub
```

➢ Key points:

- **Original string**: `originalString` contains the string to be split. In this example, it's a comma-separated list of fruits.
- **Delimiter**: the `delimiter` variable specifies the character used to split the string. Here, a comma (`,`) is used.
- **Split function**: the `Split` function divides `originalString` into an array (`substrings`) using `delimiter` as the separator.
- **Displaying substrings**: a `For` loop iterates over the resulting array, and `Debug.Print` outputs each substring to the Immediate Window.

This example illustrates a basic approach to splitting strings in VBA, allowing for efficient string manipulation and data processing within Excel macros.

Text to columns

Converting text to columns in Excel using VBA involves splitting the contents of a cell across multiple columns based on a specified delimiter. This can be achieved programmatically using the `TextToColumns` method of a `Range` object. This example demonstrates how to split data in a specific column into multiple columns using a comma `,` as the delimiter, similar to the "Text to Columns" feature available in the Excel UI.

➢ Example: Splitting text into columns using VBA

```
Sub ConvertTextToColumns()
    ' This subroutine demonstrates how to convert text in
a single column to multiple columns using a specified
delimiter in Excel VBA.
```

```
' Specify the worksheet and the range that contains
the text to be split.
' Adjust "Sheet1" to the name of your target
worksheet.
Dim ws As Worksheet
Set ws = ThisWorkbook.Sheets("Sheet1")


' Define the range that contains the text. In this
example, we use column A.
' Adjust the range as necessary. Here, "A1:A10"
assumes that your text is in the first 10 rows of column
A.
Dim targetRange As Range
Set targetRange = ws.Range("A1:A10")


' Convert text to columns using the specified
delimiter.
' This example uses a comma (",") as the delimiter.
targetRange.TextToColumns Destination:=ws.Range("A1"),
DataType:=xlDelimited, _


TextQualifier:=xlDoubleQuote, ConsecutiveDelimiter:=False,
_

                              Tab:=False,
Semicolon:=False, Comma:=True, Space:=False, Other:=False


' Notify the user that the operation has been
completed.
MsgBox "Text has been successfully split into
columns.", vbInformation, "Operation Completed"
End Sub
```

➢ Key points:

- **Worksheet and range**: the macro begins by setting a reference to the target worksheet (`ws`) and defining the range that contains the text to be split (`targetRange`). Ensure these references match your actual data.

- **TextToColumns method**: this method is applied to `targetRange`, specifying various parameters to control the text splitting behavior:
- `Destination` specifies where the resulting columns start. In this example, they start in the same location as the original data (`A1`).
- `DataType:=xlDelimited` indicates that the text is split based on delimiters.
- `Comma:=True` sets the comma as the delimiter. Adjust the delimiter settings (`Tab`, `Semicolon`, `Comma`, `Space`, `Other`) based on your data.
- **User feedback**: a message box informs the user once the operation is complete, providing clear feedback about the success of the text splitting process.

This example demonstrates a practical use of the `TextToColumns` method in Excel VBA to automate the process of splitting text across multiple columns based on a specified delimiter, enhancing data organization and preparation tasks.

TEXTJOIN

The `TEXTJOIN` function in Excel combines text from multiple ranges or strings, with each value separated by a specified delimiter. While `TEXTJOIN` is an Excel worksheet function and not directly available as a VBA function, you can achieve similar functionality in VBA by creating a custom function that mimics `TEXTJOIN`.

➢ Custom VBA function to mimic TEXTJOIN

Below is an example of how you can create a custom VBA function to join text from an array of strings, using a specified delimiter:

```
Function VbaTextJoin(delimiter As String, ignoreEmpty As
Boolean, ParamArray textValues() As Variant) As String
    ' This function mimics the Excel TEXTJOIN function in
VBA.
    ' It joins text items from a list or array, separated
by a specified delimiter.

    Dim result As String
    Dim i As Long
    Dim currentElement As Variant
```

```vba
    ' Loop through each item in the textValues array
    For i = LBound(textValues) To UBound(textValues)
        currentElement = textValues(i)

        ' Check if ignoring empty strings
        If ignoreEmpty And currentElement = "" Then
            ' Skip this iteration
        Else
            ' Add the current element to the result
string, preceded by the delimiter if it's not the first
item
            If result <> "" Then
                result = result & delimiter &
currentElement
            Else
                result = currentElement
            End If
        End If
    Next i


    ' Return the combined text
    VbaTextJoin = result
End Function
```

➤ Using the custom VbaTextJoin function

You can use this custom function similarly to how you might use `TEXTJOIN` in an Excel worksheet. Here's an example subroutine that demonstrates its usage:

```vba
Sub DemoVbaTextJoin()
    ' This subroutine demonstrates the use of the custom
VbaTextJoin function.

    Dim joinedText As String
    ' Example usage of VbaTextJoin: combining text with a
comma delimiter, ignoring empty strings.
    joinedText = VbaTextJoin(",", True, "Apple", "Banana",
"", "Cherry")
```

```
     ' Print the result to the Immediate Window (Ctrl + G
in VBA editor to view)
     Debug.Print joinedText ' Output: "Apple,Banana,Cherry"
 End Sub
```

➢ Key points:

- **Custom function**: `VbaTextJoin` mimics the `TEXTJOIN` function's behavior in Excel, allowing for flexibility in joining text with VBA.
- **Parameters**: the `delimiter` specifies the string to separate each item, `ignoreEmpty` determines whether to ignore empty strings in the list, and `textValues` is an array of the strings to join.
- **Usage**: you can call `VbaTextJoin` from any VBA subroutine or function, making it a versatile tool for text manipulation in your macros.

This example demonstrates how to extend VBA's capabilities with custom functions, providing additional text processing functionalities similar to Excel's built-in functions.

Throw error

In VBA, you can programmatically throw an error using the `Err.Raise` method. This can be useful for handling error conditions explicitly in your code, especially when writing custom functions or procedures that need to signal an error condition to the calling code.

➢ Example: Throwing a custom error

```
Sub ThrowCustomError()
     ' This subroutine demonstrates how to throw a custom
error in VBA using Err.Raise.

     ' Variable for condition check (for demonstration
purposes, this could be any condition)
     Dim conditionMet As Boolean
     conditionMet = False ' Assume condition is not met;
change as needed

     ' Check the condition
     If Not conditionMet Then
```

273

How to do this in VBA?? 202 ready-made macros: Streamline your tasks with proven expert solutions

```
        ' If the condition is not met, throw a custom
error
        Err.Raise Number:=vbObjectError + 513, _
                Source:="ThrowCustomError", _
                Description:="Custom condition was not
met."
    End If
End Sub
```

➢ Key points:

- **Err.Raise method**: this method is used to generate a runtime error. It allows you to specify the error number, source, and description.
- **Number**: the error number. It's a good practice to use `vbObjectError +` a custom number to avoid conflicts with standard VBA error numbers. In this example, `vbObjectError + 513` is used.
- **Source**: the name of the procedure or function where the error occurred. This helps identify where the error was thrown from.
- **Description**: a text description of the error. This should provide enough detail to understand the nature of the error and ideally how to address it.

➢ Handling thrown errors

To handle errors thrown by `Err.Raise` or other error-generating code, use the `On Error` statement to direct VBA to an error handling routine:

```
Sub DemoErrorHandling()
    On Error GoTo ErrorHandler

    ' Call the subroutine that might throw an error
    ThrowCustomError

    ' Normal execution continues here if no error is
thrown
    MsgBox "No error occurred.", vbInformation

    Exit Sub

ErrorHandler:
    ' Error handling code
```

```
        MsgBox "An error occurred: " & Err.Description,
    vbCritical, "Error"
        Resume Next
    End Sub
```

In this structured error handling example, any errors within `DemoErrorHandling` (including those thrown by `ThrowCustomError`) are caught by the `ErrorHandler`, allowing the program to respond gracefully rather than crashing.

This approach to throwing and handling errors in VBA enables robust error management in your applications, facilitating debugging and ensuring a better user experience by dealing with errors more predictably.

Transpose an array

Transposing an array in VBA involves swapping the rows and columns of the array. This is particularly useful when you need to rearrange data within your code for further processing or output. Below is an example that demonstrates how to transpose a 2-dimensional array manually, as VBA doesn't provide a built-in method for transposing arrays that are not Range objects.

➢ Example: Transposing a 2-dimensional array

```
    Function TransposeArray(inputArray As Variant) As Variant
        ' This function transposes a 2-dimensional array (swap
    rows and columns)

        Dim rows As Long
        Dim cols As Long
        Dim i As Long
        Dim j As Long

        ' Determine the dimensions of the inputArray
        rows = UBound(inputArray, 1) - LBound(inputArray, 1) +
    1
        cols = UBound(inputArray, 2) - LBound(inputArray, 2) +
    1

        ' Initialize the output array with transposed
    dimensions
```

```vba
        Dim outputArray() As Variant
        ReDim outputArray(LBound(inputArray, 2) To
UBound(inputArray, 2), _
                            LBound(inputArray, 1) To
UBound(inputArray, 1))

        ' Populate the output array with transposed values
        For i = LBound(inputArray, 1) To UBound(inputArray, 1)
            For j = LBound(inputArray, 2) To
UBound(inputArray, 2)
                outputArray(j, i) = inputArray(i, j)
            Next j
        Next i

        ' Return the transposed array
        TransposeArray = outputArray
End Function

Sub DemoTransposeArray()
    ' Demo subroutine to show how to use the
TransposeArray function

    ' Original 2-dimensional array
    Dim originalArray(1 To 2, 1 To 3) As Variant
    originalArray(1, 1) = "A1"
    originalArray(1, 2) = "B1"
    originalArray(1, 3) = "C1"
    originalArray(2, 1) = "A2"
    originalArray(2, 2) = "B2"
    originalArray(2, 3) = "C2"

    ' Transpose the original array
    Dim transposedArray As Variant
    transposedArray = TransposeArray(originalArray)
```

How to do this in VBA?? 202 ready-made macros: Streamline your tasks with proven expert solutions

```vba
      ' Output the transposed array to the Immediate Window
(Ctrl+G to view)
      Dim i As Long, j As Long
      For i = LBound(transposedArray, 1) To
UBound(transposedArray, 1)
          For j = LBound(transposedArray, 2) To
UBound(transposedArray, 2)
              Debug.Print transposedArray(i, j)
          Next j
          Debug.Print "------" ' Separator for readability
      Next i
  End Sub
```

➤ Key points:

- **Function `TransposeArray`**: takes a 2-dimensional array as input and returns a new array with the dimensions swapped.
- **Determining dimensions**: calculates the number of rows and columns in the input array to correctly size the output array.
- **Swapping values**: iterates through the input array, assigning values to the output array with swapped indices.
- **Demo subroutine `DemoTransposeArray`**: demonstrates how to transpose a simple 2-dimensional array and prints the result to the Immediate Window.

This example provides a generic way to transpose any 2-dimensional array in VBA, enhancing the flexibility of your data manipulation tasks.

Trim Excel

Trimming text in Excel using VBA involves removing all leading and trailing spaces from text in a cell or range of cells. While Excel has a `TRIM` function that can be used directly on the worksheet, you might need to perform trimming programmatically within a VBA subroutine to preprocess or clean data. Below is an example showing how to trim text in a specific range of cells using VBA.

➤ Example: Trimming text in a range of cells

```vba
      Sub TrimTextInRange()
```

```vba
' This subroutine demonstrates how to trim leading and
trailing spaces from text in a range of cells in Excel
using VBA.

' Specify the worksheet and range you want to work
with.
' Adjust "Sheet1" and the range as necessary for your
workbook.
Dim ws As Worksheet
Set ws = ThisWorkbook.Sheets("Sheet1")

Dim targetRange As Range
Set targetRange = ws.Range("A1:A10") ' Assuming you
want to trim text in cells A1 through A10

Dim cell As Range

' Loop through each cell in the specified range
For Each cell In targetRange
    ' Trim the text in the cell and update the cell's
value
    cell.Value = Trim(cell.Value)
Next cell

' Notify the user that the text has been trimmed
MsgBox "Text in the specified range has been trimmed
of leading and trailing spaces.", vbInformation, "Trim
Completed"
End Sub
```

➤ Key points:

- **Worksheet and range specification**: the `ws` variable is set to reference the specific worksheet, and `targetRange` is set to the range of cells where text needs to be trimmed. You should adjust these to match your specific needs.
- **Looping through cells**: the subroutine loops through each cell in the specified range using a `For Each` loop.

278

How to do this in VBA?? 202 ready-made macros: Streamline your tasks with proven expert solutions

- **Trimming text**: for each cell, the `Trim` function is used to remove leading and trailing spaces from the cell's value.
- **Updating cell values**: the trimmed text is immediately put back into the cell, effectively updating the spreadsheet with the cleaned text.

This example offers a practical approach to programmatically trimming text in Excel using VBA, enhancing data cleanliness and consistency across your worksheets.

Trim string

Trimming a string in VBA involves removing all leading and trailing spaces from the string. The `Trim` function in VBA is straightforward and easy to use for this purpose. Here's a simple example demonstrating how to trim a string:

➢ Example: Trimming a string in VBA

```
Sub TrimStringExample()
    ' This subroutine demonstrates how to trim leading and
trailing spaces from a string in VBA.


    ' Original string with leading and trailing spaces
    Dim originalString As String
    originalString = "   Hello, World!   "

    ' Use the Trim function to remove spaces
    Dim trimmedString As String
    trimmedString = Trim(originalString)

    ' Display the original and trimmed strings
    MsgBox "Original string: '" & originalString & "'" &
vbCrLf & _
        "Trimmed string: '" & trimmedString & "'",
vbInformation, "Trim Example"
    End Sub
```

➢ Key points:

- **Original string**: `originalString` contains the text to be trimmed, including leading and trailing spaces.

- **Trimming**: the `Trim` function is applied to `originalString` to produce `trimmedString`, which has no leading or trailing spaces.
- **Result display**: a message box shows both the original and trimmed strings for comparison.

This example illustrates the basic use of the `Trim` function in VBA to clean up strings by removing unnecessary spaces, which is a common task in data processing and manipulation scripts.

Try-catch

VBA does not have a `try-catch` block like other programming languages such as C# or Java. Instead, VBA uses an error handling mechanism with `On Error GoTo` statements to handle errors. You can use this to mimic a `try-catch` behavior. Here's how you can structure error handling in VBA to achieve similar functionality:

➢ Example: Mimicking Try-catch in VBA

```
Sub TryCatchExample()
    ' Mimic a try-catch block using VBA's error handling

    On Error GoTo Catch ' If an error occurs, jump to the
Catch label

    ' Try Block
    ' Your code here. For demonstration, we'll
deliberately divide by zero
    Dim result As Double
    result = 1 / 0
    MsgBox "Operation Successful: " & result,
vbInformation, "Success"

    GoTo Finally ' If no error occurs, jump to the Finally
block

Catch:
    ' Catch Block
    ' Handle the error
```

How to do this in VBA?? 202 ready-made macros: Streamline your tasks with proven expert solutions

```
        MsgBox "An error occurred: " & Err.Description,
    vbCritical, "Error"


    Finally:
        ' Finally Block (optional)
        ' Code here will run whether an error occurred or not
        MsgBox "Finally block reached.", vbInformation,
    "Finally"


    End Sub
```

➢ Key components:

- **On Error GoTo Catch**: this tells VBA to jump to the `Catch` label if an error occurs.
- **Try block**: place the code you want to "try" above the `GoTo Finally` statement. If an error occurs in this block, execution will jump to the `Catch` block.
- **Catch block**: this is labeled as `Catch` in the code. It's where you handle errors. `Err.Description` gives a description of the error.
- **Finally block**: although not a direct feature in VBA, you can simulate a `finally` block using a label (here labeled as `Finally`). This section runs regardless of whether an error occurred, making it useful for cleanup tasks. The `GoTo Finally` statement is used to ensure this block runs even when there's no error.

This setup mimics traditional `try-catch-finally` behavior found in other programming languages, providing a structured way to handle errors in VBA.

Turn off screen updating

Turning off screen updating in Excel VBA is useful for optimizing performance, especially when your macro performs numerous operations that change the appearance of the worksheet. Disabling screen updating prevents Excel from visually updating the worksheet until your macro finishes executing, which can significantly speed up the macro's execution time. Here's how you can turn off screen updating:

➢ Example: Turning off screen updating in VBA

```
    Sub OptimizePerformance()
```

How to do this in VBA?? 202 ready-made macros: Streamline your tasks with proven expert solutions

```
        ' This subroutine demonstrates how to turn off screen
updating to optimize the performance of Excel VBA code.

        ' Turn off screen updating
        Application.ScreenUpdating = False

        ' Place your code here
        ' For demonstration purposes, we'll perform a simple
operation that would normally cause the screen to update
        Dim ws As Worksheet
        For Each ws In ThisWorkbook.Worksheets
            ws.Cells(1, 1).Value = "Test"
        Next ws

        ' It's crucial to turn screen updating back on once
your operations are complete
        Application.ScreenUpdating = True

        MsgBox "Operations completed. Screen updating has been
turned back on.", vbInformation, "Screen Updating"
        End Sub
```

➢ Key points:

- **Disabling screen updating**: `Application.ScreenUpdating = False` disables the screen from updating while the macro runs.
- **Your code**: the section commented as "Place your code here" is where you would insert the operations your macro needs to perform.
- **Re-enabling screen updating**: it's crucial to set `Application.ScreenUpdating = True` after your operations are complete to turn screen updating back on. Failing to re-enable screen updating can leave Excel in a state where it doesn't visually update until you manually perform an action that forces a refresh (like switching tabs or minimizing and maximizing the Excel window).

Disabling screen updating is a common practice for improving the performance of Excel VBA macros that perform extensive manipulations on workbook data or structure.

Underline

Applying underline formatting to cells in Excel via VBA is a straightforward process. You can use the `**Font.Underline**` property of a range to set the underline style. Below is an example demonstrating how to apply a single underline to a specific range of cells.

➢ Example: Underlining text in a range of cells

```
Sub ApplyUnderline()
    ' This subroutine demonstrates how to apply underline
formatting to text in a range of cells in Excel using VBA.

    ' Specify the worksheet you're working with.
    ' Adjust "Sheet1" to the name of your target
worksheet.
    Dim ws As Worksheet
    Set ws = ThisWorkbook.Sheets("Sheet1")

    ' Define the range you want to format.
    ' In this example, we'll underline text in cells A1
through A10.
    Dim targetRange As Range
    Set targetRange = ws.Range("A1:A10")

    ' Apply a single underline to the text in the
specified range.
    targetRange.Font.Underline = xlUnderlineStyleSingle

    ' Notify the user that the operation has been
completed.
    MsgBox "Text in the specified range has been
underlined.", vbInformation, "Underline Applied"
End Sub
```
➢ Key points:

- **Worksheet reference**: the `ws` variable is set to reference the specific worksheet by its name. Ensure `"Sheet1"` matches the name of your worksheet.
- **Target range**: the `targetRange` variable specifies the cells to be formatted. You can adjust `"A1:A10"` to any range that fits your needs.
- **Underline property**: the `Font.Underline` property is used to apply the underline. In the example, `xlUnderlineStyleSingle` applies a single underline, which is the most common type. Other options include `xlUnderlineStyleDouble`, `xlUnderlineStyleSingleAccounting`, and `xlUnderlineStyleDoubleAccounting`, among others.
- **User feedback**: a message box confirms the successful application of the underline formatting.

This code provides a simple way to underline text in Excel using VBA, enhancing the visual presentation of your worksheets programmatically.

Unfilter

Removing or clearing filters from a worksheet in Excel using VBA is a common task when automating data processing. If your worksheet has filters applied, you might want to clear these filters as part of your macro's operations. Here's how you can do it:

➢ Example: Clearing all filters from a worksheet

```
Sub ClearAllFilters()
    ' This subroutine demonstrates how to remove all
filters from a worksheet in Excel using VBA.


    ' Specify the worksheet you want to unfilter.
    ' Adjust "Sheet1" to the name of your target
worksheet.
    Dim ws As Worksheet
    Set ws = ThisWorkbook.Sheets("Sheet1")


    ' Check if the worksheet has any filters applied.
    If ws.AutoFilterMode Then
        ' If filters are applied, turn off the AutoFilter
mode to remove them.
```

How to do this in VBA?? 202 ready-made macros: Streamline your tasks with proven expert solutions

```
        ws.AutoFilterMode = False
    End If


    ' Notify the user that all filters have been cleared.
    MsgBox "All filters have been cleared from '" &
ws.Name & "'.", vbInformation, "Filters Cleared"
    End Sub
```

➢ Key points:

- **Worksheet reference**: the `ws` variable holds a reference to the worksheet you're working with. Make sure to adjust `"Sheet1"` to the name of the actual worksheet you intend to clear filters from.
- **Checking filters**: the `If ws.AutoFilterMode Then` condition checks if any filters are currently applied to the worksheet.
- **Removing filters**: setting `ws.AutoFilterMode` to `False` removes all filters from the worksheet.
- **User notification**: a message box confirms that all filters have been cleared, providing clear feedback to the user.

This simple VBA subroutine provides an effective way to clear filters from a specific worksheet, ensuring your data processing or analysis can proceed without the constraints of previously applied filters.

Unhide sheet

Unhiding a sheet in Excel using VBA is a straightforward task. You can programmatically unhide any hidden worksheet within your workbook. Below is an example demonstrating how to unhide a specific worksheet by name.

➢ Example: Unhiding a worksheet

```
    Sub UnhideSheet()
        ' This subroutine demonstrates how to unhide a
    worksheet in Excel using VBA.


        ' Specify the name of the worksheet you want to
    unhide.
        ' Adjust "MyHiddenSheet" to the actual name of your
    worksheet.
        Dim sheetName As String
```

```
        sheetName = "MyHiddenSheet"


        ' Check if the worksheet exists and is hidden before
trying to unhide it.
        Dim ws As Worksheet
        On Error Resume Next ' Ignore errors if the worksheet
name doesn't exist
        Set ws = ThisWorkbook.Sheets(sheetName)
        On Error GoTo 0 ' Turn back on normal error handling


        If Not ws Is Nothing Then
            ' Check if the sheet is hidden and unhide it
            If ws.Visible = xlSheetHidden Then
                ws.Visible = xlSheetVisible
                MsgBox "'" & sheetName & "' has been
unhidden.", vbInformation, "Sheet Unhidden"
            Else
                MsgBox "'" & sheetName & "' is already
visible.", vbInformation, "Sheet Visible"
            End If
        Else
            MsgBox "Sheet '" & sheetName & "' does not exist
in this workbook.", vbCritical, "Sheet Not Found"
        End If
    End Sub
```

➢ Key points:

- **Worksheet name**: change `"MyHiddenSheet"` to the name of the worksheet you want to unhide.
- **Error handling**: `On Error Resume Next` is used to avoid errors if the specified sheet name doesn't exist. Error handling is reset afterward with `On Error GoTo 0`.
- **Check if sheet exists**: the subroutine checks if `ws` is `Nothing` to confirm that the worksheet exists.
- **Check visibility and unhide**: the sheet's `Visible` property is checked to determine if it's hidden (`xlSheetHidden`). If so, the property is set to `xlSheetVisible` to unhide the sheet.

- **User feedback**: message boxes inform the user about the action taken or if any issues were encountered, such as the sheet not being found or already being visible.

This example provides a practical way to unhide worksheets within your Excel workbooks using VBA, enhancing workbook navigation and data accessibility programmatically.

Unmerge cells

Unmerging cells in Excel using VBA involves selecting a range of merged cells and then applying the `UnMerge` method. This can be useful for reverting previously merged cells to their original, individual state for further data manipulation or formatting. Here's a straightforward example demonstrating how to unmerge a specific range of cells that are merged.

➢ Example: Unmerging merged cells

```vba
Sub UnmergeCells()
    ' This subroutine demonstrates how to unmerge
previously merged cells in Excel using VBA.

    ' Specify the worksheet you're working with.
    ' Adjust "Sheet1" to the name of your target
worksheet.
    Dim ws As Worksheet
    Set ws = ThisWorkbook.Sheets("Sheet1")

    ' Define the range you want to unmerge.
    ' In this example, we'll assume cells A1:C3 are
merged. Adjust the range as necessary.
    Dim targetRange As Range
    Set targetRange = ws.Range("A1:C3")

    ' Unmerge the cells
    targetRange.UnMerge

    ' Notify the user that the cells have been unmerged.
```

```
        MsgBox "The specified cells have been unmerged.",
    vbInformation, "Cells Unmerged"
    End Sub
```

➢ Key points:

- **Worksheet reference**: the `ws` variable is used to reference the specific worksheet. Make sure `"Sheet1"` matches the actual name of your worksheet.
- **Target range**: the `targetRange` variable specifies the cells to be unmerged. You need to adjust `"A1:C3"` to the actual range of merged cells in your worksheet.
- **Unmerge method**: the `UnMerge` method is called on the `targetRange` object to unmerge the cells.
- **User notification**: a message box confirms the successful unmerging of the cells, providing clear feedback to the user.

This code offers a simple method for unmerging cells in Excel using VBA, enabling you to programmatically revert cell merging and prepare the worksheet for further data entry or modifications.

Unprotect Excel sheet

Unprotecting an Excel sheet using VBA is straightforward but requires that you know the password if the sheet is protected with one. Here's how you can unprotect a worksheet programmatically:

➢ Example: Unprotecting a worksheet

```
Sub UnprotectWorksheet()
    ' This subroutine demonstrates how to unprotect an
    Excel worksheet using VBA.

    ' Specify the worksheet you want to unprotect.
    ' Adjust "Sheet1" to the name of your target
    worksheet.
    Dim ws As Worksheet
    Set ws = ThisWorkbook.Sheets("Sheet1")

    ' Specify the password used to protect the sheet. If
    the sheet was not protected with a password, leave this
    empty.
```

How to do this in VBA?? 202 ready-made macros: Streamline your tasks with proven expert solutions

```
    ' IMPORTANT: Using hard-coded passwords can pose a
security risk. Consider the implications carefully.
    Dim password As String
    password = "yourPassword" ' Change this to your
password or leave it as "" if there's no password.


    ' Unprotect the sheet
    ws.Unprotect Password:=password


    ' Notify the user that the sheet has been unprotected.
    MsgBox "Worksheet '" & ws.Name & "' has been
unprotected.", vbInformation, "Sheet Unprotected"
    End Sub
```

➢ Key points:

- **Worksheet reference**: the `ws` variable holds a reference to the specific worksheet you intend to unprotect. Adjust `"Sheet1"` to match the actual name of your worksheet.
- **Password**: If the worksheet is protected with a password, you need to specify it in the `password` variable. If there's no password, you can call `Unprotect` without parameters or set `password` to an empty string `""`.
- **Security consideration**: be cautious about hard-coding passwords into your VBA code, as it can be a security risk. Ensure that your Excel files are stored securely if they contain sensitive code or data.
- **User notification**: a message box confirms that the worksheet has been unprotected, providing clear feedback on the operation's completion.

This example illustrates a basic method to unprotect a worksheet in Excel using VBA, which can be particularly useful in automating tasks that require modifying protected sheets.

Unselect

In Excel VBA, there isn't a direct method like `Unselect` to deselect a cell or range that's already selected. The concept of "unselecting" doesn't directly apply because Excel and VBA always require at least one cell to be active or selected within an active worksheet. However, you can effectively "unselect" a range by setting the focus to a single cell, typically done by activating another cell, which can give the appearance of having "unselected" the previously selected range.

➢ Example: "Unselecting" by activating a single cell

```
Sub DeselectRange()
    ' This subroutine demonstrates how to "unselect" a
range by activating a single cell, effectively moving the
focus away from a previously selected range.

    ' Assuming you have a range selected or you want to
move the focus from a current range,
    ' you can activate a single cell, like A1, to give the
effect of "unselecting" the range.
    ThisWorkbook.Sheets("Sheet1").Range("A1").Activate

    ' Alternatively, if you want to ensure minimal visual
impact, you could activate
    ' a cell that's less likely to be in the way, like the
last row of the worksheet.
    ' ThisWorkbook.Sheets("Sheet1").Cells(Rows.Count,
1).Activate

    ' Notify the user that the operation has been
completed.
    MsgBox "Range has been 'unselected' by activating a
single cell.", vbInformation, "Range Deselected"
End Sub
```

➢ Key points:

- **Activating a cell**: by activating a single cell (e.g., `Range("A1").Activate`), you essentially move the focus away from any previously selected range, achieving an "unselect" effect.
- **Minimal visual impact**: if you prefer to avoid moving the focus to a commonly used area of your worksheet, you can activate a cell in an out-of-the-way location, such as the last row of the sheet (`Cells(Rows.Count, 1).Activate`). Adjust the column index as needed based on your worksheet's layout.

How to do this in VBA?? 202 ready-made macros: Streamline your tasks with proven expert solutions

- **User notification**: a message box confirms that the action has been completed, providing feedback on the operation's execution.

This method provides a practical workaround for the lack of a direct `Unselect` command in Excel VBA, allowing you to manage cell and range selections programmatically in your macros.

Use between

Using a "between" condition in VBA involves checking if a value falls within a specific range. While VBA doesn't have a built-in `Between` keyword like SQL, you can accomplish this by using logical operators. Here's an example that demonstrates how to check if a number is between two values, inclusive:

➢ Example: Checking if a value is between two numbers

```
Sub CheckIfValueIsBetween()
    ' This subroutine demonstrates how to check if a value
is between two other values in VBA.

    Dim testValue As Integer
    testValue = 15 ' The value to test

    Dim lowerBound As Integer
    lowerBound = 10 ' Lower bound of the range

    Dim upperBound As Integer
    upperBound = 20 ' Upper bound of the range

    ' Check if testValue is between lowerBound and
upperBound, inclusive
    If testValue >= lowerBound And testValue <= upperBound
Then
        MsgBox testValue & " is between " & lowerBound & "
and " & upperBound & ".", vbInformation, "Between Check"
    Else
        MsgBox testValue & " is not between " & lowerBound
& " and " & upperBound & ".", vbInformation, "Between
Check"
```

```
        End If
    End Sub
```

➤ Key points:

- **Value to test (`testValue`)**: this is the value you want to check whether it falls within a specific range.
- **Range bounds (`lowerBound` and `upperBound`)**: these variables define the lower and upper bounds of the range, respectively.
- **Logical condition**: the `If` statement uses logical operators (`>=` for greater than or equal to and `<=` for less than or equal to) to check if `testValue` falls within the range defined by `lowerBound` and `upperBound`.
- **User feedback**: depending on whether `testValue` is within the range, a message box displays the result, providing clear feedback.

This approach allows you to effectively use a "between" condition in VBA, providing a versatile method for range checking in your macros and applications.

Use Dim

In VBA (Visual Basic for Applications), the `Dim` statement is used to declare variables and allocate storage space. `Dim` stands for Dimension, and it's the most commonly used statement for variable declaration in VBA. Below is an example that demonstrates how to use `Dim` to declare different types of variables:

➤ Example: Declaring variables with Dim

```
    Sub DeclareVariables()
        ' This subroutine demonstrates how to declare
    variables using the Dim statement in VBA.

        ' Declare an integer variable
        Dim myInteger As Integer
        myInteger = 10

        ' Declare a double variable for floating-point numbers
        Dim myDouble As Double
        myDouble = 3.14159
```

```
' Declare a string variable
Dim myString As String
myString = "Hello, VBA!"

' Declare a date variable
Dim myDate As Date
myDate = DateSerial(2020, 1, 1) ' January 1, 2020

' Declare a Boolean variable
Dim myBoolean As Boolean
myBoolean = True

' Use the variables in a message box
MsgBox "Integer: " & myInteger & vbCrLf & _
        "Double: " & myDouble & vbCrLf & _
        "String: " & myString & vbCrLf & _
        "Date: " & myDate & vbCrLf & _
        "Boolean: " & myBoolean, vbInformation,
"Variable Types"
End Sub
```

➢ Key points:

- **Variable declaration**: the `Dim` statement is used at the beginning of a procedure to declare the type of each variable. This helps with code readability and ensures that variables are used as intended.
- **Data types**: VBA supports various data types, including `Integer`, `Double`, `String`, `Date`, and `Boolean`. Choose the appropriate data type for your variables based on the data they will store.
- **Initialization and use**: after declaration, variables can be initialized with values. The example demonstrates setting and then using these variables to display a message box with their values.
- **Scope**: Variables declared with `Dim` inside a subroutine or function have a local scope, meaning they are only accessible within that subroutine or function.

This example illustrates the basics of declaring and using variables in VBA, showcasing the versatility of the `Dim` statement for handling various data types.

Use Dim function

In VBA (Visual Basic for Applications), `Dim` is not used to declare functions; instead, it's used for variable declaration within procedures or modules. To define a function in VBA, you use the `Function` statement. Below is an example that demonstrates how to create a custom function using `Function`, which might be what you're looking for when you mentioned "use dim function".

➤Example: Creating a custom function in VBA

This example demonstrates how to create a simple function that calculates the area of a rectangle. This function takes the length and width of the rectangle as inputs and returns the calculated area.

```
Function CalculateArea(length As Double, width As Double)
As Double
    ' This function calculates the area of a rectangle
given its length and width.


    ' Declare a variable for the area.
    Dim area As Double


    ' Calculate the area.
    area = length * width


    ' Return the calculated area.
    CalculateArea = area
End Function
```

➤ Using the custom function in a subroutine

To use the custom function you've created, you can call it from a subroutine like this:

```
Sub UseCalculateAreaFunction()
    ' This subroutine demonstrates how to use the custom
CalculateArea function.


    ' Declare variables for length, width, and area.
    Dim rectLength As Double
```

```
        Dim rectWidth As Double
        Dim rectArea As Double


        ' Assign values to length and width.
        rectLength = 10 ' Example length
        rectWidth = 5 ' Example width


        ' Calculate the area by calling the CalculateArea
    function.
        rectArea = CalculateArea(rectLength, rectWidth)


        ' Display the calculated area.
        MsgBox "The area of the rectangle is: " & rectArea & "
    square units", vbInformation, "Area Calculation"
        End Sub
```

➢ Key points:

- **Function declaration**: the `Function` statement is used to define a custom function, `CalculateArea`, which performs a specific task.
- **Variable declaration within functions**: inside functions, `Dim` is used to declare local variables, such as `area` in the `CalculateArea` function.
- **Returning values**: functions return a value using the function name as a variable (`CalculateArea = area`).
- **Using custom functions**: you can use your custom function within any subroutine (`Sub`) or function (`Function`) in the same module or across modules if it's declared in a module with scope allowing it.

This example clarifies how to define and use functions in VBA, showing the role of `Dim` for variable declaration within those functions rather than for declaring the functions themselves.

Use e

In VBA, the constant for the base of natural logarithms, e, isn't directly available as a predefined constant. However, you can use the `Exp` function, which represents e raised to the power of a given number. Specifically, `Exp(1)` gives you the value of e, as it's $e^1 = e$.

How to do this in VBA?? 202 ready-made macros: Streamline your tasks with proven expert solutions

Here's how you can use *e* in VBA, including calculating *e* itself and using *e* in a calculation:

➤ Example 1: Calculating the value of *e*

```
Sub CalculateE()
    ' This subroutine calculates the value of the
mathematical constant e.

    Dim e As Double
    e = Exp(1) ' e^1

    MsgBox "The value of e (base of natural logarithms)
is: " & e, vbInformation, "Value of e"
End Sub
```

➤ Example 2: Using *e* in a calculation

Let's say you want to calculate e^x for a given *x*. You can use the `Exp` function directly with your desired exponent:

```
Sub CalculateEToThePowerOfX()
    ' This subroutine calculates e to the power of a
specified number.

    Dim x As Double
    x = 2 ' Example value for x

    Dim result As Double
    result = Exp(x) ' e^x

    MsgBox "e raised to the power of " & x & " is: " &
result, vbInformation, "e to the Power of x"
End Sub
```

➤ Key points:

- Value of *e*: You can calculate *e* using `Exp(1)` since $e^1 = e$.
- Using *e* in calculations: the `Exp` function allows you to calculate *e* raised to any power, making it versatile for mathematical and financial calculations that involve exponential growth or decay.

These examples demonstrate how to work with the mathematical constant e in VBA, providing a foundation for incorporating natural logarithm bases and exponential calculations in your Excel macros.

Use Excel function

In VBA, you can leverage Excel's built-in functions directly within your macros using the `Application.WorksheetFunction` object. This allows you to utilize Excel's extensive library of functions programmatically. Here's an example that demonstrates how to use an Excel function, in this case, `VLOOKUP`, within VBA:

➢ Example: Using Excel's VLOOKUP function in VBA

```
Sub UseExcelVlookup()
    ' This subroutine demonstrates how to use Excel's
VLOOKUP function in VBA.

    ' Assume you have a table in Sheet1, A1:B10, where
column A contains names and column B contains phone
numbers.
    ' You want to find the phone number for a specific
name.

    Dim lookupValue As String
    lookupValue = "John Doe" ' The name you're searching
for.

    Dim tableRange As Range
    Set tableRange =
ThisWorkbook.Sheets("Sheet1").Range("A1:B10") ' Adjust the
range according to your data.

    Dim columnIndex As Integer
    columnIndex = 2 ' The column index in the range
containing the value to return. In this example, phone
numbers are in the second column.

    Dim result As Variant
```

```
      On Error Resume Next ' In case VLOOKUP doesn't find
the lookup value.
      result =
Application.WorksheetFunction.VLookup(lookupValue,
tableRange, columnIndex, False)
      On Error GoTo 0 ' Turn back on regular error handling.


      ' Check if a matching value was found.
      If IsError(result) Then
          MsgBox "Value not found.", vbExclamation, "Result"
      Else
          MsgBox "The phone number for " & lookupValue & "
is: " & result, vbInformation, "Result"
      End If
  End Sub
```

➢ Key points:

- **Lookup value**: the value you're searching for within the table range.
- **Table range**: the range of cells that contains the data you're searching through. This includes both the lookup column and the value column.
- **Column index**: specifies the column in `tableRange` from which to retrieve the value. The index is relative to the start of `tableRange`.
- **Error handling**: since `VLOOKUP` might not find the `lookupValue`, `On Error Resume Next` is used to prevent the macro from stopping due to an error. `IsError(result)` then checks if an error occurred.
- **Result**: the phone number corresponding to `lookupValue` is displayed in a message box if found; otherwise, a **"Value not found"** message is shown.

This example illustrates how to incorporate Excel's functions into your VBA scripts, enhancing your macros' capabilities by utilizing Excel's powerful and diverse function library.

Use find

Using the `Find` method in VBA allows you to search for specific information within a range in Excel. This can be particularly useful for locating data within large datasets. Below is an example that demonstrates how to use the `Find`

How to do this in VBA?? 202 ready-made macros: Streamline your tasks with proven expert solutions

method to search for a specific value within a column and return the address of the cell containing the value if found.

➢ Example: Using the Find method to locate a value

```vba
Sub UseFindMethod()
    ' This subroutine demonstrates how to use the Find
    method to search for a specific value within a range in
    Excel using VBA.

    ' Specify the worksheet you're working with.
    ' Adjust "Sheet1" to the name of your target
    worksheet.
    Dim ws As Worksheet
    Set ws = ThisWorkbook.Sheets("Sheet1")

    ' Define the range where you want to search for the
    value.
    ' In this example, we're searching in column A.
    Dim searchRange As Range
    Set searchRange = ws.Range("A:A")

    ' Specify the value you are searching for.
    Dim searchValue As String
    searchValue = "Example"

    ' Use the Find method to search for the value.
    Dim foundCell As Range
    Set foundCell = searchRange.Find(What:=searchValue, _

After:=searchRange.Cells(1, 1), _

                                     LookIn:=xlValues, _
                                     LookAt:=xlPart, _


SearchOrder:=xlByRows, _


SearchDirection:=xlNext, _
```

```
                                              MatchCase:=False)


     ' Check if a matching value was found.
     If Not foundCell Is Nothing Then
          MsgBox "Value found in cell: " &
foundCell.Address, vbInformation, "Value Found"
     Else
          MsgBox "Value '" & searchValue & "' not found.",
vbExclamation, "Value Not Found"
     End If
End Sub
```

➤ Key points:

- **Worksheet reference**: the `ws` variable references the worksheet where the search is performed.
- **Search range**: the `searchRange` defines where the `Find` method will look for `searchValue`. Adjust this range according to your needs.
- **Search value**: `searchValue` is the value you're searching for within `searchRange`.
- Find method parameters:
  o `What`: the value to search for.
  o `After`: the cell after which the search begins. Typically, this is the first cell in your search range.
  o `LookIn`: specifies whether to search in formulas, values, or comments. `xlValues` is used here.
  o `LookAt`: can be `xlWhole` (for whole match) or `xlPart` (for partial match). `xlPart` is used in this example.
  o `SearchOrder`: specifies the order to search in (`xlByRows` or `xlByColumns`).
  o `SearchDirection`: can be `xlNext` (forward) or `xlPrevious` (backward).
  o `MatchCase`: specifies whether the search is case-sensitive.
- **Result handling**: the method returns a `Range` object representing the first cell where the `searchValue` is found. If no match is found, `foundCell` will be `Nothing`.

This example showcases how to effectively use the `Find` method in VBA to locate specific values within an Excel worksheet, providing a foundation for building more complex data search and manipulation macros.

Use immediate window

The Immediate Window in the VBA IDE (Integrated Development Environment) is a powerful tool for debugging and testing your VBA code. It allows you to execute VBA commands on the fly and to print out values of variables for immediate inspection. Here's how you can use the Immediate Window in your development process:

➤ Example: Using the immediate window for debugging and testing

1. Printing values to the immediate window

You can use the `Debug.Print` statement in your VBA code to output values to the Immediate Window. This is particularly useful for checking the state of variables at various points in your code.

```
Sub TestImmediateWindow()
    Dim sampleValue As Integer
    sampleValue = 10
    Debug.Print "The value of sampleValue is: ";
sampleValue
End Sub
```

Run this subroutine, and you'll see the output in the Immediate Window.

2. Evaluating expressions directly

You can directly evaluate expressions or execute statements in the Immediate Window. For example, type the following directly into the Immediate Window and press Enter:

```
? 2 + 2
```

Excel will evaluate the expression and return the result (`4`) in the Immediate Window.

3. Testing functions and procedures

You can call any public function or subroutine from the Immediate Window to test its output or behavior. For example, if you have a function `AddNumbers` that adds two numbers, you can test it like this:

- First, define your function in a module:

```
Sub TestImmediateWindow()
    Dim sampleValue As Integer
```

```
sampleValue = 10
Debug.Print "The value of sampleValue is: "; sampleValue
End Sub      ```
```

- Then, in the immediate window, type and Enter:

```
? AddNumbers(5, 7)
```

- You will see the result (`12`) in the Immediate Window.

4. Setting variable values

The Immediate Window can also be used to set the value of variables while paused in break mode during debugging. For instance, if your code is paused on a breakpoint and you have a variable `sampleVar`, you can set its value by typing the following in the Immediate Window and pressing Enter:

```
sampleVar = 25
```

This can be especially useful for testing how your code reacts to different values without having to modify and rerun your code each time.

➤ Key points:

- **Debugging tool**: the immediate window is an invaluable tool for printing debug information, evaluating expressions, and modifying variable values on the fly during the debugging process.
- **Accessibility**: you can open the Immediate Window by pressing `Ctrl+G` when in the VBA IDE, or by going to `View > Immediate Window` in the menu.
- **Versatility**: Its uses range from simple calculations and function tests to more complex debugging scenarios where you interact with the execution of your VBA code in real-time.

Using the Immediate Window effectively can greatly enhance your productivity and efficiency when developing and debugging VBA code.

Use Json converter

To use JSON conversion in VBA, you typically need a parser because VBA doesn't inherently support JSON parsing or serialization. A popular choice is the `VBA-JSON` library, which provides an easy way to convert JSON to and from VBA objects (like dictionaries for JSON objects and collections for JSON arrays).

First, you'll need to add the `VBA-JSON` library to your project. You can find it on GitHub (by Tim Hall) and follow the installation instructions there. Once you've added the library to your VBA references, you can use it as follows:

How to do this in VBA?? 202 ready-made macros: Streamline your tasks with proven expert solutions

➤ Example: Parsing JSON string to VBA

This example demonstrates how to parse a JSON string into VBA objects using the `VBA-JSON` converter.

```vba
Sub ParseJSONExample()
    ' Assuming you've already added the VBA-JSON library
to your references

    ' Sample JSON string
    Dim jsonString As String
    jsonString = "{""name"":""John
Doe"",""age"":30,""isEmployee"":true}"

    ' Parse the JSON string into a VBA object (Dictionary)
    Dim jsonObject As Object
    Set jsonObject = JsonConverter.ParseJson(jsonString)

    ' Access values from the parsed JSON
    Dim name As String
    Dim age As Integer
    Dim isEmployee As Boolean

    name = jsonObject("name")
    age = jsonObject("age")
    isEmployee = jsonObject("isEmployee")

    ' Output parsed values to Immediate Window (Ctrl+G to
view)
    Debug.Print "Name: "; name
    Debug.Print "Age: "; age
    Debug.Print "Is Employee: "; isEmployee
End Sub
```

➤ Example: Converting VBA object to JSON string

This example shows how to convert a VBA Dictionary into a JSON string.

```vba
Sub ConvertToJsonExample()
```

```
' Create a sample VBA Dictionary to represent as JSON
Dim dict As Object
Set dict = CreateObject("Scripting.Dictionary")
dict.Add "name", "Jane Doe"
dict.Add "age", 28
dict.Add "isEmployee", False


' Convert the Dictionary to a JSON string
Dim jsonString As String
jsonString = JsonConverter.ConvertToJson(dict)


' Output the JSON string to Immediate Window
Debug.Print jsonString
End Sub
```

➢ Key points:

- **Adding VBA-JSON**: you need to download and add `VBA-JSON` to your VBA project references for these examples to work. This provides the `JsonConverter` object used for parsing and converting JSON.
- **Parsing JSON**: the `JsonConverter.ParseJson` method turns a JSON string into a VBA object (like a Dictionary).
- **Creating JSON**: the `JsonConverter.ConvertToJson` method converts VBA objects back into JSON strings.
- **Data types**: JSON objects become `Dictionary` objects, and JSON arrays become `Collection` objects in VBA.

These examples demonstrate basic usage of JSON conversion in VBA, enabling you to work with JSON data within your Excel macros and applications effectively.

Use MsgBox Yes No

Using a `MsgBox` with Yes and No options in VBA allows you to prompt the user to make a decision, with the function returning a value based on the user's choice. You can use this return value to direct the flow of your program based on the user's response. Here's how to implement a `MsgBox` with Yes and No buttons:

➢ Example: Using MsgBox with Yes and No options

How to do this in VBA?? 202 ready-made macros: Streamline your tasks with proven expert solutions

```vba
Sub PromptUserYesNo()
    ' This subroutine demonstrates how to use a MsgBox
with Yes and No options in VBA.

    ' Display a message box with Yes and No buttons.
    Dim response As VbMsgBoxResult
    response = MsgBox("Do you want to proceed?", vbYesNo +
vbQuestion, "Confirm Action")

    ' Check the user's response and take action
accordingly.
    If response = vbYes Then
        ' User clicked Yes
        MsgBox "User chose to proceed.", vbInformation,
"Action Confirmed"
        ' Add the code to proceed with the action here.
    Else
        ' User clicked No
        MsgBox "User chose not to proceed.",
vbInformation, "Action Cancelled"
        ' Add the code to handle cancellation here.
    End If
End Sub
```

➤ Key points:

- **Displaying the MsgBox**: the `MsgBox` function is called with three arguments: the prompt message, buttons (`vbYesNo` + `vbQuestion` to show Yes and No buttons with a question mark icon), and the title of the message box.
- **Handling the response**: the user's response is captured in the `response` variable. The `If` statement then checks if the response equals `vbYes` (indicating the user clicked Yes) to proceed with the intended action, or handles the No response accordingly.
- **Customizing the Message Box**: you can customize the message, title, and even the icons by changing the parameters in the `MsgBox` function call.

This example provides a basic template for prompting users with Yes and No options in Excel VBA, enabling decision-based execution flow in your macros.

Use Or

Using the `Or` operator in VBA allows you to combine multiple conditions in an `If` statement, where the statement executes if at least one of the conditions is `True`. Here's an example to demonstrate how to use the `Or` operator effectively:

➢ Example: Using the Or operator in conditional statements

```
Sub CheckMultipleConditions()
    ' This subroutine demonstrates how to use the Or
operator to check multiple conditions in VBA.


    ' Sample variables for demonstration
    Dim temperature As Integer
    Dim weatherCondition As String


    ' Assign sample values (try changing these to test
different conditions)
    temperature = 30 ' degrees Celsius
    weatherCondition = "Rainy"


    ' Check if the temperature is above 25 degrees Celsius
OR the weather condition is "Rainy"
    If temperature > 25 Or weatherCondition = "Rainy" Then
        ' If either condition is true, execute the code in
this block
        MsgBox "It's either warm or rainy outside.
Consider adjusting your plans accordingly.",
vbInformation, "Weather Check"
    Else
        ' If neither condition is true, execute the code
in this block
        MsgBox "The weather is comfortable and not rainy.
Enjoy your day!", vbInformation, "Weather Check"
    End If
End Sub
```

How to do this in VBA?? 202 ready-made macros: Streamline your tasks with proven expert solutions

➤ Key points:

- **Multiple conditions**: the `Or` operator is used to combine two conditions: whether `temperature` is greater than 25 degrees Celsius or `weatherCondition` equals "Rainy".
- **Conditional execution**: the `If` statement evaluates to `True` if either (or both) of the conditions are met. The code inside the `If` block executes in this case.
- **Alternative action**: the `Else` block contains code that executes only if both conditions are `False`.

This example illustrates the use of the `Or` operator to make decisions based on multiple criteria, enhancing the flexibility and power of your VBA scripts.

Use VLOOKUP

Using the `VLOOKUP` function in VBA allows you to search for a value in the first column of a table range and return a value in the same row from another column. To utilize `VLOOKUP` within VBA, you typically make use of the `Application.WorksheetFunction.VLookup` method. Here's how you can implement it:

➤ Example: Using VLOOKUP in VBA

```
Sub UseVLookup()
    ' This subroutine demonstrates how to use the VLOOKUP
    function in VBA to find and return a value from a table
    range.

    ' Define the value you are looking for
    Dim lookupValue As Variant
    lookupValue = "SampleValue" ' Adjust this to the value
    you're searching for

    ' Define the range where you want to search for the
    value (the table array)
    Dim tableRange As Range
    Set tableRange =
    ThisWorkbook.Sheets("Sheet1").Range("A1:B10") ' Adjust to
    your table's range
```

```
        ' Specify which column number in the table array to
return the value from
        Dim colIndexNum As Integer
        colIndexNum = 2 ' For example, 2 if you want to return
value from the second column


        ' Specify if you want an exact match or an approximate
match
        Dim rngLookup As Boolean
        rngLookup = False ' Set to False for exact match, True
for approximate match


        ' Use VLOOKUP to find the value
        Dim result As Variant
        On Error Resume Next ' In case VLOOKUP does not find
the lookup value
        result =
Application.WorksheetFunction.VLookup(lookupValue,
tableRange, colIndexNum, rngLookup)
        On Error GoTo 0 ' Turn back on regular error handling


        ' Check if the value was found and return the result
        If IsError(result) Then
            MsgBox "Value not found.", vbExclamation, "Result"
        Else
            MsgBox "The corresponding value is: " & result,
vbInformation, "Result"
        End If
    End Sub
```

➢ Key points:

- **Lookup value**: this is the value you're searching for within the first column of your table range.
- **Table range**: the range where the `VLOOKUP` should search for the `lookupValue`. It's important this range includes both the lookup column and the return value column.

- **Column index number**: indicates from which column in the `tableRange` the matching value should be returned.
- **Range lookup**: a Boolean value where `False` specifies that you want an exact match and `True` allows for an approximate match.
- **Error handling**: since `VLOOKUP` might not find the `lookupValue`, `On Error Resume Next` is used to avoid runtime errors, and `IsError(result)` checks if an error occurred during the lookup.

This example demonstrates using `VLOOKUP` within a VBA subroutine, providing a powerful tool for searching and retrieving data based on a key value.

Use XLDOWN

Using `xlDown` in VBA is a common method for selecting a range down to the last non-empty cell in a column starting from a specific cell. It's similar to pressing `Ctrl+Down Arrow` in Excel, which jumps to the bottom of a contiguous range of non-empty cells. Here's an example of how you can use `xlDown` to select a range:

➢ Example: Selecting a range down to the last non-empty cell

```
Sub SelectRangeUsingXLDown()
    ' This subroutine demonstrates how to select a range
down to the last non-empty cell in a column using xlDown.

    ' Specify the worksheet you're working with.
    ' Adjust "Sheet1" to the name of your target
worksheet.
    Dim ws As Worksheet
    Set ws = ThisWorkbook.Sheets("Sheet1")

    ' Starting from cell A1, select down to the last non-
empty cell in the column.
    ' This example assumes A1 is not empty. If A1 could be
empty, see the note below.
    ws.Range("A1").Select
    Range(Selection, Selection.End(xlDown)).Select
```

```
        ' Optional: Print the address of the selected range to
    the Immediate Window (Ctrl+G to view)
        Debug.Print Selection.Address
    End Sub
```

➢ Note: If the starting cell (`A1` in this example) could be empty, or if there's a possibility that it's the only cell in the column that's not empty, you should add a check to prevent `xlDown` from selecting all the way down to the bottom of the worksheet. One way to handle this is by using `xlUp` from the bottom of the worksheet to find the last non-empty cell.

➢ Example: Finding the last non-empty cell and selecting range

```
    Sub SelectRangeToEndOfData()
        ' This subroutine demonstrates finding the last non-
    empty cell in column A using xlUp,
        ' then selecting the range from A1 to this cell.

        Dim ws As Worksheet
        Set ws = ThisWorkbook.Sheets("Sheet1")

        ' Find the last non-empty cell in column A starting
    from the bottom of the worksheet.
        Dim lastRow As Long
        lastRow = ws.Cells(ws.Rows.Count, "A").End(xlUp).Row

        ' Select the range from A1 to the last non-empty cell.
        ws.Range("A1:A" & lastRow).Select

        ' Optional: Print the address of the selected range to
    the Immediate Window
        Debug.Print Selection.Address
    End Sub
```

➢ Key points:

- `xlDown` and `xlUp` Usage: `xlDown` is useful for quickly selecting a contiguous range starting from a specified cell. However, when used from an empty cell or the top of a contiguous block, it might select down to the bottom of Excel's usable range. Using `xlUp` from the

> bottom of the sheet is a reliable way to find the last non-empty cell in a column.

- **Selection and debugging**: the examples above use `.Select` and `Debug.Print` for demonstration purposes. In practice, directly working with ranges without selecting them is recommended for better performance and to avoid changing the user's selection on the worksheet.

These examples provide a foundation for using `xlDown` and `xlUp` in VBA to navigate and select ranges based on the data's extent in your Excel worksheets.

VBA ^ operator

In VBA, the `^` operator is used for exponentiation, that is, raising a number to the power of another number. Here's an example demonstrating how to use the `^` operator to perform a simple calculation involving exponentiation:

➢ Example: Calculating the power of a number

```
Sub CalculateExponentiation()
    ' This subroutine demonstrates using the ^ operator to
    calculate the power of a number in VBA.

    Dim baseNumber As Double
    Dim exponent As Double
    Dim result As Double

    ' Example values
    baseNumber = 5 ' Base number
    exponent = 3   ' Exponent

    ' Calculate baseNumber raised to the power of exponent
    result = baseNumber ^ exponent

    ' Display the result
    MsgBox baseNumber & " raised to the power of " &
exponent & " is " & result, vbInformation, "Exponentiation
Result"
End Sub
```

How to do this in VBA?? 202 ready-made macros: Streamline your tasks with proven expert solutions

➢ Key points:

- **Exponentiation operation**: the `^` operator is used to raise `baseNumber` to the power of `exponent`.
- **Variables**: `baseNumber` and `exponent` are variables representing the base and the exponent, respectively. You can change these values to calculate different powers.
- **Result display**: the `MsgBox` function is used to display the result of the exponentiation to the user.

This example illustrates the basic usage of the `^` operator in VBA for performing exponentiation, a common mathematical operation in programming.

VBA AscW

The `AscW` function in VBA is used to return the Unicode character code corresponding to the first letter in a string provided to the function. This can be particularly useful for getting Unicode codes of characters, which might be necessary for various data processing tasks, including encoding or decoding data, or when working with character-specific operations.

➢ Example: Using AscW to get Unicode code

```
Sub GetUnicodeCode()
    ' This subroutine demonstrates how to use the AscW
    function to get the Unicode character code of the first
    character in a string.

    Dim sampleChar As String
    Dim unicodeCode As Integer

    ' Example character
    sampleChar = "A"   ' Change this to any character to
    find its Unicode code

    ' Get the Unicode character code
    unicodeCode = AscW(sampleChar)

    ' Display the result
```

```
        MsgBox "The Unicode character code of '" & sampleChar
& "' is: " & unicodeCode, vbInformation, "Unicode Code"
End Sub
```

➤ Key points:

- **Function usage**: `AscW(sampleChar)` is used where `sampleChar` is the string (or character) whose Unicode code you want to find. `AscW` returns the Unicode code of the first character in this string.
- **Character input**: although `sampleChar` can be a string, `AscW` only considers the first character of this string. If you pass a string with more than one character, only the code for the first character is returned.
- **Result display**: the `MsgBox` function displays the Unicode character code to the user.

This example illustrates the basic usage of the `AscW` function in VBA, allowing you to work with Unicode character codes directly in your macros for various programming needs.

Wait Excel

In Excel VBA, you can pause or delay the execution of your macro using the `Application.Wait` method. This method halts the processing of your VBA code for a specified duration. Here's how to implement a wait function in your VBA script:

➤ Example: Using Application.Wait to pause execution

```
Sub PauseMacro()
    ' This subroutine demonstrates how to pause a macro's
    execution for a specified duration using Application.Wait
    in VBA.

    ' Display the current time
    MsgBox "Current time: " & Time(), vbInformation,
    "Pause Started"

    ' Calculate the time for the pause to end (e.g., 5
    seconds from now)
    Dim waitTime As Date
```

```
waitTime = Now + TimeValue("00:00:05") ' Adjust the
TimeValue to change the duration


' Pause the macro until the specified time
Application.Wait waitTime


' Display the time after the pause
MsgBox "Resume time: " & Time(), vbInformation, "Pause
Ended"
End Sub
```

➤ Key points:

- **Current time display**: the macro starts by showing the current time using `MsgBox`.
- **Calculating wait time**: `waitTime` is calculated by adding a `TimeValue` to the current time (`Now`). In this example, `TimeValue("00:00:05")` adds 5 seconds, but you can adjust this value to your needs.
- **Pause execution**: `Application.Wait` is called with the `waitTime` argument, pausing the macro's execution until the specified future time.
- **Resumption confirmation**: after the wait period, another message box displays the time, indicating that the macro has resumed execution.

This example provides a straightforward method for implementing a delay or pause in your VBA macros, useful for timing operations, waiting for external processes to complete, or simply slowing down execution for demonstration purposes.

Worksheet function

In VBA, you can access and use Excel worksheet functions by leveraging the `Application.WorksheetFunction` object. This allows you to utilize Excel's built-in functions directly within your macros. Here's an example demonstrating how to use a worksheet function, specifically the `SUM` function, to calculate the sum of a range within a worksheet:

➤ Example: Using WorksheetFunction to calculate sum

```
Sub CalculateSumUsingWorksheetFunction()
```

How to do this in VBA?? 202 ready-made macros: Streamline your tasks with proven expert solutions

```vba
    ' This subroutine demonstrates how to use the SUM
worksheet function in VBA.

    ' Define the range for which we want to calculate the
sum
    Dim targetRange As Range
    Set targetRange =
ThisWorkbook.Sheets("Sheet1").Range("A1:A10") ' Adjust the
range as necessary

    ' Calculate the sum of the range using the
WorksheetFunction object
    Dim sumResult As Double
    sumResult =
Application.WorksheetFunction.Sum(targetRange)

    ' Display the result in a message box
    MsgBox "The sum of the range " & targetRange.Address &
" is: " & sumResult, vbInformation, "Sum Calculation"
    End Sub
```

➢ Key points:

- **Target range**: the range of cells you want to calculate the sum for is defined with the `targetRange` variable. Make sure to adjust `"Sheet1"` and the range `"A1:A10"` according to your specific needs.
- **Using WorksheetFunction.Sum**: the `Sum` method of the `Application.WorksheetFunction` object is used to calculate the sum of the specified range. This method directly mirrors the SUM function available in Excel worksheets.
- **Displaying the result**: a message box is used to display the calculated sum, showing how the result of the worksheet function can be utilized within your VBA code.

This example provides a straightforward demonstration of how to access and use Excel's worksheet functions within VBA, extending the capabilities of your macros by integrating powerful Excel functions.

Wrap text

To enable text wrapping for a specific range in Excel using VBA, you can modify the `WrapText` property of the `Range` object. This property allows text to automatically wrap within cells, ensuring that all content is visible without extending the cell's width. Here's how to apply text wrapping to a range:

➢ Example: Enabling text wrapping in a range

```
Sub EnableTextWrapping()
    ' This subroutine demonstrates how to enable text
wrapping for a specific range of cells in Excel using VBA.

    ' Specify the worksheet and the range you want to
format.
    ' Adjust "Sheet1" and the range as necessary for your
workbook.
    Dim ws As Worksheet
    Set ws = ThisWorkbook.Sheets("Sheet1")

    Dim targetRange As Range
    Set targetRange = ws.Range("A1:A10") ' Assuming you
want to enable wrapping in cells A1 through A10

    ' Enable text wrapping in the specified range
    targetRange.WrapText = True

    ' Optional: Auto-fit the rows to ensure all wrapped
text is visible
    targetRange.Rows.AutoFit

    MsgBox "Text wrapping has been enabled for " &
targetRange.Address, vbInformation, "Wrap Text"
End Sub
```

➢ Key points:

- **Worksheet and range specification**: the `ws` variable is used to reference the specific worksheet, and `targetRange` specifies the cells where text wrapping will be applied. Adjust these to match the area you're working with.

- **Enabling text wrapping**: the `WrapText` property of `targetRange` is set to `True` to enable text wrapping within the specified cells.
- **Auto-fitting rows**: after enabling text wrapping, it might be necessary to adjust the row heights to ensure all text is visible. This is done using the `AutoFit` method on `targetRange.Rows`.

This example illustrates how to programmatically enable text wrapping in Excel using VBA, enhancing the readability of cells containing more text than can typically be displayed in the cell's width.

Write a text file

To write to a text file in Excel VBA, you can use the `FileSystemObject` and its related methods. This approach gives you more control over the file handling process, such as creating, writing, and closing text files. Here's how you can write to a text file using `FileSystemObject`:

➢ Example: Writing to a text file using FileSystemObject

```
Sub WriteToTextFile()
    ' This subroutine demonstrates how to write to a text
file using the FileSystemObject in VBA.

    ' Declare variables
    Dim fso As Object
    Dim textFile As Object
    Dim filePath As String

    ' Create an instance of the FileSystemObject
    Set fso = CreateObject("Scripting.FileSystemObject")

    ' Define the file path and name
    filePath = "C:\example\example.txt" ' Adjust the file
path as necessary

    ' Create a new text file. Use True for creating a
Unicode file, False for ASCII.
```

How to do this in VBA?? 202 ready-made macros: Streamline your tasks with proven expert solutions

```vba
        Set textFile = fso.CreateTextFile(filePath, True,
    True) ' Arguments: (FileName, Overwrite, Unicode)

        ' Write a line of text
        textFile.WriteLine "Hello, this is a test."

        ' Write another line of text
        textFile.WriteLine "Writing to a text file using VBA."

        ' Close the file
        textFile.Close

        ' Clean up
        Set textFile = Nothing
        Set fso = Nothing

        MsgBox "Text file written successfully to: " &
    filePath, vbInformation, "Operation Completed"
    End Sub
```

➢ Key points:

- **FileSystemObject**: this object provides access to a computer's file system. It is used here to manage the creation and writing to a text file.
- **CreateTextFile Method**: this method is used to create a new text file. The parameters allow you to specify the path, whether to overwrite an existing file, and whether the file should be Unicode.
- **Writing text**: the `WriteLine` method of the `textFile` object writes a line of text to the file and appends a newline character.
- **Closing the file**: it's important to close the file after writing to release the file and ensure all data is flushed to disk.
- **File path**: ensure the `filePath` variable is adjusted to point to a valid directory on your system where you have write permissions.

This example provides a foundational approach to creating and writing to text files in VBA, enabling data logging, output generation, and other file-based operations.

Write write to a cell

Writing data to a cell in Excel using VBA is a fundamental operation that allows you to automate data entry and manipulation within your spreadsheets. Here's a basic example demonstrating how to write a value to a specific cell:

➢ Example: Writing data to a cell

```
Sub WriteDataToCell()
    ' This subroutine demonstrates how to write data to a
specific cell in an Excel worksheet using VBA.

    Dim ws As Worksheet

    ' Set the worksheet object to the sheet where you want
to write data.
    ' Adjust "Sheet1" to the name of your target
worksheet.
    Set ws = ThisWorkbook.Sheets("Sheet1")

    ' Specify the cell and write data to it.
    ' This example writes "Hello, Excel!" to cell A1.
    ws.Cells(1, 1).Value = "Hello, Excel!"

    ' Alternatively, you can reference the cell directly.
    ws.Range("A1").Value = "Hello, Excel!"

    ' Inform the user that data has been written to the
cell.
    MsgBox "Data written to cell A1.", vbInformation,
"Data Written"
    End Sub
```

➢ Key points:

- **Worksheet object**: the `ws` variable is set to the specific worksheet where you intend to write data. It's important to adjust `"Sheet1"` to the actual name of your worksheet.

How to do this in VBA?? 202 ready-made macros: Streamline your tasks with proven expert solutions

- **Writing data**: the `.Value` property of a `Cells` or `Range` object is used to write data to a cell. In this example, "**Hello, Excel!**" is written to cell A1. You can specify the target cell either by using the `Cells(row, column)` method or the `Range("A1")` method.
- Notification: A message box confirms that the data has been written, providing feedback to the user about the operation's success.

This code snippet is a straightforward demonstration of how to write data to a specific cell in an Excel workbook using VBA, serving as a foundational skill for Excel automation.

XLOOKUP

`XLOOKUP` is a newer Excel function that provides a more powerful and flexible way to look up data compared to older functions like `VLOOKUP` and `HLOOKUP`. As of my last update, to use `XLOOKUP` directly in VBA, you can leverage the `Application.WorksheetFunction` object or `Application.Evaluate` method, since `XLOOKUP` may not be directly accessible through the `WorksheetFunction` object in all versions of Excel. Here's an example using `Application.Evaluate` to perform an `XLOOKUP` operation within VBA:

➢ Example: Using XLOOKUP in VBA with Application.Evaluate

```
Sub UseXLookup()
    ' This subroutine demonstrates how to perform an
XLOOKUP in Excel VBA using the Application.Evaluate
method.

    Dim lookupValue As String
    Dim returnValue As Variant
    Dim formulaString As String

    ' Define the value to look for
    lookupValue = "Item1"

    ' Construct the XLOOKUP formula as a string
    ' Assuming you are looking up "Item1" in range A2:A10
and returning the corresponding value from range B2:B10
```

```
        formulaString = "=XLOOKUP(""" & lookupValue & """,
    A2:A10, B2:B10)"


        ' Use Evaluate to perform the XLOOKUP
        returnValue = Application.Evaluate(formulaString)


        ' Check if returnValue is an error (e.g., if
    lookupValue is not found)
        If IsError(returnValue) Then
            MsgBox "Item not found.", vbExclamation, "XLOOKUP
    Result"
        Else
            MsgBox "The value corresponding to '" &
    lookupValue & "' is: " & returnValue, vbInformation,
    "XLOOKUP Result"
        End If
    End Sub
```

➤ Key points:

- **Application.Evaluate**: this method evaluates a string expression as if it were an Excel formula. Here, it's used to perform `XLOOKUP` by passing the formula as a string.
- **Constructing the formula string**: the `XLOOKUP` formula is constructed as a string that includes the lookup value, the lookup array, and the return array.
- **Handling return values**: after evaluating the formula, the returned value is stored in `returnValue`. If `XLOOKUP` doesn't find the lookup value, `Evaluate` will return an error, which can be checked using `IsError`.

This method allows you to utilize the `XLOOKUP` functionality within VBA, extending your ability to perform complex lookups directly within your macros, leveraging the full power of Excel's formula capabilities.

www.ingramcontent.com/pod-product-compliance
Lightning Source LLC
LaVergne TN
LVHW051431050326
832903LV00030BD/3031